Economic and social cohesion in Europe

Discussions of a full internal market within the EC are finally reaching fruition. Regular intergovernmental talks advance ideas of economic and monetary union and perhaps eventually political union, and economic and social cohesion has become a major objective of Community policy.

Yet regional disparities remain a hard fact of Community life. Although there have been funds available since 1975 to promote regional development and training in the poorer parts of Europe, it is likely that without serious reform of the Structural Funds these disparities could become greater. There has been increasing anxiety from these countries about their ability to survive in the single market, with a risk that they might put in question their participation in the Community effort.

As a result, the EC has committed itself to new initiatives in science and technology, the environment, social policy, and economic integration. This book studies how new policy can best be designed and implemented, and explores ways in which the Structural Funds can be used to provide new opportunities for the poorer member states.

Economic and Social Cohesion in Europe will be of significant interest to those involved in European studies, particularly the economics, politics and economic geography of the Community. It will also appeal to regional economists and graduate and undergraduate students of European politics.

Achille Hannequart is Professor of Economics at the Catholic University Faculties of Mons and the Catholic University of Louvain. He is also a member of the Trans-European Policy Studies Association.

THE TRANS EUROPEAN POLICY STUDIES ASSOCIATION (TEPSA)

TEPSA is an independent scientific organisation, established in 1974 in Brussels, at the initiative of a number of European institutes. Its objective is to generate international research on European integration in order to stimulate the discussion on policies and political options for Europe. To this purpose TEPSA links affiliated national institutes from the Community member states. Through a common framework for exchange of information and coordination of activities, the participating institutes are able to give a truly European dimension to their research projects. Since integration is a multidisciplinary process, TEPSA studies invariably involve experts from various disciplines: lawyers, economists, political scientists, historians and sociologists.

TEPSA'S activities are decided upon by a Steering Group, consisting of the president and one other representative of each of the member institutes. The Steering Group is chaired by Jacques Vandamme, Chairman of the Belgian member of TEPSA and in charge of the coordination of activities. TEPSA's activities are fianced by the member institutes, by EC-subsidies and by occasional grants from other organisations and the private sector.

Member institutes

Association Française pour l'Élude de l'Union Européenne (AFEUR), Paris.
Chairman: robert Toulemon
Institut für Europäische Politik (IEP), Bonn.
Director: Wolfgang Wessels
The Federal Trust for Education and Research, London.
Director: Gary Miller
Istituto Afari Internazionali (IAI), Rome.
Director: Gianni Bonvieini
Interdisciplnaire Studiegroep Europese Integratie (ISEI), The Hague.
Chairman: Willem Molle
The Irish Association for Contemporary European Studies (IACES), Dublin.   *Chairman: Richard Sinnott*
Greek Center of European Studies & Research (EKEME), Athens.
Director: Nikos Framgalos
Spanish Group for European Studies, Madrid.
Chairman: A. Lorea Corrons
European Policy Unit of the European University Institute, Florence.
Director: Susan Strange
Centre d'Études et de Recherches Européennes R. Schuman, Luxembourg.
Director: Gilbert Trausch
Groupe d'Études politiques Européennes (GEPE), Brussels.
Chairman: Jacques Vandamme
Instituto de Estudos Estrategicos e Internacionais, Lisbon.
Director: Alvaro Vasconcelos

Economic and social cohesion in Europe

A new objective for integration

Edited by
Achille Hannequart

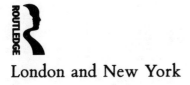

London and New York

First published 1992
by Routledge
11 New Fetter Lane, London EC4P 4EE

Simultaneously published in the USA and Canada
by Routledge
a division of Routledge, Chapman and Hall, Inc.
29 West 35th Street, New York, NY 10001

Typeset in Bembo by Witwell Ltd, Southport
Printed and bound in Great Britain by
Mackays of Chatham PLC, Chatham, Kent

A catalogue reference for this title is available from the British Library
ISBN 0–415–06617–4

Library of Congress Cataloging in Publication Data
Economic and social cohesion: a new objective of European
integration/edited by
   Achille Hannequart.
   Includes bibliographical references and index.
   ISBN 0–415–06617–4
   1. European Economic Community countries – Economic
policy.
   2. Europe–Economic integration.   I. Hannequart, Achille.
   HC241.2.E278   1992
   337.1′4–dc20   91–35859

Contents

Tables

Contributors

Dieter Biehl is Professor at the Institut für Offentliche Wirtschaft, Geld und Wahrung, Johann Wolfgang Goethe-Universität, Frankfurt am Mainz.

Alain Buzelay is Professor at the University of Nancy II and is Director of the Faculty of Economic Sciences and Management at the European Studies Centre of the University of Nancy.

Achille Hannequart is Professor at the Facultés Universitaires Catholiques de Mons and at the Université Catholique de Louvain. He is also Chairman of the research unit Systèmes Economiques, Régionaux et publics (SERP).

Eneko Landaburu ILLARRAMENDI is Director General of Regional Policy at the Commission of the European Communities.

Dennis I.F. Lucey is Professor of Food Economics, Dean Faculty of Commerce, University College Cork, Ireland.

Rory O'Donnell (BA, MA, MSc, THD) is Senior Research Officer at the Economic and Social Research Institute, Dublin.

Elvira Urzainqui and **Rosario de Andrés** are Researchers at the Instituto de Economia y Geografia Aplicadas (CSIC), Spain.

Vandamme Jacques is chairman of TEPSA (Trans-European Policy Studies Association).

Foreword

Jacques Vandamme

The enunciation of the objective of economic and social cohesion was one of the most important innovatory aspects of the 1986 Single European Act (SEA).

Informed public opinion has typically perceived the SEA as a way of facilitating and accelerating progress towards the realisation of the internal market, by changing Article 100 of the Treaty of Rome and by introducing majority voting in the Council of Ministers, notably on draft directives dealing with the harmonisation of national laws.

In fact, the internal market is but one aspect of a far broader principle enshrined in the Treaty of Rome, namely, the Common Market.

Nevertheless, the objective of economic and social cohesion was nowhere explicitly stipulated in the 1955–6 preparations for the Rome Treaty. This was because the authors of the Treaty believed that economic cohesion would automatically derive from an opening up of Europe's markets. As they saw it, investment would be attracted to countries and regions with lower manpower costs. This, it was supposed, would create more growth in those areas, leading to near equilibrium.

An analogous process was expected to occur in the social sector, and this expectation lies behind the whole philosophy of Article 117 of the Treaty of Rome, which speaks of the belief 'that such a development will ensue . . . from the functioning of the common market'.

Such expectations were to be disappointed. After more than thirty years of progress towards the realisation of the Common Market, social and economic discrepancies in regional development have increased. The enlargement of the Community to include three less-developed southern countries surely contributed to this but, even within the 'old' Community of the Six, strong divergencies are still apparent.

The insertion into the Treaties, by way of the SEA, of the principle of economic and social cohesion amounted to an implicit recognition that the original belief in the 'automatic' effects of the single market, in bringing about progressive harmonisation of living standards and more balanced economic development, had become outmoded.

Action was needed, but what could that be, and what form should it take?

The answer was provided by Article 130B of the Rome Treaty, as amended by the SEA, which indicated three basic means:

- enhanced co-ordination of the economic policies of the Member States;
- common policies and the internal market;
- structural instruments, especially the Structural Funds (regional, social, rural) and the European Investment Bank (EIB).

In this book, the Trans-European Policy Studies Association (TEPSA) has attempted an evaluation of the new policy, particularly in the field of the Structural Funds, and has also tried to set out a potentially more global approach to cohesion policy. Such cohesion would not be limited to the transfer of funds from one part of the Community to another, but would entail appropriate Community and member state budgetary policies in the framework of a federally-based Finance Union.

This would be a final challenge for reform, opening up further perspectives unenvisaged when the SEA was ratified.

Abbreviations

CAP	Common Agricultural Policy
CSFs	The Community Support Frameworks
EAGGF	European Agricultural Guidance and Guarantee Fund
EC	European Community
ECSC	European Steel and Coal Community
ECU	European Currency Unit
EEC	European Economic Community
EIB	European Investment Bank
EMS	European Monetary System
EMU	Economic and Monetary Union
ERDF	European Regional Development Fund
ESF	European Social Fund
FRG	Federal Republic of Germany
GATT	General Agreement on Tariffs and Trade
GDP	Gross Domestic Product
GDR	German Democratic Republic
IMP	Integrated Mediterranean Programme
NUTS	Nomenclature of Territorial Statistical Units
OECD	Organisation for Economic Co-operation and Development
R&D	Research and Development
SEA	Single European Act
SME	Small and Medium-sized Enterprises
TEPSA	Trans-European Policy Studies Association

Economic and social cohesion and the Structural Funds: an introduction

Achille Hannequart

As is the case with many national states or federations, the European Community (EC) is characterised by wide disparities in the development level of its regions. This problem became more acute when the Community decided to progress towards a full and unified internal market: it was feared that these disparities could become larger and so jeopardise the aims of the internal market and the cohesion of the Community itself. Furthermore, the member states had a long tradition of regional policy which could therefore be considered valid in its own right.

Economic and social cohesion is indeed recognised in the Single Act, Article 130A, as a major aim of Community policy, especially under the aspect of reducing the gap between the most-developed and the least-developed areas of the Community. Article 130B presents the instruments through which this objective shall be attained:

- the conduct and co-ordination of economic policy by the member states and the adaptation of Community policies in such a way that the objectives mentioned in Article 130A will be achieved;
- the combined use of the Structural Funds, the European Investment Bank and other structural instruments to foster economic and social cohesion in a more specific type of policy. The Structural Funds are the European Regional Development Fund (ERDF), the European Social Fund (ESF) and the European Agricultural Guidance and Guarantee Fund (EAGGF).

There are therefore two ways by which economic and social cohesion can be achieved. This justifies the division of this book into two main parts:

- the place of the Structural Funds in the general economic policies of the member states and the Community and their links to them;

- the way in which the Structural Funds are operated to reach the assigned objective.

A clear link exists between these two problems. Even if the Structural Funds are a well-integrated part of Community policy, their effect could be invalidated if they were not properly operated. Similarly, even if the Structural Funds are properly operated, their effect could be invalidated if other Community policies acted in the opposite direction.

It is worth recalling at this stage the main steps of the reform so as to keep in mind a general reference framework.

In February 1987, the European Commission presented its communication: 'The Single Act: a New Frontier for Europe' where the main guidelines for the Community's structural policy were outlined.

The reform could only make sense if the available funds were substantially increased: in February 1987, the Council decided to double the overall budget for the Structural Funds by 1993.

In June and December 1988, the Council approved the legal instruments to be used and followed in the future operations of the Funds, namely (see appendices):

- Regulation 2052/88 of 24 June 1988, which is a 'framework regulation' giving the main principles of the reform;
- Regulation 4253/88 of 19 December 1988, which is a 'co-ordination framework' measure addressing the problems of co-ordination between the Funds and with the European Investment Bank and other structural instruments;
- Regulations 4254/88, 4255/88 and 4256/88 concern the ERDF, the ESF and the EAGGF. They define the objectives to which each Fund is linked and the way each Fund has to be operated.

In this general review of the problem, I shall first look at the relation between the Structural Funds and Community policies and then discuss their nature and implementation. Finally, I will propose some tentative conclusions on the future of the system.

Structural Funds and Community Policies

Part I of this book begins with a contribution by Rory O'Donnell on the regional effects of economic integration, more particularly in the framework of Economic and Monetary Union (EMU). Although the contribution takes its inspiration from the case of Ireland, the problem is examined from a general point of view.

The author first discusses the current arguments concerning the regional effects of economic integration and takes issue on two points with the reasoning in the Delors Report:

• the conflicting views between the traditional theory and the modern theory of international trade do not warrant optimistic conclusions about the positive effects of economic integration on regional disparities:
• technical progress is not certain to make concentration of activity less likely. Radical improvements in communication may technically reduce the significance of distance but this does not mean that they reduce its economic significance.

In his conclusions, O'Donnell writes:

After consideration of all the arguments, our general conclusions must be that the long-run benefits of market completion are likely to be unevenly distributed – with the greatest benefits accruing to regions in which industries with economies of scale and highly-innovative sectors are most prevalent. Consequently, completion of the internal market should not be expected to narrow the income disparities between regions in the EC, let alone bring about convergence.

But the author insists also that this is not a sufficient reason not to proceed towards Economic and Monetary Union. The conclusion is the same if another aspect of the problem is introduced: the loss of exchange rate autonomy. The author finds the argument not to be theoretically valid. Furthermore, the argument is no longer used as such in practice.

The problem therefore remains that regional disparities in the Community may continue or may even widen. Therefore it becomes necessary to look at policies which are able to attenuate them. The author discusses four possibilities in this regard:

• structural policies;
• macroeconomic co-ordination;
• budgetary and fiscal transfers;
• differential application of policies.

Let us look rapidly at each of these possibilities, albeit in a different order to that adopted in O'Donnell's contribution.

Co-ordinated macroeconomic policy is usually needed to achieve sustained growth but nothing in it, at the logical or empirical level, makes it able to reduce substantial regional disparities.

Structural Funds are a more specific instrument to deal with the problem but it is difficult to ascertain their potential impact for two reasons:

- empirically and in the past, it has proved difficult to disentangle the specific effects of regional policies from the many factors that have influenced the European economy in the last two decades. In any case, statistical analyses available do not show a clear and definite trend towards regional convergence;
- the volume of the Structural Funds is very limited and doubts may be easily formulated concerning the efficiency of their implementation. This may be specially true if they have to foster 'indigenous growth', whose ingredients are complex and multiple.

Another possibility would be to use economic policies in a differential fashion so as to adapt them to regional peculiarities. It seems to me that there are good economic and political reasons for exploring this possibility:

- economically, differences in the structural endowments between countries or areas may call for different systems of organisation or different forms and degrees of incentives. To take only a few examples, the conditions for research and development or environmental protection differ between regions;
- politically, as the politicians of member states are elected by their regional or national constituency, they must be answerable to what people think and want. And this may be different from area to area!

O'Donnell justly underlines the practical difficulties of this sort of differentiation because it could frustrate the achievement of the internal market. It can also be added that politicians will not easily accept easier conditions for other states, with the consequence that economic activity could be made easier there. This has been the case for environmental policy for which the Single Act provides that high levels of protection must be targeted.

We face in this respect the difficult problem of the uniformity of norms and regulations. Uniformity or even similarity is not always necessary. Furthermore, it should be noted that variations among American states remain high although they are considered to form a unified internal market. Possibly, easy interstate transfers create a powerful pressure there towards 'useful convergence'. But the mobility between European states is currently weaker than in the United States and the effect of this factor of 'competitive convergence' may therefore be lessened.

I would like to return at this point to the role of the Structural Funds. If the state of affairs is as described, the Structural Funds could be considered as an instrument to foster this policy differentiation by other means, that is, through activating certain types of initiatives or lowering the costs of others. For example, research and development aids could be delivered on easier terms and environment protection costs could be covered by more generous subsidies. The link between the Structural Funds policy and other Community policies appears clearly here but the issue has mainly been considered from the point of view of competition policy.

The Structural Funds also have a budgetary dimension. But even though the volume of the Structural Funds has been increased, they remain only a part of the Community's expenditure policy and participate in its shortcomings. The main points discussed in O'Donnell's contribution are the importance of a new assignment of policy functions and the importance of having a central budget of some significance.

This link between budgetary policy and the Structural Funds is studied more extensively in Dieter Biehl's contribution. It may be said that the problem is looked upon from a federalist point of view which is based on previous works by the author (Biehl 1990).

In his contribution, the author first sets out the principles of a sound federalist budgetary policy and considers how they may apply to our problem, mainly as far as fair burden-sharing is concerned.

At the public finance level, the essence of the Structural Funds is to effect a financial transfer from the richer countries in the Community to the poorer ones. This transfer must not be considered as a zero-sum game. On the contrary, the author insists that it makes clear economic sense. Richer areas generate savings in excess of their needs. The savings may then be channelled towards the poorer countries so as to give them the resources to buy products, services and equipment in the richer ones. Therefore, the financial flows through the Structural Funds do not impoverish countries: they are the way through which an overall high rate of growth can be maintained and an international equilibrium can be preserved.

Let us also add that these financial flows may also stem from the private sector through private international investments. It is nevertheless not sure whether these funds will be sufficient, will go to the most backward areas or will cover the most appropriate fields for long-term indigenous development. It is here that the Structural Funds may play an irreplaceable role: their use would therefore have to be linked to some sort of long-term development theory.

It is now time to return to the macroeconomic problem of public finance. The central thesis of Biehl's contribution is that the Community budget has a regressive character. This regressive character comes from the nature of the revenue sources and from the nature of certain expenses, mainly those resulting from the Common Agricultural Policy (CAP).

In this framework, the Structural Funds appear as a way to redress this bias. But if they point in the right direction, their volume is too small to change the situation significantly. To give them their proper impact would require changing the general financing system of the Community, reconsidering economic policies which prove to be regressive in character and finally, but at another level, enhancing the efficiency of the Structural Funds themselves.

As for the general financing system of the Community, Biehl makes his interesting proposal for a progressive Community surcharge to national income and corporation taxes. The system should have two main advantages:

- endowing the EC with a progressive revenue source and therefore eliminating the regressive bias inescapable in the current revenue system;
- improving the decision-making process by linking the revenue and expenditure sides of the budget separately at the Community and national levels.

But Biehl introduces an interesting argument at this point by advancing that preferences are not yet sufficiently harmonised in the European Community so as to permit a mature federal system wherein each one is sure that the money will be spent in accordance with generally accepted principles. A practical consequence of this idea could be that the Structural Funds will keep their importance in the years ahead.

The argument may be related to the way in which economic theory discusses the subsidy issues in national economies (Hannequart 1985), more particularly the choice between subsidy in cash or subsidy in kind. The best economic case may be made for subsidies in cash because they increase the welfare of the recipients most. But society may be primarily interested in the recipients consuming specific types of goods, such as health or housing: it may then refuse to offer cash subsidies but agree on subsidies linked to some sort of utilisation.

The first part of this book is concluded with a contribution by Alain Buzelay on the prerequisites for Community cohesion. Community cohesion is an easy catchword but for this reason some reflection about its meaning must be in order.

At the practical level, the author looks first at the origin of the regional disparities and at their consequences. These consequences appear sufficiently far reaching to require correction. The author shows then how national and Community regional policies have, at different periods and through different instruments, intertwined to tackle the problem.

The reasoning at the theoretical level is much more difficult: on which theoretical principles is it possible to base redistribution policy? Three main theories are examined: the traditional welfare theory, the new welfare theory and the collective property theory. Their lesson is not clear cut but positive analysis reinforces the case for redistribution.

IMPLEMENTATION OF THE STRUCTURAL FUNDS

The second part of the book is devoted to a preoccupation which was frequently alluded to in the previous contributions: the fate of the reform of the Structural Funds also depends on the appropriateness of the measures and the efficiency of their implementation.

This part begins with a contribution where Eneko Landaburu gives a description of the reform of the Structural Funds. The general philosophy of the reform was to concentrate on specific areas and for specific objectives to establish an assortment of actions corresponding to Community priorities and defined in partnership between the Community, the regions and the national states so as to give the areas a greater development potential and to integrate them more efficiently in the Community market. The costs of the measures would be shared out between the Community and the regions or national states. The Community could add its own 'Community initiatives' for which specific funding was provided.

The reform of the Structural Funds may be analysed under three main headings: the objectives, the principles, the implementation system.

It is worth recalling at the beginning of this book the main objectives that were to be pursued:

Objective 1: Promoting development of regions which are lagging behind globally in comparison with some Community average;

Objective 2: Restructuring industrialised areas in decline;

Objective 3: Combating long-term unemployment;

Objective 4: Integrating young people in the labour market;

Objective 5: (a) Adjusting agricultural structures to better fit the reform of the Common Agricultural Policy;

(b) Enhancing development in the less-favoured rural areas.

Objectives 1, 2 and 5(b) are regionally-targeted: this made it necessary to define criteria for eligibility of regions or areas. The other objectives have a more horizontal character.

The principles upon which the reform is based may be listed under four main headings:

- Concentration of the Community interventions on regions or areas determined in accordance with Community criteria.
- Co-ordination of the measures under the three main Funds, the European Investment Bank and other structural instruments.
- Partnership between the Community and the regional or national public authorities for choosing the main lines of action and sharing the costs.
- Additionally, to make sure that Community appropriations result in at least an equivalent increase in the total amount of official national or local interventions.

The implementation system proceeded through two main stages: regional plans and Community Support Frameworks.

Pursuant to Article 5 of the co-ordinating regulation, the member states submitted plans where they set out the needs of the eligible areas. These plans were then discussed under the partnership principle to choose the main lines of action and to organise their financing through Community and other financial contributions. Finally, operational plans could determine how objectives would be implemented.

Three contributions analyse how the reform of the Structural Funds has been put into operation in the case of the lagging areas, the declining industrialised areas and the rural areas.

Urzainqui and de Andrés present the case of the lagging regions of the Community. There, the policies must 'on the one hand, remove the obstacles preventing take-off and, on the other hand, create suitable conditions for self-sustained growth'. Two main problems appear in this case: the low level of general infrastructure and the lack of initiative.

The problem is totally different for the declining industrialised areas whose case is presented in Hannequart's contribution. Infrastructures generally exist. Initiatives are potentially available due to a long industrial tradition, but they have to be reoriented towards new innovative capacities. The analysis is consequently focused on the necessary transformation of the productive system, the ways in which the Structural Funds respond to this need and the conditions of success.

Rural areas have been looked at by Denis Lucey. This is a new policy field for the European Community and a most difficult one. No single approach is obvious for these areas in a period of high technology and service development. Furthermore, as the author shows, these areas have to respond to various types of pressures which differ largely as to their situation and endowments. A global view across all the sectors of each rural area is absolutely necessary to overcome the compartmentalised or single-sector approaches that have been traditional in the past.

THE FUTURE OF ECONOMIC AND SOCIAL COHESION

The necessary point of departure in considering the Structural Funds is the choice by the Community, in the Single Act, of economic and social cohesion (under the aspect more particularly of some sort of regional equilibrium) as a basic aim for Community policy.

This is a political fact which reflects the way in which our society sets its values but also the way in which the Community political system is construed. This political system is still in many regards a multinational system where member states have their say and keep overall sovereignty. The poorer nations may be expected to press for the continuation of various forms of redistribution as an equilibrium price for their full participation in general Community policy and, more particularly in the achievement of the internal market. This pressure will be felt more intensively in a multinational negotiation system than in a pure parliamentary system leading generally to some 'middle-class' majority.

On the other hand, three to five years is too short a period of time to obtain tangible results. The structural transformation of regions lagging far behind, the development of rural areas on new bases and the rejuvenation of declining industrial centres are long-term processes whose take-off alone may take a longer time. The pressure may therefore be expected to stay in the years ahead.

But we also know that policies may wear out in the course of time because they were, from the beginning, token policies or because implementing them appears to be too difficult – similarly, failures in the implementation of the Structural Funds may lead donor countries to consider them as an unnecessary waste of resources and even arouse opposition to them.

Nevertheless, the abandonment of economic and social cohesion would be a great loss to the Community. It would leave whole lagging regions or areas in decline to their own fate and, more significantly, jeopardise an important element of Community philosophy. It is to be hoped that the European Parliament, which is the guardian of European democratic philosophy at the Community level, will oppose this evolution.

If the political objective of economic and social cohesion must remain a basic feature of the Community system, the endeavour will have to be continued. Some reflections on the future of the Structural Funds should therefore be in order. These reflections may in turn strengthen the feeling that the Structural Funds are an important part of the Community system, whatever form they may take.

Integrating the Structural Funds and Community policies

The first main problem is the relation between specific Structural Fund actions and general budgetary redistribution. Three reasons at least militate for maintaining a decisive role for the Structural Funds as an expression of Community policy.

First, the Commission, as a supranational body, is best placed for defining policies that correspond to current international trends or what could be called 'industrial modernity' and for associating the member states and regions in their implementation. As a counterpoint, the views in the regions may be biased by factors which originate in their traditional economic structures and are expressed in outdated demands by pressure groups. The dialogue between the Commission and the regions is a major asset, although a difficult one because it may put into question outmoded behaviour or reactions. Furthermore, the Commission has greater political autonomy *vis-à-vis* the regions than is the case for the national states.

Second, there are also specific objectives to which member states may not pay due attention beause they transcend their borders or are not politically rewarding. The main example is the internationalisation or Europeanisation of firms which is necessary both for increasing their industrial and innovative capacity and for enlarging the industrial base of the Community economic system.

This presents no problem for the largest firms which are fully equipped to engage in this trend. But for medium-sized firms, transaction costs remain high: finding a partner in another country, making the necessary arrangements, proceeding to the resulting new investments are not easy processes. If we take the poorer areas of the Community, these costs may become prohibitive.

Finally, if the achievement of the Single Market continues to progress, as will certainly be the case, and if it continues to insist on the similarity of norms between countries, some ways will have to be found to make it easier for the less-developed countries to implement these norms or to alleviate their costs to them. This could be done for each policy directly but this fragmentation would make a mess of the whole system and could be politically unacceptable to the other countries. The discussions during the negotiation of the Single Act about the proper level of environment to be maintained show how the problem may become sensitive. The Structural Funds may be a way to combine a certain uniformity of the norms with flexibility in their implementation.

The Structural Funds in their current conception and application may be very far from these conditions but, if they are right, it must be a major preoccupation to make the system responsive to them. There is another aspect to be considered. The Structural Funds are also part of the general Community redistributive system whose objectives may be achieved through the revenue side or the expenditure side. The basic fact is that the financing system of the Community is regressive and that some of the expenses are also highly regressive.

There may be a certain trade-off between Structural Funds redistribution and general budgetary redistribution. If budgetary redistribution is low, it may be compensated by the Structural Funds but their volume is too small to have an appreciable effect in this regard. If the Community decided to increase its budgetary redistribution, it could be thought that redistribution through the Structural Funds would be less needed. But, from the Community point of view, this would be counterbalanced by the loss of the Community's own objective.

Before speaking about such a trade-off, we should recognise that there is an equilibrium combination of Structural Funds redistribution and budgetary redistribution. My guess, which seems to be substantiated by some of the contributions, is that we are a long way off this equilibrium point and that the proper level of both forms of redistribution is still manifestly too low.

Implementing the Structural Funds

The volume of the Structural Funds is one problem; their use is another. There is a common interest to the Community that the Structural Funds should be used with as much efficiency as possible and in accordance with the guidelines that have been defined in partnership with the national and regional authorities.

Things are less clear at the level of the national states. These are surely interested in improved development of their problem areas: if the Community interventions are well designed, they have an interest in implementing them. But, from a more short-term viewpoint, they may also consider this supplementary funding as something they may dispose of to placate specific interests, covertly follow their own policies or simply finance developments under way. They may then run the risk that donor countries become weary of this sort of redistribution.

Furthermore, any researcher in public policy knows that there is, for many and often inescapable reasons, a large gap between policy formulation and policy implementation. This gap was highlighted some time ago in a classic study by Pressman and Wildawski (1979), whose subtitle is particularly evocative as regards our problem: 'How greater expectations in Washington are dashed in Oakland'. Nevertheless, for reasons that remain unclear, public authorities are not keenly interested in implementation studies. They prefer evaluation studies that are probably more innocuous.

We must therefore be modest when criticising the efficiency of the reform of the Structural Funds policy. The experience was nevertheless not entirely new to the Community. Even before the 1984 reform, the European Regional Development Fund (ERDF) had experimented with various forms of integrated approach upon which the Court of Auditors made a special report (OJ C 188 of 18.7.88). The 1984 Regulation (OJ L 169 of 28.6.84), which reformed the ERDF, extended its possibilities, notably through actions of 'endogenous development'. These possibilities could be joined to constitute programmes of Community interest or national programmes of Community interest, depending on the degree of relation with Community policy.

The same Regulation gave some priority to integrated development operations where the various Community Funds could combine and in which the ERDF could participate. The most well-known case is the Integrated Mediterranean Programmes (IMPs), instituted by a regulation of 1985 (OJ L 197 of 27.7.85) and whose functioning was made the object of a special report by the Court of Auditors, adopted in September 1990. The Court of Auditors' assessment of the effectiveness of the system is not very favourable. But what is of the greatest interest to us is that the Court of Auditors underlines that the main difficulties experienced with the IMPs are also to be found, *mutatis mutandis*, in the system established by the reform of the Structural Funds.

Various aspects of the efficiency problems in the management of the Structural Funds have been examined by Hannequart (1990) in a study for the Commission concerning industrialised areas in decline.

More generally, the problem of efficiency may be subdivided into two sub-problems:

- Is the nature of the measures appropriate to the transformations needed? The answer to this question depends on determining the kind of transformations, eliciting the processes through which these transformations may be achieved, designing the measures to influence the processes;
- Are the measures well implemented? The answer to this question depends on the extent to which the responsible authorities and the economic and social operators participate in the process in the way expected of them.

Implementation is concerned with the second aspect. In so far as the Structural Funds are concerned, three positive points must first be underlined:

- The Community Funds have been concentrated on rather small areas so that their effect will have more relative weight and their visibility for economic operators will increase;
- The Community Support Frameworks have given the national and regional authorities the opportunity to discuss their common needs, to adjust to each other and to integrate their actions;
- The monitoring committees have introduced into the process a monitoring and evaluation system that is designed to follow the experience on the ground.

The success of the Structural Funds will probably depend on overcoming two difficulties.

The first one is the grass-root co-ordination of the measures contained in the plans. A co-ordination has been made at the Community level in that resources are channelled to the areas for innovation, training, investment, and so on. But the problem at the grass-root level is more individual: it may be a specific firm that needs, at the same time, an innovative breakthrough, new forms of training, venture capital, and so on. The problem remains as to how the various interventions may be channelled to the point of demand. This may be difficult because the potential user is not aware of these possibilities and because responsibility for the various instruments is inevitably shared out among various institutions.

The second difficulty comes from the fact that there is also a link here between supply and demand. Through instruments provided for in the Structural Funds, the Community increases the supply of interventions. But this supply has to be met by an increasing new demand if it is to have any effect. However, that demand is often lacking in these areas!

A main condition is therefore to increase demand and this can best be conducted in the actual area where economic operators live and make their plans. But the area may cover many local authorities and, at a higher level, be only a part of the area covered by regional authorities. It is therefore not at all sure that the appropriate information will be disseminated to frame new initiatives towards the proper objectives and to reduce the transaction costs of participating in them for economic operators. Had they greater awareness and information, they could undertake the grass-root co-ordination by themselves with the help of the administrative organisations responsible.

Another way to proceed is to develop the intermediation system as a link between supply and demand. But this may be difficult in our field. Intermediation develops best for high-cost transactions (high-technology transfers) or numerous standard transactions (financial transactions). The advantage of a market system is nevertheless to increase the number of people interested in spreading the process and to give them an interest in doing so. The manner in which the Sprint programme operates may be taken as an example: it gives the consultants working for medium-sized enterprises in various countries the opportunity to meet and discuss possibilities of co-operation between the firms they are working with. Some sort of market system could also be fostered in our field through consultants or banks.

Co-ordinating the measures at the grass-root level, making people conscious of new needs and possibilities and activating the demand are tasks that require the setting up of some sort of management system which must be endowed with resources, continuity of action and responsibility. This simultaneously raises technical and financial considerations. The best way to introduce them is to have recourse to two remarks by the Court of Auditors in its annual report for the financial year 1989:

- Point 7.95 (page 134): 'The Commission should do more to ensure that integration is real, in particular by ensuring that effective management structures are set up and by granting them definite preferential treatment. This approach appears more likely to convince the national authorities involved of the need for greater coordination';
- Point 7.122 (page 137): 'As regards financial management . . . Neither the system of commitment nor that of payment, nor consequently the Community accounts enable the Commission to have an accurate idea of the extent of its obligations and of the level of implementation of its operations'.

The flaws in the management system probably explain the Community's insistence on monitoring and assessment. This insistence becomes still more understandable when responsibility for management and control is known to lie primarily with the member states. But monitoring and assessment are probably very poor substitutes for efficient management design, save when conditions for effective monitoring are present.

It is at this point that the monitoring committees intervene. The Commission stressed in its decision that these committees should be set up to monitor the programmes but doubts may be raised as to the efficiency of the system.

First, monitoring committees must meet in principle twice yearly. Their role and composition may vary from place to place according to circumstances, initiatives of the member states, delays or difficulties in the programmes, and so on. There is therefore much uncertainty and vagueness in the process.

Second, monitoring implies the control of physical indicators to be monitored in relation to what was provided for. Regrettably, as the actions are multiple and complex, and as the rules are cumbersome and the standards ill defined, uncertainty and vagueness are again present.

But when uncertainty or vagueness are present, sanctions for noncooperative behaviour are difficult to apply and it may even be difficult to assess the degree of co-operation. Regional and national authorities are fully aware of the process and they could use it to justify their own reticence. In these circumstances, the deceptive assessment which the Court of Auditors formulated for the Integrated Mediterranean Programmes in its annual report is possibly inescapable: 'In fact, in practice, the work of the monitoring committees usually consists in noting the problems encountered, without really promoting the execution of the programmes' (point 7.75, page 132).

Enlarging the field of structural action

The reform of the Structural Funds has co-ordinated for specific objectives and on specific areas a rich diversity of economic instruments. On the other hand, there are many policy measures in the European Economic Community (EEC) that have a similar structure but which, as special programmes, do not fall under the Structural Funds. These programmes (examples are the Comett or Sprint programmes) have often been designed by the Community to reflect the newest developments in industrial restructuring and innovative behaviour.

It is therefore paradoxical that, for institutional reasons, these programmes are almost totally absent from the Community Support Frameworks while they are recognised at the same time as catalysts to economic modernity!

Let us take an example. Almost by definition, eligible regions or areas suffer from inadequacies or inefficiencies in their productive system. These inadequacies or inefficiencies can be reduced or reversed through links with foreign firms. This form of co-operation would also lead to a much-needed technological and financial transfer, supplementing the pure budgetary transfers. Now, the Community operates several programmes of this kind such as Euro-partnership or Sprint. It would seem normal and even necessary that an effort be made under these headings in the eligible areas but it is not understood as such under the Structural Funds policy.

Surely these independent policies have to be pursued in their own regulatory framework. Furthermore, associating them with the action would make the co-ordination task even more burdensome.

Nevertheless, Article 130B provides that member states will conduct and co-ordinate their policies, taking into acount the objectives of Article 130A, that is, economic and social cohesion. Similarly, the Article provides that common and internal market policies will have to be operated in the same framework.

The problem comes from the fact that 'common' policies have different effects in various regional environments because structural endowments and transaction costs are different. A programme to contribute to the Europeanisation of small and medium-sized firms may succeed in an active and dynamic environment because there are many of them and decision systems are flexible and information flows are dense. In a less-developed area, these conditions may not obtain: as a result, what are now called 'transaction costs' will be high and will curb initiatives. The link of the 'functional policies' with the Structural Funds appears to be not necessarily to adjust them according to circumstances but to reduce the associated transaction costs at the appropriate points.

Sound reflections in this field will only be rewarding if we succeed in bringing some order to this mass of Community instruments which are constantly increasing in number. The only way to gain some reassurance would be to regroup them under general headings referring to categories of strategies.

If we look in this way at the upgrading of industrial capacity in a given area, we could use the following headings (for each one we briefly comment on some Community programmes related to the heading):

- stirring up the level of information and stimulation: as examples, we could offer the 'Euro-Info Centres' and the action programme to prepare small and medium-sized firms for the internal market of 1993;
- raising the technological and organisational level of the firms: we could cite here the Enterprise and Innovation Centres, the Comett programme, the co-financing of innovation and technology transfer;
- diffusing the recourse to high-level producer services, in fields such as management consultancy, marketing, accounting;
- increasing transnational co-operation between firms: the programmes which can be listed under this heading include Euro-partnership, Sprint, Business Co-operation Network;
- financing investments: various types of grants or loans may be offered for investment but also in the form of capital venture or seed capital funds.

Such a grouping could help understanding and controlling the way an area copes with its development problem in a larger framework than the one given by the Structural Funds themselves.

REFERENCES

Biehl, D. (1990) 'Financing the EC budget' in Remy Prudhomme (ed.) 'Public finance with several levels of government', International Institute of Public Finance, 46th Congress, Brussels.

Hannequart, A. (1985) *Economie des interventions sociales*, Economica.

Hannequart, A. (1990) 'Stratégies managériales et coordination des Fonds Structurels dans les zones de vieille industrialisation', Rapport pour la Commission des Communautés Européennes, Trans-European Policy Studies Association (TEPSA), Brussels.

Pressman, J.L. and Wildawski, Q. (1979): *Implementation*, 2nd edn, University of California Press, Berkeley.

Part I

Economic and social cohesion: Community policies and the Structural Funds

Chapter 1

Policy requirements for regional balance in economic and monetary union

Rory O'Donnell

This chapter considers the regional effects of economic integration and the range of policies which are available to achieve regional balance in a European economic and monetary union. The first section identifies some conflicting views on the regional effects of integration and argues that benefits of market completion are likely to be unevenly distributed – with the greatest benefits acccruing to regions in which industries with economies of scale and highly innovative sectors are most prevalent. In addition, it is argued that it would be dangerous to assume that macroeconomic shocks with asymmetric regional effects will not occur in economic and monetary union (EMU). The second section is concerned with the broad outlines of a Community system of policy to achieve regional balance. Four possible types of Community policy to assist convergence are identified – structural policies, macroeconomic co-ordination, budgetary transfers and differential application of other Community policies – and their merits assessed. The central conclusion is that all four types of policy are necessary in the Community now. In the final section these arguments are used to assess the discussion of cohesion and cohesion policies in the recent Delors Report on Economic and Monetary Union.

THE REGIONAL EFFECTS OF INTEGRATION

The regional distribution of economic activity and income in the Community is clearly of great importance to all member states and regions. Not surprisingly, it has played a significant role in deliberations on the costs and benefits of economic and monetary union.

In textbook discussions on this subject, it is considered that the allocation of economic activity between the member states would differ depending on whether the states had formed a customs union, a common market, or an economic and monetary union. This is because, in the textbook approach, the degree of mobility of goods, labour and capital is distinctly different in each model. This difference is often considered by some to have implications for the pattern of economic activity in different states of a monetary union. In particular, it has been argued that adherence to a single monetary standard will impose costs on economically weaker states and regions. We discuss this question in more detail later. The relevant point is that, given these textbook definitions, the forces influencing the pattern of activity are likely to be different in the three cases – customs union, common market and economic and monetary union.

In a recent assessment of the relative regional implications of a customs union and an economic and monetary union, Ireland's tripartite National Economic and Social Council did not place major emphasis on the macroeconomic dimension of the regional effects of EMU. In particular, in its Report *Ireland in the European Community*, it did not place great emphasis on the traditional argument that EMU would be especially difficult for weaker regions because of the deflationary effects of adhering to a uniform monetary standard. Consequently, it departed somewhat from the textbook view in arguing that there are a number of reasons why the effects of market forces in shaping the pattern of activity across various member states and regions may not, in fact, be very different at different stages of integration.

It is most important to stress, however, that this view did not imply that no regional difficulties or imbalances are likely to arise in the integration process viewed as a whole. In fact, there is every reason to believe that the effects of integration have been, and will be, regionally uneven and that other forces in the world economy also create regional imbalances. Consequently, in formulating a policy system for the European Community, an important question is: what are the policy requirements for regional balance in a European economic and monetary union? In this section we briefly discuss the conflicting arguments concerning the regional effects of economic integration and proceed in the next section to indicate what policy approaches and systems seem necessary to secure regional balance.

Tendencies for regional convergence and divergence

One reason why the textbook theory of economic integration viewed monetary integration as more likely to exacerbate regional problems was that the relative costs and benefits of a customs union, a common market and an economic and monetary union were assessed by applying the traditional theory of international trade. That traditional theory was based on very restrictive assumptions and these had a major role in generating the benign view of trade in the conventional literature. In recent years, significant developments have occurred in the theory of international trade and integration. The new approaches take account of important real world phenomena such as economies of scale, external economies, the market power of firms and learning by doing. The important point is that these new approaches alter somewhat our views of the gains from trade and integration (see NESC 1989).

Limitations of space preclude a detailed discussion of how these new trade theories alter our views of the gains from trade. However, for a reason that will emerge presently, the issue is an important one and a brief summary of the position is warranted.

In general, the new approaches to trade indicate that the overall gains from trade and integration are potentially larger than in the conventional analysis. In addition, the new theories provide some reasons to believe that the costs of adjusting to free trade will be *more evenly* distributed between regions, and some reasons why the long-run benefits of trade will be *less evenly* distributed. Krugman summarises this difference by saying that trade based on economies of scale, the market power of firms and product differentiation 'probably involves less conflict of interest *within* countries and more conflict *between* countries than conventional trade' (Krugman 1987; this statement is explained in a non-technical way in Chapter 2 of NESC 1989).

The theory of regional economics contains a formidable list of reasons why advanced economic activity will tend to concentrate in certain regions. Among the facts making for concentration are economies of scale, economies of agglomeration and the division of labour, advantageous labour market characteristics, innovation leadership and external economies associated with the generation of knowledge. There are also forces for diffusion of manufacturing and other activities. Among these are the emergence of a new spatial division of labour, improvements in transport and telecommunications in peripheral regions and congestion in central regions. However, our analysis suggests that, in the coming years, these forces, while they will certainly be at work, will not be sufficiently strong, nor sufficiently convergence-generating, to overcome the forces for concentration.

Now, this *general* view of regional developments is one which finds a clear echo in the theory of *trade* and the study of European market *integration*. Robson (1987) says that 'the formation of an economic grouping is likely to enhance the forces of polarisation at country level'. Eaton (1987) considers that 'the benefits of trade may not be shared symmetrically . . . with the country exporting the commodities whose production involves greater scale economies typically benefitting more'. Krugman (1987) tells us that while scale economies and oligopoly increase the *potential* gains from trade, 'they also open up some possible ways in which trade can have adverse effects'. Padoa-Schioppa (1987), in his important study of the Community system, considers that 'the spatial distribution of such gains is less certain and is unlikely to be even'. Finally, and specifically on the completion of the internal market, Pelkmans and Robson (1987) say that the structural problems of the less-advanced member states 'will almost certainly be accentuated by an approach to fully-fledged industrial market integration'.

A different view of the likely regional distribution of gains from integration generally, and internal market specifically, was put forward in the 'Cecchini Report' (Emerson *et al.* 1988). There it is said that the *traditional* theory of international trade predicts vicious and virtuous cycles of regional decline and growth, and that the *new* approach predicts a more even distribution of the gains from trade and integration (pp.139–40). This argument assumes considerable importance because it is restated by President Delors (1989b). Indeed, having stated the view, Delors refers the reader to 'The economics of 1992' 'for a fuller presentation of these arguments and further references' (Delors 1989b: 83).

While there is some truth in the idea that in the new theories of trade, regional effects are *less predictable*, there is, in my view, no basis for the statement that an uneven distribution of benefits and costs is less likely. It can be shown that the view put forward in the Cecchini Report, and restated by Delors, is based on a misrepresentation of the traditional trade theory and a highly selective account of the new approach (see NESC 1989: 344–8). In fact, the new theory of trade takes account of those very features of the modern economy – increasing returns, external economies, the advantages of experience, monopoly power and the barriers to entry created by high capital and research and development (R&D) requirements – which were originally used to explain regional inequality and divergence. Contrary to the impression created by the Cecchini Report, it is those new theories which include the possibility of cumulative processes of growth and decline.

Another argument advanced by Delors in his essay on the regional implications of economic and monetary integration is that changes in technology and demand make concentration of economic activity less likely. He argues that, because of technical change, 'transport costs are becoming, on average, less important in the location of industrial production'. To some extent, this focus on transport costs reflects an equal emphasis on infrastructure, distance and access transport by some of those who argue that integration will bring about further concentration of economic activity (Doyle 1989: 75). However, two wrongs do not make a right; and the argument that technical and organisational change unambiguously reduce the forces making for geographic concentration of economic activity is highly debatable. For example, in discussing the regional implications of 1992, Pelkmans and Winter (1988) note that 'Although improved communications reduce the economic distance between the periphery and the core, they also currently generate economies of agglomeration'.

Overall, a more detailed consideration of the issues and a wider reading of the literature strongly suggests that it is too simplistic to infer that radical technical telecommunications and transport improvements, because they *technically* reduce the significance of distance, also reduce its overall *economic* significance, or cause a wider dispersal of activity and a convergence of regional economies. There is considerable evidence that the effects of the new technologies on the *scale* of firms and plants is highly complicated and depends on very *specific* features of the industry. It should come as no surprise that a similar conclusion applies to the effect of technical change on the *location* of activity (see Wadley 1986; Padoa-Schioppa 1987; Ergas 1984; Kaplinsky 1984; Borris *et al.* 1987; Sayer 1986; Cooke and Imrie 1989; Perez 1983; Dosi 1988 and Stopford and Turner 1985).

After consideration of all the arguments, our general conclusions must be that the long-run benefits of market completion are likely to be unevenly distributed – with the greatest benefits accruing to regions in which industries with economies of scale and highly-innovative sectors are most prevalent. Consequently, completion of the internal market should not be expected to narrow the income disparities between regions in the EC, let alone bring about convergence.

Having rejected President Delors's view on the likelihood of concentration of economic activity, I should add that one of the central propositions in his essay, 'Regional Implications of Economic and Monetary Integration', seems absolutely correct. He correctly took issue with the view that the existence of substantial structural differences between European regions was a reason *not to proceed* to economic and monetary union, as was suggested in some quarters. In advising their governments, social partners took a very similar view to President Delors and the Delors Committee on this issue. However, this has implications for the kinds of policies and policy frameworks which are needed *in* EMU if regional imbalances are to be minimised (see below).

Monetary union and the loss of exchange rate autonomy

It was stated at the beginning of this section that, in assessing the regional distribution of economic activity and income, little emphasis would be put on the regional effects of loss of exchange rate autonomy in an economic and monetary union. It is now necessary to say something about this issue.

The possible cost of losing discretion over the exchange rate was, for many years, the major issue in analyses of the costs and benefits of economic and monetary union (Corden 1972; Coffey 1977; Robson 1987). It is clear that, to some extent, the issue of whether monetary union would impose costs on weaker regions turns on the question of whether exchange rate devaluation can address the real problem of these regions. Initially, this was widely thought to be the case. However, the effectiveness of devaluation was subsequently questioned for both theoretical and empirical reasons. It is important to distinguish between the theoretically- and empirically-based scepticism about the ability of exchange rate devaluation to increase output and employment. The theoretically-based scepticism derived, in many cases, from adherence to the notion that the real economy in each country has a natural tendency to full employment and, consequently, it would be logically impossible for devaluation of the exchange rate, or any other macroeconomic policy, to increase output and employment. This is *not* the position which underlies the argument of this author. While we must share this scepticism about power of exchange rate policy to address regional problems, we must also note that both the theory and evidence on exchange rate changes and their real effects, if any, have, once again, become quite uncertain.

In the face of this considerable uncertainty, consideration of the costs and benefits of monetary union for a weaker region should take the following factors into account:

1 an adequately structured and rationally organised *economic* and monetary union would have a set of budgetary mechanisms which,

because of their interregional redistributive effects, would cushion regions from macroeconomic fluctuations and shocks at least as effectively as exchange rate movements do (see below);

2 without necessarily rejecting the notion that monetary integration, specifically adherence to a hard currency peg, can impose costs on weaker regions, a modern and flexible approach to trade and integration qualifies traditional views of the pattern and timing of the overall costs and benefits of integration. Specifically, it suggests that even *free trade* can generate large and unevenly distributed costs and benefits in both the short and long run. At the very least, this would take the emphasis off monetary integration as the step which raises problems for weaker economies;

3 many of the major forces which cause long-run regional concentration and diffusion will operate on an open economy, regardless of the monetary regime in place.

These points play an important role in the argument that leaders in less-developed member states, and states with serious regional problems, should strongly support moves to build a European economic and monetary union.

It is most important to realise that the arguments for the establishment of adequate budgetary mechanisms in an economic and monetary union do *not* depend on the argument that, in the absence of monetary union, exchange rate devaluation can generate an increase in output and employment in weaker countries and regions. It is sometimes thought that evidence of the limited effectiveness of exchange rate devaluation in increasing output and employment constitutes proof of the validity of the theory that the economy has a natural tendency to full employment and that balance of payments deficits are temporary and *purely* monetary phenomena. That idea is a logical fallacy. Regardless of the effectiveness or ineffectiveness of exchange rate devaluation in a customs union, there can, in an economic and monetary union, be both long-run and short-run problems which affect different regions differently, and which therefore generate regional macroeconomic imbalance. This, and the many other arguments considered in this chapter, justifies the establishment of a central system of public finance (see below).

In recent debates on European EMU, there is noticeably less discussion of the role of invisible and automatic shock absorbers than there was in previous periods of interest in EMU. This has recently been defended on the grounds that asymmetrical regional macroeconomic shocks are now much less likely than in the past. The convergence of national approaches to macroeconomic policy in recent years, and the success of the EMS, is cited as evidence in support of this view. The implicit assumption in this argument is that asymmetric shocks occurred in the past because of divergent macro-policy responses to external shocks such as the oil crises of the 1970s.

There are a number of reasons why it seems dangerous to assume that asymmetric shocks are altogether a thing of the past; perhaps that assumption should be viewed in the same light as the periodic notion that the trade cycle is dead. External shocks surely have asymmetric effects independent of policy responses to those shocks. Even if we were to accept, for the sake of argument, that asymmetric effects of *external* shocks are unlikely, this would not rule out differential macroeconomic experiences. As Katseli (1989) points out, intra-EC trade and financial flows are highly unbalanced. Alteration of these imbalances, without the use of exchange rate changes must, almost by definition, induce opposite effects in different EC countries. Indeed, more generally, differences in economic structures can imply that different countries respond differently to the same macroeconomic changes (Katseli 1989).

Furthermore, it can be argued, with some plausibility, that the experience of the EMS to date has depended on circumstances, such as the overvaluation of the dollar, which are very special indeed. Thus De Cecco (1989) sees great contradictions within the EMS which have, to date, been hidden, due to a uniquely favourable set of circumstances. Likewise, the extensive literature on the asymmetry of the EMS must surely support the view that asymmetric real macroeconomic experiences cannot be ruled out by assumption.

The burden of all these arguments is that, while limited weight should be put on arguments based on the loss of exchange rate autonomy and, in particular, the loss of the possibility of devaluation, earlier views on the necessity of a balancing fiscal mechanism in economic and monetary union retain a considerable part of their validity. As Samuel Brittan says in a recent article on economic and monetary union,

> The sense in which an element of common fiscal policy is required is best described by the term 'fiscal federalism' . . . A monetary union does not need a fully fledged federal government, but it will work best if there are enough EC-level taxes and transfers to provide a cushioning mechanism.
>
> (Brittan 1988)

Conclusion on the regional effects of integration

Our general conclusion must be that the benefits of market completion and monetary union are likely to be unevenly distributed – with the greatest benefits accruing to regions in which industries with economies of scale and highly innovative sectors are most prevalent. Consequently, completion of the internal market, or introduction of EMU, should not be expected to narrow the income disparities between regions in the EC, let alone bring about convergence. This conclusion is derived from an exhaustive analysis of traditional regional economic theory and the more recent developments in the theory of trade – only the bare bones of which were stated above (see NESC 1989). Our next task is to assess what this implies for Community policy.

COMMUNITY POLICIES FOR CONVERGENCE AND COHESION

Given these arguments about the tendencies to regional convergence and divergence in economic and monetary union, it seems clear that both the Community and the member states need to devise policies which will preserve regional balance and, if possible, create regional convergence. This chapter is concerned with Community rather than national policy and asks, in particular, what system of Community policy is necessary to achieve a regionally-balanced economic and monetary union.

We can identify four kinds of Community policy which could address regional issues and assist convergence and cohesion:

1 structural policies;
2 macroeconomic co-ordination;
3 budgetary or fiscal transfers;
4 differential application of other Community policies, such as agricultural policy or internal market policy.

It is important that both member states and the Community take a broad and realistic view of what can be, and is likely to be, achieved by each of these types of policies in the attempt to pursue economic and social cohesion. In the following subsections we consider each of these policies in order to assess its potential role. We conclude by outlining an overall system of Community policy.

Structural policies

In identifying the potential role of Community structural policy in an overall system of Community policy, we need, first, to analyse the effectiveness of past structural policy and then to assess the likely impact of structural policy in the coming years.

Empirical evidence on regional development

We begin our analysis of the effectiveness of Community structural policy with a brief review of the empirical evidence on regional disparities in the EC in recent years. The reports on the evolution of regional disparities which are cited below cannot, in general, be taken as a rigorous test of the effectiveness of Community structural policies and regional policy in particular. This is because the period under review, roughly the 1970s and 1980s, has seen a number of economic changes of major proportions – all of which are likely to have regional impacts. First, the period since the early 1970s has been one of severe economic disruption internationally, and this has prompted varied *national* responses. Second, there have been distinct alterations in the international division of labour following the rise of several Asian economies. Third, European economic integration deepened and widened. Finally, but on a scale which is incomparable with these three, there has been a Community regional policy in operation since 1975. All of these will certainly have influenced regional disparities and we cannot hope to disentangle their separate effects. Nevertheless, the broad trends identified in the empirical research on regional development provide a significant background against which to judge the effectiveness of regional policy.

A comprehensive statistical profile of the regions of the Community can be found in the second and third *Periodic Reports on the Social and Economic Situation and Development of the Regions of the Community*, produced in 1984 and 1987 respectively. Our concern here is merely the overall level of regional disparities and the trend towards convergence or divergence.

The 'Third Periodic Report' gave the following description of the pattern of *regional income disparities* in the Community after the enlargement to include Spain and Portugal: about half the Community population lives in regions whose per capita incomes lie within a band of ± 15 per cent around the Community average. *Below* this band, there are some forty regions, comprising about one-quarter of the

Community population. Closer examination reveals that this group is made up of *two* very unequal subgroups. About a dozen regions, accounting for 6 per cent of the Community population, have an income gap of 15 to 25 per cent, this group being a heterogeneous one that includes a number of regions with particular problems in the northern part of the Community. Clear signs of lagging development typify the second and larger subgroup, whose incomes are more than 25 per cent below the Community average. These regions comprise just under one-fifth of the Community population. They are all regions on the extreme southern and western periphery of the Community, with low average population density, a young and strongly-growing population and production that is still heavily geared towards agriculture. If one compares the ten weakest with the ten strongest regions in the Community as a whole, the disparity in incomes generated is a ratio of 1:3. There is, however, less homogeneity in recorded unemployment between these backward regions; on the one hand, there are considerable differences due to national structures and policies; on the other, there are forms of underemployment, in some cases substantial, due to agricultural structures and the lack of alternative employment.

The Commission has developed a composite measure of the intensity of regional problems. This measure, known as the 'synthetic index', combines measures of a region's economic strength and its labour market situation.[1] From its calculation of the synthetic index for the early to mid-1980s, the Commission has identified a group of regions with the highest intensity of regional problems. These are Greece, Ireland, the Mezzogiorno in Italy (excluding the Abruzzi), Portugal, Spain and Northern Ireland. A second smaller group of regions, also with relatively high levels of problem intensity was also identified. This consisted of the Abruzzi, six regions in the UK and two in Belgium. The first group of most disadvantaged regions are largely agricultural and are located on the southern and western periphery of the Community. By contrast, the second group are confronted with particular industrial adjustment problems.

Trends in regional disparities

For our present purposes, the most important questions concern the trends in regional and national disparities in the period since the inception of Community regional policy. The main indicators which have been used in the empirical literature are income per head, unemployment, employment and industrial structure. We now briefly report the trends which have been identified.

Studies of the evolution of national and regional incomes per head from 1969 to the present have identified two phases. From 1969 to approximately 1974, disparities between *national* levels of income (GDP) per head narrowed, but from 1975 onwards, these disparities widened slightly. By and large, disparities between *regional* income levels followed a similar pattern – though the narrowing of disparities in the early period was fairly limited. The turnaround from convergence to divergence was even more marked when unemployment rates are considered. Much of the convergence in the earlier period was the result of very strong growth in Spain, Portugal and Greece between 1960 and 1970 – though these countries were not members of the Community during that period.

More detailed analysis of the pattern of regional development has been undertaken by Keeble, Owens and Thompson of Cambridge University. Their report *Centrality, Peripherality, and EEC Regional Development* (1981a) was designed specifically to assess 'whether there exists a significant tendency towards increasing concentration of people and industry in the more central areas of the Community' and, consequently, it forms an important but by no means conclusive test of some of the arguments outlined above. In order to investigate this, they were asked to answer three related questions:

1 Do significant economic differences exist between the central and peripheral regions of the Community?
2 Are these different categories of regions evolving differently over time?
3 How far may observable differences be explained by, or related to, relative location within the Community?

Using a measure of *accessibility* or economic potential, they classified each EC Level-II region as 'central', 'intermediate' or 'peripheral'. These classifications were then used to investigate regional variations in economic performance and structure within the EC in the 1970s and early 1980s.

This analysis confirmed a clear trend towards widening centre–periphery disparities in economic performance during the 1970s. Subsequent research by Keeble, Offord and Walker (1986) repeated this analysis using 1983 data. This revealed that, unlike the period 1965 to 1979, between 1977 and 1983 the periphery was characterised by slightly *higher* rates of GDP growth than central regions. However, notwithstanding higher growth *rates* in peripheral regions, the absolute gap in *levels* of GDP per head between peripheral and central regions *widened* appreciably during this period.

These trends in income growth were related to a marked and intensifying centre–periphery difference in *regional economic structures* during the 1970s. After 1973, the demographic trends in the peripheral regions were markedly different to those in the central regions, with substantial population growth in the former but virtually no increase in the latter (see the Commission's Annual Economic Report 1988–89: 117–30). The economies of peripheral regions are significantly more dependent than central regions on agriculture, whereas central regions are significantly more specialised than peripheral regions in manufacturing and producer service industries.

Analysis of employment change revealed that, during the 1970s, *total* employment grew more rapidly in the periphery than in the centre. Moreover, this general finding masked significant differences within the periphery, which may have a bearing on policy. Specifically, the northern periphery succeeded better in maintaining employment than the southern (especially Italian) and, in their view, this suggests that national, and particularly Irish, regional policies have had some impact on the location of mobile manufacturing investment. Second, they note that 'Ireland has made considerable strides to improve its manufacturing structure' between 1973 and 1979 – something that was found also in Scotland and Northern England.

The more recent research by Keeble, Offord and Walker (sponsored by the European Commission's Directorate-General for Regional Policy) confirmed many of the results cited above. In particular, the differences in population growth, dependence on agriculture, specialisation in manufacturing and specialisation in producer and consumer services all remained true in the early 1980s. However, the relative rates of *change* in some of these variables were different in the later period. Trends in total employment in the years 1979–83 reveal a clear centre–periphery gradient, with virtually no growth in employment in the centre, but 14 per cent growth in the periphery. (However, the periphery was not homogeneous in this; there was above average growth in the Italian periphery and declining employment elsewhere.) Manufacturing employment decline was slower in the periphery (-2.7 per cent) than that in the intermediate (-6.6 per cent) or central (-11 per cent) regions.

One other new trend of considerable significance emerged. Although the peripheral regions were still found to have manufacturing structures significantly biased towards traditional industries, compared with intermediate or central regions, the *direction of change* in these structures was new. Unlike the situation in the 1970s, in the 1980s central regions recorded rapidly falling ratios of modern to traditional manufacturing industries, whereas peripheral regions have experienced increasing ratios, albeit from a very low base. In their view, 'both sets of EUR 10 regions are thus apparently now converging towards intermediate region values and the Community average' (Keeble, Offord and Walker 1986).

The empirical evidence cited in this section provides evidence of the extent of structural differences between the regions of the Community. It also provides evidence of the possibility of increasing disparities in incomes and unemployment and, at the same time, convergence in relative manufacturing structures.

Community regional policy to date

We cannot infer from absence of economic convergence that the Community's structural policies have failed altogether to influence the regional pattern of economic activity or income. However, it is now widely agreed that the Community's structural policies had a number of characteristics which severely limited their effectiveness in removing regional disparities. In this section we briefly outline these, drawing particular attention to the problems in Community regional policy.

One important feature that the three Structural Funds have in common is their small size relative to the total Community budget, relative to total Community GDP and, most significantly, relative to the scale of inequalities and structural problems in the European economy. Table 1.1 gives a breakdown of the Community budget in some representative years: 1972, 1980 and 1986. It shows, first and foremost, the extent to which the Community budget has been dominated by agricultural spending. Furthermore, only a very small fraction of that spending was on *structural* measures in agriculture – the vast bulk being price guarantee. Row no. 10 shows the total share of the Structural Funds – ERDF, ESF and Guidance Section of EAGGF – in the Community budget. The three Funds have increased from 4.1 per cent of Community spending in 1972, to 16.3 per cent in 1986, and are set to increase to 25 per cent in 1992. It should be recalled, however, that there was no Regional Development Fund until 1975, and it was its introduction which accounts for so much of the increased share of the

Table 1.1 Structure of the Community budget

		Shares in total expenditure (%)			Shares in Community GDP (%)		
		1972	1980	1986	1972	1980	1986
1	Agriculture and fishing of which	76.2	73.6	65.3	0.42	0.61	0.64
	1.1 price guarantee	75.0	69.7	62.4	0.42	0.58	0.61
	1.2 fishing	—	0.3	0.5	—	0.00	0.01
	1.3 structural guidance	1.2	3.6	2.4	0.00	0.03	0.02
2	Other sectoral policies R&D, transport, energy and other industries	3.6	1.9	2.3	0.02	0.02	0.02
3	Social Fund	2.9	4.7	7.2	0.02	0.04	0.07
4	Regional Fund	—	6.7	6.8	—	0.06	0.07
5	Mediterranean Programmes	—	—	0.4	—	0.00	0.004
6	Development and co-operation	6.1	3.1	3.3	0.03	0.03	0.03
7	General administration, etc.	5.9	5.0	5.2	0.03	0.04	0.04
8	Repayments	5.3	5.1	9.4	0.03	0.04	0.09
9	Total (1 to 8)	100.0	100.0	100.0	0.56	0.83	0.97
10	Structural Funds (1.3 + 3 + 4)	4.1	15.0	16.3	0.02	0.13	0.16

Source: The Regions of the Enlarged Community, EC Commission, 1987.

Structural Funds.

The structural policies and Funds are put in further perspective when the Community budget, and its component parts, are measured against Community GDP. The right-hand side of Table 1.1 shows each item of the budget as a percentage of total Community GDP. By 1986 the total EC budget amounted to under 1 per cent of Community GDP. The total share of the Structural Funds in Community GDP has increased considerably but, by 1986, still accounted for less than a fifth of 1 per cent of income generated in the Community. The Regional Funds, on which we concentrate in this chapter, absorbed only 0.07 per cent of Community GDP in 1986. These data confirm the first common feature of the Community's structural policies – their small scale.

A second common feature of these structural policies is that payments from the Community Funds must be accompanied by outlays from national governments. The percentage of the cost of projects or programmes provided by the Community varies across the three policies and has changed over time.

These two common features – small-scale and co-financing – are related to a third. The Community's structural policies have to date left considerable control in the hands of member states in devising approaches to structural problems. However, as we will see in the case of regional policy, the Community has acquired a greater role in policy formulation in recent years.

These features of the Community's structural policies generally were strongly reflected in Community regional policy. Both the Commission and the European Parliament identified the following drawbacks in early Community regional policy:

1 The total ERDF was too small in relation both to the scale of regional problems and to the level of regional expenditures by member states.
2 The system of national quotas meant that the Funds were spread over too many Community regions.
3 The three Structural Funds were not adequately co-ordinated and, in general, other Community policies had substantial regional effects which needed to be checked for consistency with the Community's regional policy objectives.
4 The ERDF could respond only to *national* initiatives in regional policy, and payment of Funds to national governments meant that direction of policy was too centralised.
5 One of the effects of this system of payments was that it was difficult to ensure that Community Funds were truly *additional* to national regional aid (see Armstrong 1978; Mawson et al. 1985; Robson 1987).

These problems go some way to explaining why the existence of Community structural policies and, in particular, Community regional policy has not been sufficient to achieve regional convergence. However, lest this be read as a criticism of the Community *per se*, or of the Commission, a number of other points should be noted. First, in order to overcome these problems, the Commission has, since 1975, put forward many proposals for the reform of the ERDF. These changes were consistently resisted by member states – in order to prevent the involvement of subnational authorities (Mawson et al. 1985) or to forestall the emergence of an independent Community policy (Wilson 1980). Nevertheless, changes in this important aspect of Community policy have been introduced in a series of disputed and belated reforms. Second, while retaining considerable control of regional policy, most member states implemented a type of regional policy which, if it ever was effective, had certainly become much less effective in the new economic environment of the late 1970s and the 1980s. We explain this problem when we discuss the future of regional policy.

Overall, the conclusion seems unavoidable that the aspiration in the Preamble to the Treaty of Rome did not prevent what Padoa-Schioppa has called 'tokenism' in the scale of intervention in the Community's regional and social policies. Thus, on the evidence of the past, there is little reason to believe that the Structural Funds, on their own, will bring about convergence.

Future Community regional policy

However, the Community's structural policies will not be identical in the future. We have seen that, following the review called for in the Single European Act, the Structural Funds are to be doubled in size, to be somewhat more concentrated on priority regions and objectives, and to be administered on the basis of more rigorous regional development plans (see Chapter 4). These reforms certainly create the *possibility* that these Community policies could have *greater* impact than they did during the period 1975 to 1986.

However, even after their recent doubling, the Structural Funds will still represent less than one half of 1 per cent of Community GDP. We have argued in the second section that the benefits and cost of the completion of the internal market are likely to be distributed unevenly and to exacerbate regional inequalities. Taking all these factors into account, it seems necessary to conclude that the Structural Funds as currently constituted will not be sufficient to create convergence let alone establish equality in regional economic structures and income.

It is important to note that this conclusion does not arise only because of the *size* of the Funds. It reflects also two other substantive problems confronting regional policy – first, the limited effectiveness of traditional regional policy and, second, our limited knowledge of the determinants of regional development. Consider first the effectiveness of traditional regional policy. A number of considerations have each independently led researchers and policy-makers to be sceptical of the value of using regional policy funds to attract mobile manufacturing projects to designated regions. Prolonged recession has meant that the effectiveness of conventional regional policy in influencing the location of manufacturing industry was greatly reduced since there were few mobile investments available (Martins and Mawson 1982; Armstrong and Taylor 1985). Analysis of changes in the world economy indicates that there has been a secular slowdown in demand for standardised manufactured products and that the success of regional policy in the 1960s was probably contingent on a set of conditions which no longer hold (Ewers and Wettman 1980). Research on the economic impact of grant-aided branch-plant investments on the regions in which they are located demonstrated that they had not greatly stimulated industrialisation (NESC Reports, no. 56 (1981) and 64 (1982)). Work in development economics and economic history revealed that industrialisation depended in large part on the indigenous social and economic structure (Bagchi 1987; Kriedte 1981). Together, these developments have stimulated interest in what has been called an 'indigenous' growth approach to regional policy (Wadley 1986).

However, our second point is that this new approach does not yet offer a comprehensive alternative to conventional regional policy. The reason is that knowledge of the nature and processes of regional development has not yet reached the stage where plans capable of really reversing regional decline, or initiating regional growth, are available to member states or the Commission. Until more effective regional development plans are designed, further increases in the volume of the Structural Funds would be of definite but limited value. When such plans have been developed, then significantly larger Structural Funds are likely to be necessary to implement them.

Macroeconomic co-ordination

It is sometimes argued that the key to regional convergence is the pursuit of sound macroeconomic policies by less-developed member states. The achievement of national and regional convergence during the period of rapid growth from 1960 to 1973 is often cited in support of this view. While sound macroeconomic policies are warranted to avoid inflationary balance of payments and fiscal problems, there is no validity to the notion that the independent pursuit of low inflation, current account balance and fiscal balance by member states will reduce regional disparities. Indeed, independent pursuit of these objectives is likely to lend a deflationary bias to overall macroeconomic management in Europe – and this tends to make reduction of regional disparities more difficult.

The view that rapid growth of the European economy is generally conducive to reduction in regional disparities almost certainly has some validity. However, we do not see it as capable of supporting the proposition that prudent macroeconomic policy at national level or completion of the internal market will *of themselves* start a process of regional income convergence. There are two reasons for this.

First, even if we accept that the fragmentation of the market has *inhibited* European growth and that the completion of the internal market will give a boost to growth, there are strong reasons to believe that co-ordinated growth-oriented macroeconomic policy is a *necessary* adjunct to the market completion policy (Padoa-Schioppa 1987; Lawrence and Schultze 1989; Commission of the European Communities 1985; Emerson *et al.* 1988). Indeed, this analysis led Professor Dreze of the Centre for European Policy Studies (CEPS) in Brussels to the conclusion that 'If the EC's internal market programme is not realised during a period of faster growth then the costs will outweigh the benefits'.

Second, although co-ordinated macroeconomic policy is necessary to achieve sustained growth, it does not follow, either logically or historically, that rapid growth of the European economy, however achieved, is *sufficient* to bring about a significant reduction in regional disparities. The reason is that the relationship between high European growth in the period 1960–73 and an element of convergence of regional and national incomes in those three years, on the one hand, and low growth in 1974–86 and slight divergence, on the other, has not been analysed in nearly enough detail. From the simple correlation highlighted by the Commission, it is not possible to identify *how* EC growth affects national or regional growth. A research project on the scale of the 'Cecchini Report' would be required before knowledge of the nature and strength of the relationships involved could be confidently acquired.

Evidence of the possible complexity of the relationships involved can be found in an intriguing analysis of the relationship between national/ union growth and regional growth formulated by Burns using US data (1987). He argues that national, in this case US or Europe-wide, growth does indeed influence regional growth, but in a *cyclically uneven* way. Specifically, the disparity between central incomes and regional or peripheral ones widens as central/national growth accelerates and narrows as central growth slackens. In the acceleration stage of the cycle, the growth-effects are spatially concentrated in the *core* regions; the result is a *widening* of regional differences. As acceleration of growth stops and high growth is achieved, the growing imbalance characterising the acceleration stage begins its reversal. High growth establishes linkages which cause the positive effects to spill over into peripheral regions. As the number of linkages increases, the dominance of the core diminishes. When national growth *slackens* and enters a deceleration phase, the gap between the centre and periphery *narrows* most. As deceleration gives way to low growth, the linkages between core and periphery weaken, and the vitality of the peripheral economy disappears. Thus Burns identifies an integration cycle that follows the national/union growth cycle, but runs *inverse* to it. Note that this hypothesis is consistent with the simple relationship between European growth and convergence highlighted by the Commission. Consequently, when reviewing policies available to pursue cohesion, there are very strong arguments for the co-ordination of macroeconomic policy. However, statement of these arguments, and implementation of co-ordinated macroeconomic policy, does not undermine the case for other policies to reduce regional disparities.

Budgetary transfers

The limited ability of either structural policies or co-ordinated macroeconomic policy to achieve convergence naturally focuses attention on the possibility of regional redistribution by means of Community taxes and expenditure. Examination of this subject reveals two striking facts. First, in existing economic and monetary unions, normal budgetary contributions and expenditures constitute much the most significant redistributive mechanism between persons, regions and member states. Second, there are very strong arguments, in the principles of public finance, for development of the Community budget and reassignment of policy functions between the tiers of Community government. Here we briefly explain each of these findings.

Existing economic and monetary unions

In-depth study of the four largest EC States (Germany, France, Italy and the UK) and four federations outside the EC (Australia, Canada, Switzerland and the US) reveal some very important facts (McDougall 1977; Padoa-Schioppa 1987):

1 Per capita incomes between the nine EC countries are at least as unequal as they are between the various regions of the countries studied.

2 The public finance systems of the countries studied provide a very substantial redistribution between regions. On average, these systems reduce income differences by 40 per cent.

3 The redistributive power of the Community's finances, by comparison, is very small indeed (1 per cent) – partly because the Community budget is so small and partly because the expenditure and revenue of the Community have a weak geographical redistributive power per unit of account.

4 The instruments of interregional redistribution consist in all countries of the main public expenditure programmes. Thereafter, a difference between unitary states and federations emerges. In the former, a large part of the total redistribution between regions arises automatically and is invisible. In federations, intergovernmental grants and tax-sharing play a much more important part. Regional policy, narrowly and explicitly defined, provides only a minor component of the overall financial redistribution process.

5 These interregional flows tend to finance a current account deficit on the 'balance of payments' of poorer regions and to sustain current account surpluses in richer nations.

6 As well as redistributing income regionally on a continuing basis, public finance in existing economic unions plays a major role in cushioning short-term and cyclical fluctuations.

It does not follow, of course, that these federal and unitary states are rational in using the public finance system as a major instrument to ensure regional balance. This is where our second conclusion comes in.

Arguments for a new assignment of policy functions

Our second conclusion is that there are strong arguments on integration, macroeconomic, public finance and equity grounds for considerable and early development of the Community budget and for its use as an instrument to maintain regional balance. Here we briefly state the public finance and integration considerations which support this conclusion.

In devising an effective system of policy formation and implementation for the new Europe, we can draw to some extent on the theory of public finance and, in particular, on a particular branch of it – the theory of fiscal federalism. While there are undoubtedly limits to the applicability of this theory to the European Community, and this limited applicability must be taken into account, there is, in my view, much that can be learned from it.

This theory of public finance provides guidance on the assignment of various policy functions to the local, regional, national and federal levels of government. In suggesting the correct assignment, the theory uses technical, economic and political criteria, such as economies of scale, externalities and spillovers, and political homogeneity (for a clear non-technical explanation of the reasons for these criteria, see Robson 1987). Here, we simply wish to draw the reader's attention to the main conclusions of this approach in its most comprehensive formulation, the theory of fiscal federalism.

These conclusions are, first, that the resource *allocation* function should be shared amongst upper and lower tiers of government, according to the particular 'public good' characteristics of the services to be provided and the homogeneity or diversity of the preferences for them. Second, both the *redistribution* function and the stabilisation function should be carried out at the highest level (Oates 1977). When using these concepts, it is appropriate to invoke the principle of *subsidiarity* – which states that functions should be assigned to the lowest tier of government which can conduct them efficiently and effectively. The integration consideration which supports the argument, that a more developed Community budget and direct budgetary transfers should be among the approaches to regional convergence, arises from application of this theory of public finance to the EC. Pelkmans has pointed out that, more than anything else, that application must take account of the fact that the Community is a group of *modern mixed economies* (Pelkmans 1982). One of the central themes of Pelkmans' work on integration is that establishing a genuine common market between mixed economies has many more profound implications than was traditionally appreciated. This is because the numerous domestic government interventions – in areas such as industry, technology, training, social provision, education, pensions, transport and finance – are, conceptually, *similar in their effects to border interventions*. In particular, they influence competitive conditions between member states. It follows that, to achieve genuine product market, labour market and financial market integration, these interventions must be harmonised to a considerable extent. If they are not to be harmonised by deregulation, or by the market power of the largest and richest member states, then they require to be harmonised by the formulation of Community policies in these areas of intervention.

This fundamentally important observation about the integration of modern mixed-economy democracies was well explained by Pelkmans and Robson in their review of the Commission's Internal Market White Paper:

> An undiluted application of the principles of free movement for factors and products – which would involve not merely the negative abolition of restrictions but the elaboration of many 'positive' measures – would inevitably, through its impact on the 'effective jurisdiction' of Member States, drastically undermine the delicately balanced packages of public policy regulation, market intervention, income redistribution measures and macroeconomic policies that are at present determined at the level of national politics. Nevertheless, if markets are not subjected to a harmonisation of public policy interventions that significantly affect competitive conditions in Member States, the benefits from a common market will remain smaller than is technically feasible, and the operation of the market itself could be seriously impaired. In its absence, movements of goods, factors and services within the Community would respond to distorted price signals and the outcome would be an inferior allocation of resources.
>
> (Pelkmans and Robson 1987)

This puts into perspective what is involved in creating a genuine common market and implies that, to all intents and purposes, it requires creation of an economic and monetary union. Furthermore, it gives us some idea of how policies must be assigned to the Community, national and local tiers of government if that economic and monetary union is to achieve genuine integration and microeconomic efficiency.

These insights into the economies of integration can be expressed by reference to the distinctions between *negative* and *positive* integration (Tinbergen 1954; Pinder 1968). *Negative* integration refers to the *removal* of obstacles to the movement of goods, labour or capital. *Positive* integration refers to the establishment of common policies and institutions in order to achieve economic integration or to pursue other objectives of the group or union.

These arguments strongly suggest that the existing economic and monetary unions, studied by McDougall, Padoa-Schioppa and others, are far from irrational in having a central budget of some significance – since this is necessary for the execution of the many policy functions which need to be conducted at the highest tier, if they are to be conducted effectively. It is an additional advantage that this approach also provides them with their most powerful regional policy instrument.

The suggestion that a more developed system of Community public finance should be one of the instruments to achieve regional balance frequently raises fears about disincentive effects, administrative inefficiency, or worse. These fears are understandable but, in my view, do not undermine the strong analytical and empirical arguments for this proposal. In saying this, I would stress that nothing I have said so far provides a case for *intergovernmental* financial transfers. Indeed, the most general argument relates to the need for certain policies to be conducted at Community level. The choice between direct Community expenditure and Community-member state transfers depends on the specific policy area under consideration. Having said this, it is entirely appropriate that the incentive and disincentive effects of *all* regional policy approaches be scrutinised and policies adapted accordingly.

Differential application of other Community policies

From as early as 1977, attention was drawn to the marked regional impact of certain Community policies which were not explicitly concerned with regional matters. By far the most important of the policies cited was the Common Agricultural Policy. It was demonstrated that, in general, the CAP *increased* rather than decreased regional disparities within the Community (Cuddy 1982). In any event, only limited progress has been made in having the regressive regional impact of the CAP, and the unknown or uncertain regional impact of other Community policies, taken into account.

However, Article 130B of the Treaty states the following:

> Member States shall conduct their economic policies, and shall coordinate them, in such a way as, in addition, to attain the objectives set out in Article 130A. The implementation of the common policies and of the internal market shall take into account the objectives set out in Article 130A and in Article 130C and shall contribute to their achievement.

This raises the possibility of Community policies being formulated and applied in a *differential* fashion in order to assist cohesion and convergence. To date, this has occurred to a quite insufficient degree.

In my view, there are a number of policy areas where it is possible, and extremely desirable, that the cohesion objective be taken into account by means of differential implementation of Community policy.

Examples are the allocation of agricultural quotas, the implementation of transport regulation and deregulation, the implementation of competition policy (especially the monitoring of regional aid), and the allocation of resources for technological research and development. It should be noted that, in some cases, the implementation of these policies in a differential fashion will merely serve to make *equal* the regional impact of Community policy. A good example was provided by Padoa-Schioppa. The attempt by the Community to stimulate European R&D is likely, other things being equal, to favour firms in the more advanced regions (Padoa-Schioppa 1987).

However, it would seem that there is a definite but *finite* number of policy areas where it is feasible or advantageous to seek differential application of Community policy under Article 130B. In particular, the major elements of the internal market programme cannot be applied in a differential fashion without frustrating the Community's basic aims. Furthermore, a widespread application of this or other policies on a differential basis would ultimately amount to a 'two-speed' or 'variable geometry' Europe and neither of these is in the interest of less-developed regions or member states.

Conclusion on policy approaches to avoid regional imbalance and achieve convergence

In conclusion, it seems that all four policy approaches – structural policy, macroeconomic policy, public finance policy and differential implementation – are necessary. We should be aware, however, that the greatest direct contribution to convergence is likely to arise from the development of the Community budget.

It must also be noted that if member states are to argue that regional convergence is a shared Community objective and responsibility, and to advocate that Community policies to achieve it be adopted on a realistic scale, then they must be capable of making a leading contribution to the formulation of those policies. Both the objective and the policies to achieve it must be advocated by argument of the highest quality.

THE DELORS REPORT ON ECONOMIC AND MONETARY UNION

In this final section, we use the analysis developed above to examine the 'Report on Economic and Monetary Union in the European

Community', (Delors 1989a), submitted to the European Council in April 1989. Given that the focus throughout this chapter has been on the regional distribution of activity and income, rather than macroeconomic management, we will look at the Delors Report in the same way – ignoring many issues concerning the institutional arrangements for the management of macroeconomic and, especially, monetary policy.

The Delors Committee's general approach

The Delors Committee argues convincingly that the completion of the internal market will increase the interdependence of the European economies and, consequently, will reduce the room for independent policy manoeuvre and amplify the cross-border effects of developments originating in each member country. An important implication of this is that the

> success of the internal market programme hinges to a decisive extent on a much closer coordination of national economic policies, as well as on more effective Community policies. This implies that in essence a number of the steps towards economic and monetary union will already have to be taken in the course of establishing a single market in Europe.

Indeed, the Committee says that EMU is at once a 'natural consequence' of the commitment to create a market without frontiers and a 'quantum jump' which goes beyond the single market programme.

A very significant aspect of the Delors Committee's Report is its insistence that 'economic and monetary union form *two integral parts of a single whole* and would therefore have to be implemented in parallel'. This is an important and well-founded rejection of the extreme view that all that is required is monetary union and that this, plus the financial markets, will impose sufficient fiscal policy discipline on the governments of member states.

On the side of economic union, the Committee also begins with the 1992 programme and insists that 'Community policies in support of a broadly balanced development are an indispensable complement to a single market'. Furthermore, in explaining the more advanced integration associated with EMU, it is stated – in accordance with the principle of 'subsidiarity' – that 'all policy functions which could be carried out at national (and regional and local) levels without adverse repercussions on the cohesion and functioning of the economic and monetary union would remain within the competence of the member countries'. Indeed, it is said that, in order to create an EMU, the single market would have to be complemented with, among other things, 'arrangements . . . to design an overall economic policy framework for the Community as a whole'.

On the cohesion and functioning of the Community economy, the Committee is quite clear that the 'adjustment and restructuring set in motion' by the 1992 programme 'is unlikely to have an even impact on different regions'. Indeed, it is agreed that historical experience suggests that economic and monetary integration generally can, in the absence of countervailing policies, have a negative impact on peripheral regions. In explaining this, the Committee cites some of the same arguments which were used in our analysis of the regional dimension. These tendencies would expose the economic union to 'grave economic and political risks' unless sufficient consideration were given to regional imbalances. Indeed, it is stated bluntly that 'the process of achieving monetary union is only conceivable if a high degree of economic convergence is attained'.

From these points it can be seen that there is a considerable degree of congruence between general ideas in the Delors Report and the analysis reported in this chapter. However, some very significant differences emerge when the Delors Committee's precise definitions of economic and monetary union are considered and when policies to ensure regional balance in EMU are discussed. Here, we concentrate on the latter area.

Policies for regional balance in EMU

Despite the argument that integration can reinforce tendencies to regional divergence, and the emphatic statement that 'the process of achieving monetary union is only conceivable if a high degree of economic convergence is attained', virtually the only countervailing policy measures proposed to deal with this are structural policies. Indeed, it is said that the 'foundations for a more effective Community role in general regional and structural development has recently been established'. The Committee adds that 'depending on the speed of progress, such policies might have to be strengthened further after 1993 in the process of creating economic and monetary union'.

A realistic view shows that convergence will *not* be attained by the internal market plus the existing Structural Funds.

In the Delors Report, it is explicitly said that 'the principal objective of regional policies should not be to subsidise incomes and simply offset inequalities in standards of living, but to help equalise production conditions through investment programmes . . .' (p.15).

Our analysis, and that of others who have studied this subject, suggests that achievement of convergence requires four types of policy measures: Structural Funds, macroeconomic co-ordination, differential application of Community policy, *and interregional redistribution through an enlarged Community budget*. Indeed, analysis and plain observation suggest that, as in existing economic and monetary unions, the greatest contribution will arise from the tax and expenditure system.

The policy system of economic management outlined by the Delors Committee ignores the role which the central budget plays in maintaining regional macroeconomic balance in existing economic and monetary unions. The point has been well made by Robson:

> In these contexts, what limits the impact of adjustment problems and provides a mechanism for their alleviation, although regions, like the member states in a monetary union, cannot devalue, is not the fact that foreign currency deficits and surpluses cannot arise, but the interregional fiscal adjustment mechanism that is built into their systems of public finance as a result of the combined operation of progressive taxation and the character of public expenditures. Such a mechanism would be absent in a monetary union unless at the same time there were a strong Community fiscal authority disposing of a relatively large budget and significant tax powers. Since the emergence of asymmetrical adjustment problems can never be excluded, complete monetary union may thus be recommendable and feasible only if it is accompanied by a degree of fiscal integration that would suffice for dealing with them.
>
> (Robson 1987)

It is important to note that these mechanisms serve to maintain macroeconomic stability, not only for regions experiencing 'balance of payments' deficits, or the equivalent, but also for regions experiencing surpluses, which would be unsustainable in the absence of balancing mechanisms.

Despite assigning remarkably few policy decisions to the Community tier in EMU, the Delors Committee, rather oddly, lays down that in the system of economic management envisaged, 'Governments . . . would refrain from direct intervention in the wage and price formation process'.

This is to succumb to a very narrow, and highly questionable, view of the approaches which are available for macroeconomic adjustments or for achieving other economic and social aims. It is a particularly restrictive proposition in a situation where exchange rate policy is to be voluntarily but irrevocably abandoned, where forces making for regional divergence are acknowledged to be at work, but where balancing interregional budgetary mechanisms are not to be available. Some of the most successful states and regions, both within and outside the Community, have built their economic success on a consensual approach to economic and social management and this frequently includes income distribution.

NOTE

1 In constructing the synthetic index of regional problems, two measures of economic strength are used: gross domestic product (GDP) per head of population and GDP per person employed – the latter intended to indicate the productivity of the region's economy. Likewise, two measures of the labour market situation are included – the first is the unemployment rate adjusted for estimated underemployment. Second, in order to include a dynamic or forward-looking element, consideration is given to prospective labour force change to 1990. This indicates the job requirements of a region. The above four variables are combined using the following weights: GDP per head of population, 25 per cent; GDP per person employed, 25 per cent; unemployment adjusted for underemployment, 40 per cent; prospective labour force change till 1990, 10 per cent. Finally, in the *Third Periodic Report*, the index was calculated for 1981, 1983 and 1985 and an average of these three years taken.

REFERENCES

Albrechts, L., Moulaert, F., Roberts, P. and Swyngedouw, E. (eds) (1989) *Regional Policy at the Crossroads*, London, Jessica Kingsley.

Armstrong, H. W. (1978) 'Community Regional Policy: a survey and critique', *Regional Studies*, 12.

Armstrong, H. W. (1983) 'The assignment of regional policy powers within the EC', in A.M. El-Agraa (ed.) *Britain Within the European Community: The Way Forward*, London, Macmillan Press.

Armstrong, H. and Taylor, J. (1985) *Regional Economics and Policy*, Oxford, Philip Allan.

Bagchi, A. K. (1987) 'Industrialisation', in J. Eatwell, M. Milgate and P. Newman (eds) *The New Palgrave – A Dictionary of Economics*, London, Macmillan Press.

Borris, M., Tyson D'Andrea, L. and Zysman, J. (1987) 'Creating advantage: how government policies shape international trade in the semiconductor industry', in P.R. Krugman (ed.) *Strategic Trade Policy and the New International Economics*, Cambridge, USA, Massachusetts Institute of Technology.

Brittan, S. (1988) 'A single currency for the EC', *The Financial Times*, 23 June 1988.

Burns, L. S. (1987) 'Regional economic integration and national economic growth', *Regional Studies*, 21.

Coffey, P. (1977) *Europe and Money*, London, Macmillan Press.

Commission of the European Communities (1985). EC Commission White Paper, *Completing the Internal Market*, Brussels, European Commission, June.

Cooke, P. and Imrie, R. F. (1989) 'Little victories: local economic development in European regions', paper read to European Conference on *Strategies for Local Economic Development*, Trinity College, Dublin.

Corden, W. (1972) 'Monetary integration', in *Essays in International Finance*, no. 93, Princeton University.

Cuddy, M. (1982) 'European agricultural policy: the regional dimension', *Built Environment*, 7 (3).

De Cecco, M. (1989) 'The European Monetary System and national interests', in P. Guerrieri and P. C. Padoan (eds) *The Political Economy of European Integration*, London, Harvester Wheatsheaf.

Delors, J. (1989a) 'Report on Economic and Monetary Union in the European Community', report to European Council by Committee chaired by J. Delors. Brussels, European Commission.

Delors, J. (1989b) 'Regional Implications of Economic and Monetary Integration', paper submitted to the Delors Committee for the Study of Economic and Monetary Union, published with *Report on Economic and Monetary Union in the European Community*, Luxembourg.

Dosi, G. (1988) 'Sources, procedures, and microeconomic effects of innovation', in *Journal of Economic Literature*, 26, September.

Doyle, M. (1989) *Regional policy in European economic integration*, paper submitted to the Delors Committee for the Study of Economic and Monetary Union, published with *Report on Economic and Monetary Union in the European Community*. Luxembourg.

Eaton, J. (1987) 'Credit policy and international competition', in D. R. Krugman (ed.) *Strategic Trade Policy and the New International Economics*, Cambridge, USA, Massachusetts Institute of Technology.

EC Commission (ed.) (1977) Report of the Study Group on the Whole of Public Finance in European Integration (the so-called 'MacDougall Report'), Brussels.

Emerson, M. *et al.* (1988) 'The economics of 1992', *European Economy*, no. 35. Brussels, European Commission, March.

Ergas, H. (1984) 'Corporate strategies in transition', in A. Jacquemin (ed.) *European Industry: Public Policy and Corporate Strategy*, Oxford, Clarendon Press.

Ewers, H. J. and Wettman, R. W. (1980) 'Innovation-oriented regional policy', *Regional Studies*, 14.

Kaplinsky, R. (1984) *Automation: the Technology and Society*, London, Longman.

Katseli, L. (1989) 'The political economy of macroeconomic policy in Europe', in P. Guerrieri and P. C. Padoan (eds) *The Political Economy of European Integration*, London, Harvester Wheatsheaf.

Keeble, D., Offord, J. and Walker, S. (1986) 'Peripheral regions in a Community of twelve Member States: summary of final report', mimeo,

Department of Geography, University of Cambridge.

Keeble, D., Owens, P. L. and Thompson, C. (1981a) *Centrality, Peripherality and EEC Regional Development*, Commission of the European Communities, Directorate General for Regional Policy, and United Kingdom Department of Industry.

Keeble, D., Owens, P. L. and Thompson, C. (1981b) 'Regional accessibility and economic potential in the European Community', *Regional Studies*, 16, (6).

Keeble, D., Owens, P. L. and Thompson, C. (1982) 'EEC regional disparities and trends in the 1970s', *Built Environment*, 7, (3/4).

Kriedte, P. (1981) 'Proto-industrialisation and de-industrialisation', in P. Kriedte, H. Medick and J. Schlumbohn (eds) *Industrialisation before Industrialisation: Rural Industry in the Genesis of Capitalism*, London: Cambridge University Press.

Krugman, P. (1987) 'Economic integration in Europe: conceptual issues', in T. Padoa-Schioppa (ed.) *Efficiency, Stability and Equity: A Strategy for the Evolution of the Economic System of the European Community*, Oxford, Oxford University Press.

Lawrence, R. Z. and Schulze, C. L. (eds) (1989) *Barriers to European Growth: A Transatlantic View*, Washington DC, Brookings Institution.

MacDougall Report (1977), see EC Commission (ed.).

Martins, M. R. and Mawson, J. (1982) 'The programming of regional development in the EC', *Journal of Common Market Studies*, 20, (3).

Mawson, J., Martins, M. R. and Gibney, J. T. (1985) 'The development of the European Community regional policy', in M. Keating and B. Jones (eds) *Regions in the European Community*, Oxford, Clarendon Press.

NESC (National Economic and Social Union) (1981), *Industrial Policy and Development: A Survey of Literature from the Early 1960s to the Present*, Report no. 56, Dublin, NESC.

National Economic and Social Union (1982), *A Review of Industrial Policy*, Report No. 64, Dublin, NESC.

National Economic and Social Union (1989) *Ireland in the European Community: Performance, Prospects and Strategy*, Dublin, NESC.

Oates, W. E. (1977) 'An economist's perspective on fiscal federalism', in W. E. Oates (ed.) *The Political Economy of Fiscal Federalism*, Lexington, Massachusetts, D.C. Heath.

Padoa-Schioppa, F. (1987) *Efficiency, Stability and Equity: A Strategy for the Evolution of the Economic System of the European Community*, Oxford, Oxford University Press.

Pelkmans, J. (1982) 'The assignment of public functions in economic integration', *Journal of Common Market Studies*, 21, (1 and 2), September/December.

Pelkmans, J. (1986) *Completing the Internal Market for Industrial Products*, Luxembourg, Office for Official Publications of the EC.

Pelkmans, J. and Robson, P. (1987) 'The aspirations of the White Paper', *Journal of Common Market Studies*, 25, (3).

Pelkmans, J. and Winters, L. A. (1988) 'Europe's Domestic Market', Chatham House Papers 43, The Royal Institute of International Affairs, London, Routledge.

Perez, C. (1983) 'Structural change and assimilation of new technologies in the economic and social system', *Futures*, 15.

Pinder, J. (1968) 'Positive and negative integration: some problems of economic union in the EEC', *World Today*, 24.

Robson, P. (1987) *The Economics of International Integration*, 3rd edn, London, Allen & Unwin.

Sayer, A. (1986) 'Industrial location on a world scale: the case of the semiconductor industry', in A. J. Scott and M. Storper (eds) *Production, Work, Territory*, Boston: Allen & Unwin.

Stopford, J. M. and Turner, L. (1985) *Britain and the Multinationals*, London, John Wiley & Sons.

Tinbergen, J. (1954) *International Economic Integration*, Amsterdam, Elsevier.

Wadley, D. (1986) *Restructuring the Regions: Analysis, Policy Model and Prognosis* Paris, OECD.

Wilson, J. (1980) 'The European Community's regional policy', in *Local Government Studies*, 6, (4).

Chapter 2

Structural Funds and budgetary transfers in the Community

Dieter Biehl[1]

THE ISSUES INVOLVED

The preamble to the European Economic Community (EEC) Treaty of 1957 contained a statement that the contracting parties intended to integrate their economies by reducing the disparities between their regions and the backwardness of the least-favoured areas. The Single European Act, in amending the EEC Treaty, subsumed this statement into Article 130A of the new Title V, dealing with economic and social cohesion. Article 130B specifies the means of achieving these objectives in the form of policy co-ordination, common policies and the Structural Funds. Article 130C explicitly incorporates the already existing Regional Fund and states that it has to contribute to redressing the principal regional imbalances. The next Article calls for the reform of all structural funds, which include the Regional Fund, the Social Fund and the Guidance section of the EAGGF, through the medium of a new framework Regulation aimed at co-ordinating the activities of the Funds with those of the European Investment Bank (EIB) and the other financial instruments of the European Community (EC).

Using the Structural Funds in an efficient way, in order to achieve economic and social cohesion, presupposes that the causes of regional disparities and underdevelopment are well understood and that the programmes based on these objectives are well prepared. That this implies a broad notion of resources, including geographical location, urbanisation and concentration of economic activities and population in space, as well as a growth-oriented sectoral structure and, last but not least, an adequate endowment of infrastructure, has been explained elsewhere.[2] The new system of action for the Structural Funds is also discussed elsewhere, in Chapter 4 of this book. We shall concentrate in this chapter on the role of the Structural Funds in the EC budgetary system and their financing.

THE STRUCTURAL FUNDS AND THEIR ROLE IN THE EC BUDGETARY SYSTEM

According to the Medium-term Financial Perspective 1988–92, structural operations will almost double in terms of 1988 prices, increasing from ECU7.8 to ECU13.5 billion during that period.[3] This corresponds to a rise of the share in total EC expenditure from 17.2 to 25.6 per cent. The Structural Funds are to serve five main objectives:[4]

- promoting the development and adjustment of lagging regions (Objective 1);
- converting regions, frontier regions or parts of them seriously affected by industrial decline (Objective 2);
- combating long-term unemployment (Objective 3);
- facilitating the occupational integration of young people (Objective 4);
- adapting production, processing and market structures in agriculture and forestry (Objective 5a) and promoting the development of rural areas (Objective 5b).

The main reform elements are that the Structural Funds have been increased and their deployment has been focused on specific objectives.

That the doubling of the Structural Funds was finally accepted may be partly attributable to the fact that the declining industrial areas were included in the list of regions entitled to be assisted. However, this not only diverts a part of the total funds for these regions, but also affects competition between enterprises in the truly lagging regions and those that, although suffering unemployment and restructuring problems, are nevertheless still relatively rich, mostly highly urbanised and well endowed with infrastructure. On the other hand, the 'classical' backward regions will have to demonstrate that they are capable of efficiently exploiting the improved aid to increase employment and productivity. The challenge to these regions is greater than for the old industrialised areas, as they usually suffer from a complex syndrome of problems: peripheral location, low density of population, deficits in infrastructure endowment as well as, frequently, disadvantages as to climate and fertility of soil for agriculture, and sometimes even a low attractiveness for new investors.

The significance of these regional and structural policies does not rest upon a pure redistributive philosophy, to the effect that the amounts that richer regions and member states contribute to Community finances reduce their own prosperity and growth. This would result in a zero-sum game only. Fortunately, there is another positive-sum logic: growth in rich regions depends also on the export demand for their goods and services. Within the EEC, less-developed areas are actual and potential buyers for these goods and services; they are not yet necessarily strong demanders for various reasons, such as low purchasing power or lack of infrastructure. On the other hand, it is well known that richer countries generate a savings surplus that will have to be invested outside their borders in order to maintain growth and international equilibrium.

As has been shown by the MacDougall Report,[5] richer regions within national economies are normally net exporters and therefore gainers from interregional and international trade, and, at the same time, are net payers in the overall national public finance systems. These richer regions 'retransfer' a part of their gains from trade via public finance channels to those less-developed regions within their national economy; the less-developed regions contributed to the formers' welfare by not protecting their markets so that, in other words, these less-developed regions are net receivers in the public finance field and net importers at the same time. By analogy, the funds provided by the more prosperous regions through the EC Structural Funds, retransfer a part of the actual and future gains from trade due to the already realised Common Market and the future Internal Market.

Indeed, as the Cecchini Report has demonstrated,[6] there are considerable potential gains from abolishing the still-existing barriers to trade and factor mobility. The political issue is how these potential gains are distributed. For the Community as such, it is sufficient to show that realising the Internal Market will increase welfare – for the member states and their regions, it is important to know whether at least a part of these gains will be channelled through the Community budget into the net importer regions so that they become net receiver regions. Admittedly, this also requires a serious reform of the Common Agricultural Policy, as redistributive effects are not in line with this concept.

From the point of view of the receiving countries, the effect of the transfers will depend on:

- the net amount of transfers received;
- the efficiency with which these transfers are used.

The present contribution is focused on the first of these points. From a macroeconomic perspective, the Structural Funds represent a very important element in the whole system of public finance with its expenditure and revenue sides.

The best way to tackle the problem is to make reference to the functioning of a federal system. The EC may be considered at least as a prefederal order where functions are subdivided between the Community, the member states and, partly, the regions. But, as Biehl has argued,[7] there are federalist principles that should be respected for a well-ordered system. These principles are the following:

• optimal assignment of competences to various levels of government;
• optimal differentiation of competences;
• optimal combination of competences;
• subsidiarity;
• correspondence between payers and receivers;
• fair burden-sharing and fiscal equalisation.

This approach is based on the idea that the traditional economic analysis, which only takes resource cost into account, is inadequate for dealing with problems of fiscal federalism. As a second major cost category, preference or frustration cost (Biehl, Pennock) has to be considered too. Extending economic analysis in this way allows us to conceive a representative democratic system with separation of powers as a minimum cost solution between resource and preference cost maxima.

Preference costs, however, are difficult to measure; basically, they have to be revealed in the process of political decision-making. But again, the analogy with the structures of existing national public finance systems helps to delineate, at least qualitatively, the main features of a Community finance system as well. All member states dispose, not only of regressive and proportional taxes but of progressive taxes, as well; and they distribute their expenditure not according to the principle of just return, as has already been explained with reference to the findings of the MacDougall Report. One of the fundamental judgements that seems to be accepted in all member states is that the citizens belonging to a national economy and society should be entitled to benefit from a sort of equal minimum supply of public services, independently of the fiscal capacity of their region and municipality. This, again, is not only a purely redistributive position as the potential productivity, and therefore wealth, is determined also by the overall resource endowment of which publicly provided infrastructure is an important part. This means that richer regions are rich because inter alia they are much better equipped with infrastructure capacities through public investment. As the Infrastructure Study mentioned above has shown, there are disparities in infrastructure endowment that are as large as 20:1 if the best and the worst-equipped regions in the EC are compared.

As a consequence, regions with a peripheral location, a low degree of urbanisation, an inadequate sectoral structure and, in particular, a poor infrastructure endowment, can only have a very low fiscal capacity. Too low a level of productivity and of public services will then cause inefficiently high migration of labour and of unemployed people, leading to excessive agglomeration in the better-off regions and in underagglomeration and depopulation in the emigration areas. It is in this context that the principle of fair burden-sharing deserves special attention.

FAIR BURDEN-SHARING AND THE STRUCTURAL FUNDS

The principle of fair burden-sharing establishes the basic rules for distributing the burden of financing government activities in relation to the advantages they offer. Different theoretical points of view may be held in this regard but, for our purpose, it is sufficient to consider two aspects:

- a financial system should be progressive in that the percentage to pay increases with the revenue per capita;
- there should be some fiscal equalisation by which revenues are better balanced at a regional level.

Given that the major proportion of EC funds comes from agricultural levies, tariffs and, especially, from the revenue sharing in VAT, the overall impact of this financing system must be classified as being regressive. The reason for this is obvious: not only do poorer individuals spend a higher percentage of their income on consumption compared with richer households, but poorer member states in general have a higher percentage share of consumption compared with savings or investment in their national income. In relation to their average national income, the poorer member states pay relatively more than the richer ones. The Community financing system may therefore be considered as regressive.

This argument of regressivity has already been developed by the MacDougall Report, recognised later by the Commission and the

European Parliament and finally accepted, in that the share of VAT finance has been fixed at 1.4 per cent and an additional proportional GDP levy has been introduced. In order to avoid excessive regressivity, it was decided in 1988 to apply a cut-off maximum rate of participation in VAT revenue sharing at 55 per cent.

However, it is quite clear that, even if this new revenue source was to be much more heavily relied on for the financing of the budget, the regressivity would at best be reduced, but it would not be possible to arrive at proportional burden-sharing and obviously impossible to realise progressive financing in this way.

The principle of fiscal equalisation is not realised in a reasonable manner either. Admittedly, it can be argued that systems of horizontal fiscal equalisation in particular certainly presuppose that there is a highly-developed and mature federal system, so that those who pay transfers to other groups or regions within that federation can be sure that the money will only be spent in accordance with the generally-accepted principles of the federation as a whole. As long as the EC has not yet developed so far as to become that sort of federation, the preference cost would be extremely high if one were to try to establish a unified horizontal fiscal equalisation system.

The consequence is that only implicit equalisation can be realised: the instruments for this are the Structural Funds. According to the new Regulation on the Structural Funds, in particular the Objective 1 regions that is, the really less-developed regions, are almost exclusively to be found in the poorer member states so that there is a clear net transfer into these economies. As far as Objective 2 regions are concerned, namely the declining industrialised regions, they are partly to be found in richer countries. Nevertheless, the net effect of Structural Fund expenditure is still in the desired sense.

However, given the small share of these expenditures within the total EC budget (roughly 17.2 per cent in 1988), they cannot determine the overall redistributive effect. Furthermore, it must be recalled that the CAP has a highly-regressive influence for reasons that will be seen later.

As a consequence, the EC is confronted with a dilemma. On the one hand, the homogeneity of preferences is not yet strong enough to allow a fair and efficient system of direct and explicit equalisation to be introduced; on the other hand, the implicit redistributive effects of regressive financing here and some expenditure policies with undesirable redistribution effects there cause a sort of 'perverted' system of implicit fiscal equalisation. The combination of the two effects was particularly strong in Great Britain and caused the so-called net-payer/net-receiver discussion within the EC.

We may conclude at this point that the action through the Structural Funds would be enhanced by a better-designed overall budget system. Let us look at this both from the revenue and the expenditure side.

The revenue side

As has been said, the financing of the European Community has a regressive character that has to be changed if the Community's economic and budgetary policies are to contribute to economic and social cohesion, as is required by Article 130B of the Single Act. This part of the reform cannot only consist in endowing the EC with a progressive revenue source but must also allow for an improved decision-making process through which further initiatives in this field may be taken. Two main proposals have been made in this regard.

The first possibility is to apply a progressive key to the existing resources of the Community, especially VAT. The MacDougall Report of 1977 already contains a proposal for a progressive key.[8] The basic idea is to use the present VAT system (in which the EC shares the revenues with the member states up to 1.4 per cent) and to apply to it a sort of progressive multiplier based, for example, on income per capita. A similar proposal was developed by the European Parliament in 1980.[9]

These two solutions, in general, are in line with the principle of fair burden-sharing, but they are not compatible with the correspondence principle. The reason is that they basically remain systems of contributions that will have to be paid out of the national treasuries and, therefore, do not allow joint decision-making on taxation and spending and do not create a direct link between the EC politicians and the European citizens who elect them.

As a second possibility, Biehl proposed a two-stage procedure aiming at endowing the EC with a new progressive revenue source:

1 In the first stage, member states are considered as contributors and the overall amount to be paid by them via the progressive instrument is fixed in relation to the income per capita of each country. Similar to the idea of the MacDougall Committee, progressive multipliers could be calculated in order to determine the overall amount to be paid by each member state. The first stage corresponds closely, therefore, to a system of progressive national contributions.

2 In the second stage, this overall national tax burden is redistributed

on the total national revenue from income or income plus corporation taxes so that a uniform percentage surcharge on the individual national tax payments results. This percentage surcharge is to be explicitly shown on each tax declaration and each national tax invoice so that the taxpayer knows exactly what he has to pay in order to co-finance European expenditure.

This proposal is in line with the principle of fair burden-sharing, as each member state is assessed on the basis of a common European scale, whereas the national citizens are charged according to a combination of this European scale and the existing set of national rules that determine the individual income or corporation tax to be paid. :

In addition, the correspondence principle is also realised if the Council and the European Parliament are given the legislative competence to fix the conditions for this European tax. It is also possible to proceed in two stages, in that all decisions to be taken at Stage One fall within the competence of the EC, whereas the execution and application of the criteria necessary to fix the individual national surcharge rate could also be decided within the framework of a European tax law by national authorities. At any rate, EC politicians would then be in the same position as national ones: if they need additional funds, they would have to decide simultaneously on expenditure and taxes. This implies that they would have to defend their decisions *vis-à-vis* their voters – the only way to obtain budgetary discipline.

Such a proposal would at the same time achieve the double objective of greater progressivity and a more sensible decision-making process in the field of budgetary responsibilities.

This proposal for a progressive surcharge is meant to be a second-best solution for the time being, that is, for a period of up to 15–20 years. In the long run, a uniform European income and corporation tax system would be the best solution. However, given that the actual system is regressive and that the existing national income and corporation tax systems differ in many respects, one has to admit that a uniform European tax would not be feasible, due to extremely high preference costs. Therefore, to have a progressive instrument of finance implies the use of (different) national progressive taxes as long as they exist with their differences, as they are apparently in line with national structures, on the one hand, and with national preferences, on the other.

The expenditure side

With the aid of these proposals, the Community can be endowed with a true tax competence of its own and its progressive design would reduce the actual regressivity of EC financing. But, to reach a better financial equilibrium, action is also needed on expenditure. At this level, three main points may be brought forward:

- the distribution of expenditure;
- the link between national and EC expenditure patterns;
- the efficiency of expenditure.

The distribution of expenditure

As has already been explained above, the overall redistributive effects of the EC budget also depend on the distribution of expenditure. Obviously, it would not be possible to modify the character of each EC policy so that it always becomes compatible with an accepted redistributive goal for Community activities in general. In the first place, all these policies must preserve their character, be it an allocative one or a redistributive one. What is possible, however, is to try to obtain a better balance between the overall effects of the different types of policies.

CAP (Common Agricultural Policy) expenditure, in particular, still works frequently in the opposite direction of an equitable distribution. The basic reason for this is that when the CAP started to become expensive, notably in the 1960s and later on, the most expenditure-intensive market systems were for those products produced by the relatively better-developed agricultural regions. They produced the largest part of the surplus and were strong exporters so that they obtained higher amounts of export subsidies. In the meantime, this lopsided preference for 'northern' products has been partly outweighed by new market systems for 'southern' products, such as fruit, wine and olive oil. Furthermore, in the current situation, with the world-wide General Agreements on Tariffs and Trade (GATT) negotiations and pressure from the Americans and the Cairns Group to abolish or at least substantially reduce agricultural subsidies, there are favourable conditions for engaging in a reform of the CAP.

This reform would have to consist of two sets of measures: reducing the degree of protectionism of the present CAP, notably by reduc-ing the internal agricultural prices, as already proposed by the

Commission, and to add at the same time policies that can help to compensate the negative impact of the price reductions on farmers' income. The instruments are to be positive payments for agricultural environment protection (instead of a tax, for example, on fertilisers and pesticides) and of subsidies in case of overindebtedness of farmers, if necessary complemented by income support measures designed to be neutral in relation to production.[10]

The link between national and expenditure EC patterns

Regional and structural disparities do not only have a Community dimension but also a national and regional one. Therefore, it is not sufficient simply to look at Community-wide disparities. Regional disparities within a single member state are politically and economically as important as regional disparities across Europe. The issue is to help to decrease Community-wide disparities across Europe as a whole, without ruling out national and regional policies within member states. This problem can be solved if regional disparities are judged from a double perspective:

- from the Community-wide perspective, with the aim of subsidising public infrastructure and private investment in a restricted number of clearly less-developed regions and at high matching rates;
- from a national perspective – and, in the case of countries like Belgium, Spain and Germany, from a provincial, regional or Länder perspective too – as far as similarly restricted numbers of regions are concerned that are lagging within the national context, but possibly not in the Community context, and where only low subsidy rates are admitted.

This double strategy is meant to give priority through Community funds to those less-developed regions that will not otherwise be able to catch up, whereas regional subsidies for only national but not Community less-developed regions should be financed by national means. However, in order to ensure that these national subsidies do not counteract the effects of the Community subsidies for the worst-off regions, the admissible rates of national and Länder subsidies have to be considerably lower.

In both cases, national and Community aids should be allocated only on the basis of well-designed and supported regional development programmes. The new Structural Funds Regulation clearly states this principle for all regions that are eligible for Community aids. In addition, these programmes have to be developed in close co-operation with decentralised units of government.

The efficiency of expenditure

As has already been stressed, redistribution, even in this broader sense, is not the only effect of the regional and structural EC funds. What is crucial is the purposes for which the funds are spent. In general, lasting welfare and growth can only be expected if the funds are used within the assisted regions in order to increase the regional development potential or production capacity.

Given that, besides geographical location, agglomeration and sectoral structure, regional infrastructure endowment represents one of the main determinants of regional growth, Community support for infrastructure programmes is important. As was shown by the Report of the Infrastructure Study Group on the Contribution of Infra-structure to Regional Development, infrastructure disparities are considerably larger than income disparities across the Community's regions. However, infrastructure represents the 'public' part of the overall national and regional capital stocks. As it would be too costly to try to substitute lacking infrastructure capacities and qualities by private investment and capital, the lagging regions within the Community can only catch up with the already well-developed areas if they are assisted in reducing the differences in infrastructure endowment.

On the other hand, a better infrastructure capacity only represents higher potential income and employment. In order to exploit this potential, private investment is needed. Private business will invest in backward regions only if, despite disadvantages as to location, urbanisation and sectoral structure, the ratio of labour cost to productivity is not distorted. This implies that the Community and the national governments concerned have to watch carefully that the potential benefits of the Structural Funds are not consumed by wage increases which are out of line with productivity.

NOTES

1 The author wishes to thank Achille Hannequart for his help in preparing the text of this chapter which summarises a number of contributions to earlier TEPSA conferences and some more recent papers.
2. See D. Biehl (ed.) (1986) 'The Contribution of Infrastructure to Regional Development', 'Document' Series of the EC Commission, Luxembourg.

3. See EC Commission (ed.) (1989) *The 'ommunity Budget: The Facts in Figures*, Luxembourg, 101.
4. See EC Commission (ed.) (1989) *Guide to the Reform of the Community's Structural Funds*, Luxembourg, 14.
5. See EC Commission (ed.) (1977) *Report of the Study Group on the Role of Public Finance in European Integration* (the so-called 'MacDougall Report'), Brussels.
6. See (1988) *European Economy*, (the so-called 'Cecchini Report') March.
7. See D. Biehl (1991) 'Financing the EEC Budget' in Rémy Prud'Homme (ed.) *Public Finance with Several Levels of Government*, Proceedings of the 46th Congress of the International Institute of Public Finance, Brussels.
8. See MacDougall Report (Note 5 above), 64–6.
9. See European Parliament (1980) 'Report on behalf of the Budgetary Committee on Own Resources' (the so-called 'Spinelli Report'), Doc. no. 1–772, 5 January.
10. See, for such a comparison of measures, the proposals of a European group of experts presented in D. Biehl *et al.* (1987) *Common Agricultural Policy, European Integration and International Division of Labour*, CEPES/IEP, Bonn.

Chapter 3

Restructuring European industry and redistributing regional incomes: prerequisites for Community cohesion

Alain Buzelay

The attempt to co-ordinate and achieve coherence between different national and Community policies, which is called for by the Single European Act in the name of economic and social cohesion, has as its aim the harmonious growth of the Community already envisaged in the preamble to the Treaty of Rome. The objective is to create a macroeconomic environment conducive to the equitable distribution of the increased prosperity expected as a result of the implementation of the Single Market.

For reasons which must be sought in the member states and in the way that the integration process has operated over the last thirty years, this objective was never fully achieved and the recent enlargement of the Community has indeed set it back. Not one region belonging to the new member states exceeds the – statistically reduced – European median income level. The increase from ten to twelve member states has doubled the population living in regions where per capita income is 25 per cent or more below the Community average. This situation will only be aggravated, in the short term, by including the German Democratic Republic, in the light of German reunification.

Renewed European growth through the achievement of the Single Market will be more effective if it is more geographically widespread, since the current disparities hinder its spread and intensification. This explains why the Community and its member states have undertaken schemes to balance the geographical spread of activities. If, according to the works of Colin Clark, J. Fourastié and D. Bell, the changes which mark our post-industrial societies are a consequence of growth, they are also a prime cause in cases such as regional industrial restructuring.

Industrial regeneration runs directly into the problem of finance, since those countries and regions in the Community which stand most in need of such development are those least able to afford it. It is for this reason that this regeneration necessitates financial redistribution between member states, a tangible aspect of economic and social cohesion.

REGIONAL DISPARITIES AND RESTRUCTURING

The origins and their effects

Interregional disparities originate from national causes which can be linked to the enlargement of the Community; this bore heavily on transport costs but not on the economies based on the major population centres, which reduced the competitive position of the periphery. They can also be traced to the decline of traditional industrial activities and to the inadequacies of local infrastructure which acts as a disincentive to industrial start-ups. They can also, as in France, be the result of a tradition of centralisation, which creates its own disequilibria.

To these national causes may be added those linked to the integration process as it has been carried out over the past thirty years. The larger market that has been created as a result has increased the problems of regions whose rivals are no longer other regions in the same state but all the regions of the member states. The obligation to maintain fixed exchange rates may force a country with an unfavourable external balance to impose deflationary policies which do less harm to the country overall than to certain regions which, due to their specific situation, are already in the grip of a recession. Without adequate harmonisation of policies and structures, the mobility of factors of production – and most markedly capital – will seek profits in those regions which are already favoured.

None of the theories analysing regional disparities and their impact on growth seem to me to have won general acceptance up to now. The empirical approach calls for three observations:

- regional disparities may restrain growth inasmuch as the inequalities of income which they engender risk slowing down the multiplier effect of the expense incurred and thus blocking the development of large internal markets;
- disparities are factors of inflation, given the close correlation observed between the level of economic development of a given region and the average productivity of its enterprises. Thus, the highest productivity in the most favoured regions could finance a

potential increase in the costs of production which could only be translated into higher selling prices in the least-developed and productive regions;

• finally, regional disparities justify the deterioration of terms of trade for developing areas, thus underpinning their recessionary processes. Empirical studies[1] reveal that it is not the deterioration which causes disparities but the reverse. The reversal of causes is explained by the low level of productivity and specialisation, themselves dictated by insufficient technology, under-equipment and so on.

The development and significance of national and Community regional policies

Regional policies, aimed at creating a better geographical spread of industrial activities within member states, were originally practised at the national level. The first country to implement regional policies was the United Kingdom in 1945, followed by Italy and the Federal Republic of Germany in 1950 and France in 1954. The means or instruments traditionally deployed until recently were industrial location assistance (in the form of investment and employment subsidies, tax breaks, interest rate subsidies and setting-up assistance), financing of infrastructure likely to attract or retain local people and to open up the region (communications, housing, public utilities, and so on) and the creation of poles of activity (industrial zones, rehabilitation areas, and so on).

National action was complemented by Community action following the creation of the ERDF (European Regional Development Fund) in 1975, to which were added the EAGGF (European Agricultural Guidance and Guarantee Fund), the ESF (European Social Fund), European Coal and Steel Community (ECSC) loans and European Investment Bank loans. However, up to 1986, ERDF aid was 95 per cent dependent upon aid allocated by member states and the distribution of the range of Structural Funds and loans suffered frequently from incoherences brought about by a lack of co-ordination.

The effectiveness of the actions undertaken is not easy to assess. Whatever the choice of models used (Shift, Moore, Rhodes), one comes up against the choice of which variables to select, of the difficulty of knowing with certainty whether the results obtained are or are not effectively optima, of the problem of obtaining information, of the ways of taking into account and measuring the secondary effects, of the problem of time lapses . . .

However, the fact is that, the results achieved notwithstanding regional disparities continue to exist within the member states: the United Kingdom remains in the grip of the difficult problem of industrial reconversion; the gap between the north and the south of Italy remains very large indeed; in the Netherlands, work is still needed to redress the balance between the west and the rest of the country; the progress made in France conceals some new disparities behind their apparent overall reduction . . .

At the Community level, these disparities have become more marked because of sectoral crises which struck a very concentrated number of regions and because of the enlargement of the Community to include Greece, Spain and Portugal.

This is the reason behind the continuing change in the way Community and national regional policies have evolved, not only through the increase in the Structural Funds scheduled for the 1987–92 period but also in a search for increased effectiveness.

The reform of the ERDF has reinforced the effectiveness of Community regional policy by giving it greater coherence, flexibility and firmness.

The increase in coherence stems from the experience of co-ordination obtained through the implementation of the Integrated Mediterranean Programmes (which require better meshing between regional policy and other Community programmes with an impact on the regions), the 'Community Initiative Programmes' (which retain their 'outside the quota' status, being linked directly to Community decisions) and national programmes of interest to the Community (which require smooth interaction between national and Community policies).

The increased flexibility in the system itself results from the introduction of selectivity into proposals for Community action, proposals which were hitherto too generalised. Regional under-development will henceforth be analysed and remedied according to more specific norms (or objectives). Regions where the per capita GDP is less than 75 per cent of the Community average will benefit from development aid (Objective 1). Those whose unemployment rate is higher than average and whose industrial employment level is equal to or higher than the Community average will receive aid to combat industrial decline (Objective 2). Regions suffering from long-term unemployment and problems concerning the integration of young people into the work-force will be granted assistance in the framework of national plans (Objectives 3 and 4). Finally, there is aid for regions which are forced to undertake swift adaptation of their agricultural structures in the light of the reform of the Common Agricultural Policy (Objectives 5(a) and 5(b).

The greater rigour in the system is the result of the changeover from a system of quotas to one of upper and lower limits. This has the effect of spurring competition between various requests for assistance, since member states have every interest in framing their requests in a manner consistent with Commission requirements while the lower limit guarantees a minimum level of support to each state so long as there is an adequate number of eligible requests for assistance addressed to the Commission.

In parallel with the reform of the ERDF, the reform of the Structural Funds reinforced the effectiveness of Community regional policy by putting emphasis on geographical and functional concentration in its implementation, by setting up multi-annual programmes in place of *ad hoc* projects and by encouraging the participation of states and regions in the drawing up and implementation of Community programmes.

Thus, reorientation of European regional policy has communicated itself to regional and national policy-makers who have adopted, to varying degrees, the techniques of programming and partnership. The principle of Community Support Frameworks, the response of the Commission to the needs expressed in national plans, is leading to the regionalisation of national plans. The achievement of the internal market requires more collaboration and increased delegation at the Community level. Participation at all levels is in line with the principles of subsidiarity and partnership which are becoming the key elements of regional policy at national and Community level.

Through the influence of the Community and based on experience acquired, the regional policies of the member states have been focused on the causes of underdevelopment rather than its effects, that is to say, on the effectiveness of the productive process and its environment rather than on job creation, which can be regarded as a consequence of that. Thus, in contrast to past practice, there is no longer any concentration on employment-creation by employment subsidies or by creating or keeping companies afloat. Rather than giving grants whose inspiration was created by an opportunity, the opportunity itself is being created, without which national and Community expenditure risks being useless and simply a burden on the exchequer. Thus, the accent is now on modernisation using own funds, on making fuller use of human resources, on developing research and innovation networks.

In order to receive and assimilate innovation, the region needs a high educational level. Its future development rests on its ability to adapt its structures to accommodate high-productivity sectors and new technologies.

This approach is in line with the factors that influence business location, which are, in decreasing order of importance: economic development and opening-up of the region, size and proximity of upstream and downstream markets, quality of manpower, financial assistance, tax advantages and real estate prices.

REGIONAL RESTRUCTURING AND INTRA-COMMUNITY REDISTRIBUTION

Theoretical justification

Community financing of the redistribution of resources needed to reduce disparities in growth between regions implies a transfer of resources from favoured to less-favoured regions. The redistributive effect is all the greater since the level of decision-making is independent of member states and they have no power to seek a 'fair return' on their money. The process of redistribution is usually justified by various theoretical analyses.[2]

The first arises from welfare theory. With the state replacing the private individual, Pigou was able to write that any transfer from a relatively rich to a relatively poor state could increase the sum of total satisfaction. This approach runs into the problem of comparing interpersonal utility relative to public resources, a simple transposition of interpersonal comparisons. It also comes up against the problem of decreasing marginal utility of income, which is even more dubious at the level of national income since the process of industrialisation implies new forms of organisation and new requirements which can only be met by constantly increasing public expenditure.

A second approach is the new-welfare school, represented by J. R. Hicks, N. Kaldor and T. Scitovsky. While for Pigou, redistribution is a means of evening out marginal utility of income to maximise welfare, for these authors, it is a form of compensation aimed at raising the Pareto optimum above its limits to achieve welfare. When viewed as a dynamic process and applied to intra-Community transfers, this approach leads one to note that the growth of one state and its resources must occur to the detriment of another. Viewed in this light, redistribution is a form of compensation paid by a favoured state to a relatively less-favoured one. However, this analysis accepts, more or less explicitly, the hypothesis of initially unbalanced growth, which again is open to question.

A third approach associates redistribution with the theory of collective property. Viewed from this angle, redistribution is considered as one of the goods which can be directly integrated into individual functions of satisfaction. Applied to our theory, the taking into account by member states of the transfer variable in their order of preferences shows recognition of the principles of utility interdependence and reciprocity, and is all the better accepted by those who bear the cost when they suspect that one day they might be the beneficiaries. But, as with preceding theories, this approach is not without its critics. The specific nature of collective welfare which redistribution represents makes the Samuelson approach to the problem impossible since, according to the paradox of universal externality, one cannot, using a public good offered for indiscriminate and general consumption, satisfy the Pareto optimum conditions in the simple form of marginal rates of substitution. Let us add here that the justification for redistribution, through its assimilation with a collective good integrated into the function of a state, supposes that its consumption would not be incompatible with another collective good, such as national independence, for example.

If these normative approaches do not always furnish an adequate basis for justifying redistribution, more positive analysis reinforces it. By offering new resources to relatively deprived states and regions, and by enabling them to improve their infrastructures in order to attract industrialisation sensitive to external economies, intra-Community redistribution improves production structures and, by virtue of this, primary income distribution, whose ultimate adjustment depends on the fiscal policy of each state. This is consistent with Scitovsky's thesis, which rejects total dependence on the market economy and predicates the need for the creation of externalised economies by public agencies in less-favoured areas in order to even out geographical disparities in growth rates.

Redistribution within the Community and the reduction in regional disparities which should result from this can only aid monetary integration. At the level of trade flows, it leads to their balancing out by improving the average productivity, and thus the competitiveness of less-favoured regions. At the level of capital flows, it diminishes structural deficits to the extent that only permanent public transfers can do something to remedy chronic disequilibria and supplement insufficient private transfers in helping to overcome the problem of external deficits.

More efficient redistribution through Community enlargement

The reform of the ERDF, by making the Commission less dependent upon the member states, has given it greater power to redistribute, a power increased by the enlargement of the Community to cover underdeveloped regions and countries and the doubling of the Structural Funds.

Since intra-European disparities have grown, and since redistribution is aimed at the least-developed regions, some former beneficiaries may be more or less overlooked and become net contributors to the Community budget.

Since in the years up to 1992, the contribution of member states to the Community budget will move from 0.8 per cent to 1.4 per cent of General Domestic Product (GDP), their allowable receipts from the Structural Funds could become much higher or much lower, as is indicated in Table 3.1.

This new redistribution, which aims at reducing the major discrepancies in the enlarged Community at the expense of the smaller, historic ones, must be more effective. Apart from reasons linked to the microeconomic approach, which tend to lead to greater efficiency in the use of funds deployed, other reasons stem from the macroeconomic approach and are linked to two kinds of effect:

1 The induction effect: this is linked to the principle of additionality which, according to Article 9 of the Community Regulation, states that the Commission and the member states must ensure that, following the implementation of 'Community Support Frameworks', the increase in the Structural Funds, as a result of their doubling, is matched by a similar increase in real terms, in overall programme financing from national sources.

Thus, Community financing is designed not to replace national funding but to act as an incentive for its increase by at least an equal amount. In giving their approval to the Community Support Frameworks, member states are pledging themselves to do just that.

This induction effect will be all the greater for being concentrated, as the Structural Funds are, on those regions below the new Community average.

Table 3.1 Structural Funds - Expenses

Country	In national GDP terms % 1987	1992	In % of total Community funding 1987/92[1]
Portugal	1.4	3.6	15.0
Ireland	1.8	2.7	8.0
Greece	1.3	2.6	14.0
Spain	0.3	0.7	24.0
Italy	0.2	0.3	19.0
United Kingdom	0.21	0.18	7.6
Luxembourg	0.19	0.12	0.5
France	0.10	0.12	6.0
Belgium	0.08	0.09	0.8
Denmark	0.07	0.06	0.3
The Netherlands	0.05	0.06	0.8
West Germany	0.03	0.04	3.7
			100

Note 1 Not including sums spent on 'Community Initiative' programmes.
Source for table: calculations and estimates made by J. Van Ginderachter and A. Buzelay on the basis of the Annual Reports of the Court of Auditors and statistics provided by the Directorate General for the Co-ordination of the Structural Funds.

2 The multiplier effect: this applies to investment aimed at increasing output and employment in the regions aided and at external trade favouring intra-Community growth following the principles of positive retroactivity.

Community aid, which mainly concerns investment in physical and human capital, has an impact all the more powerful for being concentrated in regions suffering from insufficient gross capital formation. Since it amounts to 15 to 20 per cent of investment expenditure in the poorest states and regions, it can make a substantial contribution to reducing regional per capita revenue disparities. Thus, if, according to Community estimates, the lagging regions stand at 62.6 in 1989 (Community average: 100) and if, thanks to aid from the Structural Funds and the achievement of the Single Market, their per capita revenue could grow at 2 per cent above the Community average, they would find themselves at around 75 in the year 2000.

By improving living standards in the underdeveloped regions, Community and national funds will result in an expansion of trade which will be all the more significant, given that these regions are below the European average. This is consistent with post-Keynesian interpretations, according to which reduction in disparities between incomes is all the more important where income distribution is highly biased, since it allows a considerable increase in the overall propensity to consume amd thereby an increase in the multiplier effect.

Thus, the lagging regions need no longer act as a brake on the growth of their partners but will participate in that growth instead. The underlying inspiration for this approach is that of the economies of scale anticipated from distribution carried out in a wider geographical and income-level framework.

Community enlargement and the implementation of the Single Market require a reorientation of growth patterns so that their impact does not accentuate current disparities. The increased competition linked to the post-1992 period will be less between nations than between regions where productivity differentials will be more marked for more or less similar input costs.

The financing of this reorientation, once purely a national concern, will now entail a redistribution policy that reflects national cohesion. As a result of the reforms and increases in volume, Community financing, which sees itself more and more as having an induction effect, will become more redistributive in the name of the economic and social cohesion that is one of the themes underlying the Community's philosophy. This geographically and quantitatively wider redistribution responds to the requirements for greater and more painstaking cohesion. There is the example of the Common Agricultural Policy. At the beginning, it stressed redistribution from consumers to producers in the member states, but it is now progressively abandoning this line to arrive at a redistribution from the industrialised to the less-industrialised countries through using, among other things, lower intervention and indicative prices.

The question which is now before us is whether there are limits to the use of economies of scale in the redistribution process.

NOTES

1. Compare, in this regard, the report written under our supervision: 'Regional inequalities and deterioration of terms of trade: an inter-European analysis', by Arnauld Bourgain, Centre Européen Universitaire de Nancy, 1989.
2. See, for example: A. Buzelay (1989) 'Convergences et redistributions dans la perspective 1992', *Revue français d'économie*, IV, (3), 108–27.

Part II

The Structural Funds: implementation and efficiency

Chapter 4

The reform of the Structural Funds: the first year of implementation

Eneko Landaburu

The entry into force of the Single European Act marked the start of a new phase for the Community's structural policies. Unlike the Treaty of Rome, the Single European Act went beyond the stimulation of free trade to make provision for greater 'economic and social cohesion' within the EEC. This cohesion, hitherto inadequate, is now of particular importance in view of the impending completion of the internal market.

Although the simulation exercises now in progress cannot yet show incontrovertibly whether completion of the single market will have a positive or negative effect on the regions of the Community, the possibility that some of them will experience difficulties must be borne in mind. The extent to which the development of southern Europe is lagging behind, for example, makes it ill placed to compete. In the north, certain declining industrial regions are now in too deep a crisis to benefit fully from the new upsurge in activity. This means that completion of the internal market and a solution to these specific problems are closely connected.

THE SINGLE ACT AND THE REFORM OF THE STRUCTURAL FUNDS

By signing the Single European Act in 1986, the heads of state and government laid the basis for a significant advance in the development of the Community's structural policies, and its regional policy in particular. The European Regional Development Fund (ERDF) took its place in the Treaty alongside the other Structural Funds (the European Agricultural Guidance and Guarantee Fund (EAGGF) Guidance Section for agricultural structures and the European Social Fund) with the stated aim of reducing regional imbalances within the Community (and not simply, as before, within the individual member states). Finally, the Single Act provided for a thorough revision of the rules under which the three Funds operated and, here, the lengthy negotiations resulted in a framework regulation, a co-ordinating regulation and the updating of the regulations governing the ERDF, the European Social Fund and the EAGGF Guidance Section.

The agreement reached in Brussels in February 1988 represented a further important advance. The European Council decided to double structural expenditure in real terms from European Currency Unit (ECU) 7 billion in 1987 to ECU14 billion in 1993 and to concentrate it on the Community's most disadvantaged regions.

The reform of the Structural Funds rests on three key principles: greater selectivity, increased resources and improved methods of intervention.

In future, interventions will be concentrated on a limited number of objectives, five of which have been selected as priorities. Some apply to the Community as a whole while in other cases, a geographical definition has been required.

Objective 1: Promoting development in regions where it is lagging behind. This involves helping to revive productive investment and achieving a higher-than-average growth rate in regions whose per capita Gross Domestic Product (GDP) is less than 75 per cent of the Community average. These regions, home to one-fifth of the Community's population, include the whole of Greece, Ireland and Portugal, a large part of Spain, southern Italy, Corsica, the French overseas departments and Northern Ireland.

Objective 2: The conversion of industrial areas in decline so that they can be fully integrated once again into the economic development process. These areas have been defined on the basis of their degree of industrialisation, the decline in industrial employment and the unemployment rate.

Objective 3: Combating long-term unemployment, which requires action throughout the Community.

Objective 4: The occupational integration of young people, which also concerns the whole of the Community.

Objective 5: The adjustment of agricultural structures, linked with the general reform of the Common Agricultural Policy (Objective 5 (a)) and the development of less-favoured rural areas (Objective 5 (b)). These areas have been defined on the basis of the economic and social difficulties which they face, the degree to which they are rural in nature, the extent to which they are peripheral, and so on.

To achieve these objectives, the European Structural Funds have to co-ordinate their interventions. Hence, although it is concerned primarily with Objectives 1 and 2, the ERDF also has to support rural development (Objective 5 (b)). The important role played by human resources in economic expansion means that the Social Fund, which is solely responsible for Objectives 3 and 4, must also provide assistance for regional and rural development while the Guidance Section of EAGGF has to assist in the general reorganisation of agriculture by paying particular attention to less-favoured regions. It is also stipulated that the three Funds will co-ordinate their action with intervention by the Community's other financial instruments and with the operations of its lending instruments, such as the European Investment Bank. It should be recognised that, compared with the previous situation, the principles of the reform represent a considerable effort to improve the effectiveness of the Community's structural measures. The following aspects are particularly worthy of note:

- concentration of assistance from the Funds in the least-favoured regions whose development is lagging behind (southern Europe and Ireland) or which are in industrial decline (United Kingdom, France, Germany and the Benelux countries), selected on the basis of Community criteria;
- a Community bias to national development priorities;
- greater partnership with national, regional and local authorities in the preparation and implementation of measures;
- greater co-ordination of measures under the three main Funds with development priorities financed (following negotiations with member states and the region) in the context of multi-annual regional development programmes;
- simplification of procedures, particularly by the use of programme financing and the provision of global grants to regional intermediaries to avoid direct management of an excessive number of projects and dispersal of effort;
- development of new ideas and measures on regional planning at the European level.

Table 4.1 Appropriations from the Structural Funds for 1989–93

Objectives	million*		ECU
1	Regions whose development is lagging behind		38,300
2	Regions affected by industrial decline		7,205
3 and 4	Long-term unemployment and the occupational integration of young people		7,450
5(a)	Adjustment of agricultural structures		3,415
5(b)	Development of rural areas		2,795
	Transitional and innovatory measures		1,150
TOTAL			60,315

*At 1989 prices

IMPLEMENTATION OF THE REFORM

The Community Support Frameworks (CSFs)

Those were the principles behind the reform. Implementation began in 1989. First of all, at the beginning of the year, the Commission took a number of decisions defining the areas eligible under Objectives 2 and 5(b) and fixing the indicative allocation among the member states as 85 per cent of the ERDF's resources. The Commission also approved a note on Objectives 1 and 2 setting out guidelines for the member states on the principles and priorities for the various phases of implementation.

However, the greatest challenge was the preparation of the Community Support Frameworks (CSFs) involving Community expenditure totalling more than ECU60 billion between 1989 and 1993. Table 4.1 shows the allocation of the appropriations.

The CSFs for the Objective 1 regions were formally adopted by the Commission on 31 October 1989, that is less than seven months after the submission of the national development plans. Those for Objective 2 were adopted before the end of 1989 and those for rural areas (Objective 5(b)) followed in March or April 1990.

More than 60 per cent of the resources of the Structural Funds were earmarked for Objective 1 regions affected by serious problems and there was further concentration within that category on the least-favoured countries, Portugal, Greece and Ireland. CSFs will run for a period of five years.

Table 4.2 Allocation of appropriations for Objective 1

Country	ECU million
Greece	6,667
Spain	9,779
France	888
Ireland	3,672
Italy	7,443
Portugal	6,958
United Kingdom	793
TOTAL	36,200

Table 4.3 Allocation of appropriations for Objective 2

Country	ECU million
Federal Republic of Germany	280
Belgium	160
Denmark	21
France	555
Italy	209
Luxembourg	7
Netherlands	74
Spain	650
United Kingdom	1,289

The detailed allocation of appropriations is shown in Table 4.2.

Similarly, in the case of Objective 2, the Commission applied the principle of concentration by reducing the number of eligible regions. Initially, the eligible population amounted to about 25 per cent of the Community total, but this figure was later reduced to about 15 per cent in accordance with the guidelines of the framework Regulation. The indicative breakdown of the resources available under Objective 2 is biased towards regions where industrial decline is most acute. The CSFs will run for three years. The breakdown of appropriations is as shown in Table 4.3.

Partnership is one of the main innovations of the reform and is of decisive importance for its implementation. In general, the Commission is pleased with the relations which it has recently established with the regional authorities. Even though the constitutional structure of certain member states means that the three-cornered relationship between the Commission and the national and regional authorities has sometimes been difficult to set up, the objective of associating the regional authorities has been achieved in most cases.

During the preparation of the CSFs, the Commission organised successful negotiations with both regional and national authorities. These resulted in:

• the inclusion of regional aspects in the CSFs for Objective 1;
• the establishment of regional CSFs for Objective 2.

Another result of negotiations was that the priorities selected reflected Community development priorities more closely.

In the case of Objective 1 regions, the selection of these priorities normally stressed infrastructures which would combat the disadvantages of remoteness and increase the competitiveness of economic sectors such as telecommunications, research and development and services to businesses. Particular attention was paid to vocational training measures.

In the case of Objective 2, the main aim was to create alternative employment to compensate for jobs lost in traditional sectors now in decline. Accordingly, stress was laid on measures to assist small and medium-sized businesses, improve the environment and assist research and development, tourism and, once again, vocational training.

During the implementation of the CSFs, there will be no diminution in the importance accorded to partnership (importance of the committees to monitor the CSFs at regional level; preparation, implementation and monitoring of the operational programmes).

Consultation with the two sides of industry took place through the Social Fund Committee. In addition, in Portugal, Italy, Spain and Ireland, the Commission organised measures to inform management and labour at regional level. Similar meetings will be organised in the other Community countries.

Operations are better co-ordinated because the CSFs constitute a link between the Structural Funds and the financial instruments. With the exception of the earlier Integrated Mediterranean Programmes, this is the first time that all parts of the Community's structural measures have been planned and negotiated together. In order to meet the particular needs of the various regions, the breakdown between the Funds is specific to each individual Community Support Framework.

When the legal framework for the reform of the Funds was adopted at the end of December 1988, some doubts were expressed about whether the new structures could actually be introduced in time to ensure continuity in the work of the Funds.

While grant decisions had already been taken in respect of all the Social Fund's 1989 appropriations, a large number of operational programmes will be approved by the Commission following the adoption of the Objective 1 and 2 frameworks. Here, two major points should be emphasised. First of all, the Commission has done all in its power to provide finance for measures proposed earlier which were in line with the reform and now form part of the Support Frameworks. This work continued throughout the year. Second, the Commission departments were instructed to examine draft programmes and other applications for finance as swiftly as possible to ensure a smooth transition to the new methods of intervention. This means that the doubts referred to above proved unfounded: the reform is in place and the work of the Funds has continued satisfactorily.

Following the introduction of the Community Support Frameworks and the first grants of assistance under them, the member states and the Commission agreed on effective monitoring of measures. This will involve regular progress reports on priorities and related measures, incuding the proposing of amendments where necessary. Like the establishment of the first Community Support Frameworks, this is a new task for the member states and the Commission. Since, so far, partnership has taken place in a satisfactory fashion, the Commission has high hopes in this regard too. In particular, the monitoring of measures will enable the Commission to carry out regular checks to ensure that the resources made available are genuinely additional and so really result in an enhanced economic impact in the assisted regions. This point should be emphasised since it is of prime importance for the Commission, being the key to the credibility of the Community's structural measures.

Community initiatives

Following the exceptional effort to achieve a multi-annual approach to programming with implementation at operational level, it is now time to prepare for the future by means of specific initiatives at Community level. Accordingly, certain financial resources have been reserved for Community initiatives. These are expected to total ECU3.1 billion; the Commission will ensure that 15 per cent of the ERDF is used for Community initiatives, of which about 80 per cent will go to Objective 1 regions.

Table 4.4 Indicative breakdown of funds allocated to Community
              initiatives

Initiative	ECU million
Rechar	300
Envireg	500
Stride	400
Transfrontier co-operation	700
Remotest regions	200
TOTAL	2,100

In its 1989 action programme, the Commission paved the way for
three initiatives, Rechar, Envireg and Stride. Rechar, which is intended
to assist the conversion of coal-mining areas, was adopted in principle
by the Commission in 1989 and Envireg, which (particularly in
conjunction with the Medspa programme in the Mediterranean area) is
concerned with environmental improvement, will be adopted shortly.
The Stride programme seeks to combine regional development with
research and development work so as to improve the access of less-
favoured regions to the new technologies. Preparatory work is also in
progress on transfrontier co-operation and ways of assisting the
remotest regions.

The indicative breakdown of the funds allocated to these five
Community initiatives is shown in Table 4.4.

Studies and pilot projects

The Commission recently launched the first pilot projects intended to
stimulate regional development at Community level and implement
new ideas. Their special feature is that they are not geographically
restricted so that initiatives can be launched in any of the Community's
regions.

The projects and studies begun cover, in particular:

• measures to be taken in areas adjacent to both the Community's
  internal and external frontiers to remove physical obstacles, develop
  co-operation and contribute to the creation of a Europe without
  frontiers;
• exchanges of experience and greater co-operation between regions

and towns to develop the ability of local and regional authorities to participate in the development process.

THE IMPENDING SINGLE MARKET

The impending single market requires a long-term vision of the development of Europe over the next decades and of the contribution which the various regions can make to that progress. In terms of the single market, every region has its advantages and its handicaps and, obviously, the question is how to maximise the former and reduce the latter. To achieve this goal, the Community's regional policy operates in a number of ways, both by varying its objectives in the light of the problems to be dealt with (development lagging behind, industrial conversion, rural adjustment) and by making specific adjustments to meet the particular problems of a given region through new implementing procedures (regional development plans and Community Support Frameworks). In addition, the flexibility and variety of forms of assistance (programmes for one or more sectors, whether integrated or not, individual projects, global grants) should enable a complex and diversified range of regional requirements to be satisfied.

This new flexibility in the Community's regional operations augurs well for its effectiveness in the future, which is all the more essential since the appropriations available to the Funds give them an important role in the development process of most of the regions concerned.

The extent of the efforts required to enable weak regions not simply to absorb the shock of the single market, but to benefit from the new growth it engenders, means that all those concerned in development must pool and co-ordinate their efforts and eliminate any duplication and inconsistency. It should be possible to achieve that objective by implementing the master development plans represented by the Community Support Frameworks and by applying the two principles underlying the reform, partnership and subsidiarity.

As stressed above, the aim of partnership is for all those involved in development to define together the measures which they are going to undertake jointly. It is the guarantee of full understanding of all the objectives sought and the methods to be used and of the most rational utilisation of the funds available. The goal of subsidiarity is to permit each level of political or administrative responsibility to carry out the tasks which it is best fitted to undertake. In the case of regional development, this means that responsibility for implementation of the Community Support Frameworks is shared between local, regional, national and Community authorities. Each of these can and should concentrate on its own responsibilities, so enhancing the overall efficiency of the system. Some methods of intervention, such as the management of global grants by intermediaries, constitute a direct application of this principle.

Finally, management of a large integrated economic area must be accompanied by consideration of the use to be made of it so as to provide a context for long-term planning, whether with regard to the design of large communications and telecommunications networks, the development or maintenance of complementary initiatives (for example, in the field of energy), the prevention of imbalances (excessive concentrations, the environment) or the promotion of major works on a scale exceeding the purely regional or national.

This overall vision, which is essential to the smooth operation of the single market, was expressly incorporated in the reform. A series of preparatory studies have been launched and the first conclusions and guidelines should be available at the end of this year. For instance, a start has been made on a prospective approach to regional planning on a European scale.

CONCLUSION

The first year of operation of the reform of the Structural Funds has shown clearly that the member states and the Commission are well able to meet the challenge posed by more effective Community structural measures. The Community has succeeded in concentrating its contributions, developing an overall vision and improving considerably the programming of its intervention. The various stages of the reform have been met without undue difficulty: the member states have drawn up excellent development and conversion plans to meet extremely tight deadlines and the Commission has been able to reply, thanks to the successful operation of partnership, by establishing Community Support Frameworks within a reasonable period of time.

The Community has met the problems of the regional impact of the single market and the need to take action in preparation for the future by equipping itself with principles, means and money. The reform of the structural policies and the Structural Funds, a key factor in securing economic and social cohesion, has enabled the regions concerned to take a decisive step forward. The future should demonstrate that the reform, together with their own dynamism, offers these regions the best means of tackling the 1993 deadline.

Chapter 5

The implementation of the reform of the Structural Funds in the lagging regions of the Community

Elvira Urzainqui and Rosario de Andrés

THE IMPLEMENTATION OF THE REFORM OF THE STRUCTURAL FUNDS IN THE LAGGING REGIONS OF THE COMMUNITY

The reform of the Structural Funds, encouraged by the entry into force of the European Single Act, marks the start of a new phase in European Economic Community (EEC) regional policy, the purpose of which is to reinforce the economic and social cohesion of the Community once the Single Market is implemented. The extensive regional differences already existing in the European Community could increase, causing a serious threat to the benefits which are expected to accrue from the disappearance of internal frontiers, since the market mechanism has not the capacity to distribute the benefits of integration equally.

In this context, Article 130A of the Single Act establishes that the Community will attempt, in particular, 'to reduce the differences amongst its different regions and also develop the lagging regions'.

The aim of regional development policy is to reduce the existing differences both in the level of income and in employment between specific areas. Where one of these areas has the levels of the parameters (income and employment) which are considered acceptable and the other has not, it is expected that the interventions contemplated by the Community's regional policy will have differentiated spatial effects. This implies an accurate delimitation of the area in which there are specific conditions that determine its level of development in terms both of income and employment.

Concerning the 'lagging regions' contemplated in the Community's regional policy and considered as the main aim of the Structural Funds, the policies must, on the one hand, remove the obstacles preventing take-off and, on the other hand, create suitable conditions for self-sustained growth. The aim of regional action is to reduce the differences, which are at the same time the cause and effect of the situation of underdevelopment preventing the implantation of activities which generate employment and income, and also to transform the characteristics of the location of the activities, making them more attractive to the economic and social agents that make investment decisions.

The objectives aimed at by the reform of the Structural Funds for these lagging regions have to be considered from two different points of view:

* a quantitative perspective in terms of volume of resources used (sufficiency);
* a qualitative perspective expressed in terms of adequacy (efficiency) of the actions contemplated in the objective. The objective also has a double aim: to stimulate economic take-off and to maintain it in a self-sustained way, the latter being an essential condition needed to reduce the backwardness of the lagging regions.

It is necessary for the lagging regions in the EEC to take advantage of the Single Market and to attain a level of economic growth above the EEC average. To achieve this, an increase and a diversification of economic activities whose objectives are to generate income and employment are essential. It is important to point out that the reform does not establish any quantitative norms to be achieved in the catching-up process.

The points of view expressed above call for an analysis of the appreciation of the reform on the basis of a knowledge of the nature of the obstacles preventing the progress of lagging regions.

PROBLEMS OF THE LAGGING REGIONS

The reform of the Structural Funds, the instrument of the Community's regional policy, establishes as the main objective of the co-ordinated intervention of the three funds (ERDF – European Regional Development Fund, ESF – European Social Fund, and EAGGF – European Agricultural Guidance and Guarantee Fund) the promotion of the development and structural adjustment of the lagging regions, defined as 'Objective 1', and delimits these regions as those where the GDP (Gross Domestic Product) is less than 75 per cent of the average in the EEC.[1] These regions together contain 21.5 per cent of the Community population (about 70 million people), located in Spain, France, Greece,

Ireland, Italy, Portugal and the United Kingdom (Northern Ireland),[2] that is to say, in the peripheral areas of the Community.

On the other hand, the lagging regions show common characteristics in their demographic and macroeconomic make-up, and also in their socio-economic nature.

A synthesis of the features common to them all appears as follows.

Demography and labour market

The population of the lagging regions (at present 21.5 per cent of the total in the EEC) shows a progressive decrease in relation to the rest of the EEC's population.

From a territorial point of view, the backward regions that cover a major part of the territory of the Community show a population density (inhabitant/per km^2) lower by far than the average for the rest of the EEC.

This population imbalance is due to profound structural transformations caused by emigration not compensated for by the natural growth of the population.

From the territorial point of view, the distribution of population in the regions shows a lack of medium-sized towns which constitute the urban structure of regional territory in the more developed regions and which transmit the advantages derived from the big urban centres. These are very scarce in the lagging areas.

Concerning the distribution of population by age, the backward regions have a high proportion of young people, that is, above the Community average, and this factor, very often, results in a rapid increase in the working population.

The regions included under Objective 1 show rates of activity lower than the average in the Community, with the peculiarity that the number of people employed in primary production is well above this average (8 per cent).

The qualifications and skills of the working population are inadequate. The level of unemployment is above the Community average and the level of underemployment gives cause for concern.

Income, productive structure and productivity

The low contribution of these regions to Community GDP results in a GDP per inhabitant lower than the 75 per cent of the average in the EEC. This difference from the Community average is closely related to the productive structure of these regions in which agricultural production is more important than industry and services. Productivity per person is lower than the average in the Community, thus effectively discouraging competitiveness.

The agricultural component in the lagging regions makes their development dependent upon their geographical and climatic peculiarities and also their productive structure. Agricultural income is not complemented by industrial activity and services. Most of the regions included in Objective 1 have strong rural characteristics. Due to this, their development and structural adjustment cannot be separated from the development of rural areas (see Chapter 7).

Economic and social infrastructure

The infrastructures which condition the development of productive activity and the stability of the population so profoundly are underfunded in the backward regions, both in economic infrastructure (roads, railways, electrification, etc.) and social infrastructure (health, education, housing, etc.). Ireland and Portugal are the countries with regions with the highest indices of lack of infrastructure.

The dispersal of population, low levels of income, high rates of unemployment and lack of communications (isolation) can be found in the regions included in Objective 1. They form local markets of a reduced size that prevent enterprises from taking advantage of economies of scale.

In addition to all these factors, there is the psychological impact that the condition of underdevelopment has on the inhabitants of these regions; lack of confidence in the future, together with the incapacity to face it, necessitates external help to stimulate and complement the development of their internal potential. The latter requires a minimum of local initiative but, unfortunately, a great number of lagging areas show a lack of any initiative. In this sense, the reform of the Structural Funds seeks to provide an answer to the problem. It attempts to deal with the structural problems which are at the root of the low level of development with a true Community policy, promoted by the Commission. This policy has to be complementary to the efforts made at national level and to a long-term strategy to create well-articulated social and economic structures in the regions included in Objective 1.

Scientific literature on regional development clearly shows that, in order to generate dynamic development in a lagging region, the existence of a minimum threshold of economic and social infrastructure is necessary, together with help towards entrepreneurial productive investment (agricultural, industrial or services). This assistance is not sufficient unless we add other qualitative measures and incorporate them in the planning of regional development, so that they contribute towards the creation of a regional culture which is adapted to the needs of the economy and modern society.

On the other hand, we think that this 'qualitative' aspect is essential to attain the goals set for the zones included in Objective 1.

Regional policy aimed at lagging regions must remedy the considerable lack of infrastructure and basic equipment in order to reach a minimum which could make these regions attractive to productive entrepreneurial investments and encourage population stability at the same time. This means arriving at a favourable balance between the infrastructure of services available to the population (such as education, hospitals, housing) and the technical infrastructure of communications (transport, telecommunications). This equilibrium should be reached, as Araujo points out,[3] before aid (incentives) is granted to enterprises. Without this prior condition, entrepreneurial incentives could be inefficient.

Both the technical and social infrastructure should be developed simultaneously with the aim of satisfying economic and social needs linked to the regional activitity which is going to be promoted. As far as entrepreneurial incentives granted to lagging regions are concerned, they must be – as Araujo also points out – very large and proportional to their economic lag in order to compensate for the spontaneous advantages found in urban-industrial areas as economies of scale.

In the regions covered by Objective 1, the articulation of regional instruments should produce a high rate of aggregated growth which, on the one hand, could increase internal demand, employment and income and, on the other, could facilitate the transfer of productive activities from other regions.

SOME REMARKS ABOUT THE IMPLEMENTATION OF THE REFORM OF THE STRUCTURAL FUNDS IN THE LAGGING REGIONS

The reform of the Structural Funds is fundamentally based on:

- an increase in budgetary resources;
- the modification of the system of operation and application of the funds.

In the first case, the increase has meant the doubling of the amount of the Structural Funds. Compared with 7,000 million ECUs in 1987, the final amount will be 14,000 million by 1993 (20 per cent of the EEC budget) and, with regard to the regions covered by Objective 1, this doubling will take place in 1992.

In the second case, the reform aims at introducing more efficiency as regards the application of the different funds, by implementing a whole range of qualitative changes. The lagging regions are the main beneficiaries of the redoubled structural effort. Concerning this point, it must be emphasised that most of the resources of the ERDF (80 per cent) will be destined for these regions.

No doubt the efficacy of the reform will depend both on the correct selection of the instruments to be used and the intensified co-operation and co-ordination of the different agents who will participate in the whole process, that is to say, the Commission, the member states, regions, and other territorial entities and local organisations.

The application of the basic principles contained in the reform should be very effective, as long as they are adhered to. The basic principles are:

- concentration of effort, the basic aim of which is to achieve a strong economic impact;
- implementation of comprehensive programmes which replace existing projects;
- co-operation of the Community with all interested parties;
- co-ordination of the different financial instruments of the Community. In the case of Objective 1, the three funds, (ERDF, ESF, EAGGF) would all contribute towards its attainment;
- improvement in the methods of evaluation and control.

Without doubt, the doubling of the Structural Funds and their concentration on the less-favoured regions are extremely important because it is clear that such a financial effort is essential to attain their development. The regions included in Objective 1 have been given 38,300 million ECUs for the period 1989–93, 63.5 per cent of the total amount of these funds in the distribution agreed by the Commission (60,315 million ECUs in all) (see Table 5.1). From these 38,300 million ECUs, 2,100 million ECUs are reserved for the Community initiative programmes. The 36,200 million ECUs are distributed as Table 5.1.

The reform of the Funds gives priority to the regions included in Objective 1 and this is expressed in the percentage, already indicated, of resources destined for these regions. This priority is reinforced by

Table 5.1 Allocations of appopriations for Objective 1

Country	Million ECUs	%	ECUs/Inhabitant
Greece	6,667	18.4	69.4
Spain	9,779	27.0	437.2
France	888	2.5	574.0
Ireland	3,672	10.1	1,036.5
Italy	7,443	20.6	358.5
Portugal	6,958	19.2	681.7
United Kingdom	793	2.2	506.1
TOTAL	36,200*	100.0	517.5

Note: *2,100 million ECUs are reserved for Community initiative programmes.

the previous decision that established the regulations of the ERDF (the main instrument of Community regional policy): 80 per cent of its credits would be applied to these regions.

However, it is also true that a greater effort is needed from the Community in this field since we cannot forget that the assignment of the Structural Funds was not increased in 1986 and 1987, as was needed. As a result, the foreseen doubling of the funds available could be insufficient.

In 1987, structural aid represented 0.3 per cent of the GDP of the member states and it is estimated that the Structural Funds will not reach 20 per cent of the Community budget in 1992. This, compared with the great problems experienced in the Objective 1 regions, makes us doubt the sufficiency of the financial effort made. Besides, the probable impact of the increase of the funds could be seriously reduced if co-ordination among the different parties involved does not occur, and if the policy of each member state does not allocate an increase equivalent to the total volume of national public aid. The additional help by the Community must help to avoid a return to the status quo, as has happened previously. It could become common practice for central governments or even local governments to include a whole range of programmes current in their planning, present them to the Community and, once they have been approved, use the resources assigned to these programmes for other programmes.

Greater control over central government and regional government by the Commission could be highly beneficial in this regard.

The carrying out of the second basic principle of the reform, the substitution of projects by five-year programmes, may also have important results.

There is a need for a debate on regional policy in which all the different groups could co-operate, in order to help understand the problems of each region. By this means, it would be easier to pinpoint special measures which facilitate the process of development. Another positive effect will be the probable simplification of bureaucracy.

The need to co-operate among the different interested groups is highlighted in the presentation of the 'Regional Development Plans' by member states. These plans will form the basis for 'Community Support Frameworks' negotiated by the Commission and the member state concerned.

The development priorities and the types of measure requiring financing (the so-called axes of development) are determined within that framework.

Throughout this process we must bear in mind the different instrumental policies contained in the Community measures which, for the regions included in Objective 1, are basically the following:

- infrastructure: due to the importance of productive investment and the deficiencies of the existing economic structure, it is considered vital that a major part of the investment of the ERDF be devoted to these types of investments;
- incentives for location of economic activities;
- evaluation and stimulation of the internal potential, of economic encouragement and of the diffusion of social opportunities in the territory;
- urban policy, to direct the growth of economic activities in the context of demographic stability and an urban system;
- environmental policy, in order to guarantee a rational use of national resources and their restoration or improvement in the case of existing damage.

The Single Market must be considered as a Community reference framework to avoid the danger of having what has been called a two-speed Europe and also the concentration of both economic activities and population in the developed regions of the EEC. It is crucial to attain adequate competitivity in the non-developed regions in order to achieve a Community which is strongly interconnected both politically and socially. Regional policy can play a primary role in attaining this objective and it will thus be necessary to act on different variables in all these regions in order to achieve these objectives:

- to increase productivity;
- to diversify the organisation of production;
- to make the system flexible.

Co-ordination of the different funds will allow a choice as to the type of aid according to each case. Grants for projects with a low or zero rate of return and loans or subsidies for those that could generate profits would be the best solution.

Finally, evaluation and control will permit, in the first case, the definition of the correct objectives before the approval of both the Community Support Frameworks and the programmes, establishing the degree of control needed to attain the proposed objectives. It might be convenient to increase the executive capacity of the Commission in relation to the application of each member state's aid measures, since the new regulations establish that the capacity of control and evaluation regarding application of the different measures is subordinated to the decisions of the different states.

Another positive aspect which appears in the reform of the ERDF is the possibility of spending 15 per cent of its funds on Community initiative programmes. The Commission could facilitate the access of enterprises in the lagging regions to a whole range of programmes dedicated to the assistance of advanced technology projects. Access could be facilitated by the regional policy because these enterprises cannot afford these programmes themselves. Co-operation could be encouraged among the different enterprises of these developing regions in order to produce projects which deal with the application of technology more suited to their specific characteristics. Once again, effective co-ordination could be a decisive factor for the success of this concept.

NOTES

1 EEC Regulation no. 2052/88 of 24.6.1988.
2 See Annex to EEC Regulation no. 2052/88 of 24.6.1988.
3 Araujo, L. L. (1989).

FURTHER READING

Araujo, L. L. (1989) 'Las infraestructuras y el Desarrollo Regional', *Boletín de Información sobre la CEE* no. 22–23, 10–26.
Vela Sastre, I. (1989) 'La reforma de los Fondos Estructurales y el Mercado Comunitario de Apoyo: Reflexiones para una valoración crítica', *Boletín de*

Información sobre la CEE, no. 22–23, 93–108, Universidad de Oviedo, Spain.

Bowles, R. and Jones, P. (1987) 'La España de las regiones y el presupuesto comunitario', *Castilla y Léon en Europa*, no. 19, 1–15.

Castillo, J., Larrañaga, P. G. and Leza, A. S. (1989) 'La reforma de los Fondos Estructurales', *Situación*, no. 3, Madrid.

EEC Regulation no. 4253/88 of 19.12.88.

EEC Regulation no. 4254/88 of 19.12.88.

EEC Regulation no. 4255/88 of 19.12.88.

Ministerio de Economia y Hacienda (1990) *Politica regional en 1989*, Madrid.

Plan de Desarrollo Regional de España 1989–1993, Madrid, 1989.

Plan de Reconversión Regional y Social de España 1989–1993, Madrid, 1989, 262 pp.

Politica regional en la Europa de los años 90, Madrid, 1989, 630 pp.

Rodriguez Cañas, E. (1989) 'Aspectos presupuestarios de la reforma de los Fondos Estructurales', *Boletin de Información sobre la CEE*, no. 22–23, 33–5, Universidad de Oviedo, Spain.

Chapter 6

The implementation of the reform of the Structural Funds in old industrialised areas

Achille Hannequart

INTRODUCTION

Among the objectives that have been laid down in the reform of the Structural Funds, Objective 2 concerns regions in industrial decline. The objective is to renovate the regions, employment areas and urban communities seriously affected by industrial decline and to facilitate the restructuring of declining industries.

Under the system that has been set up, regions eligible under Objective 2 have transmitted regional plans to the Community through the member states. These regional plans set out the analysis of the situation, the general strategy to be followed and the priorities to be implemented. The Community has responded to these plans by elaborating 'Community Support Frameworks' (CSFs) in partnership with the regions. Following on from this, the member states have put forward 'operational programmes' (in which various types of action consistent with the priorities are defined and the implementing agency is identified) or other forms of proposals.

The first section will offer some general remarks on the nature of the system: it will be shown to have very specific features at the constitutional, political and organisational level. It is from these features that the reform draws its importance.

The second section will determine how the needs of these areas may be defined at a theoretical level and will make some comments on the contents of the regional plans in this regard.

In the third and fourth sections, the whole process of producing the Community Support Programmes is analysed in order to highlight and assess the role played by the Commission in partnership with the affected areas and member states.

Operational Programmes, after being approved, have to be implemented at the grass-roots level. As is often the case with public policy, mainly when a great number of social actors are operating the same scheme from different perspectives, a good or bad implementation may make all the difference. The fifth section will analyse the conditions of success for the Community Support Frameworks and Operational Programmes.

THE NATURE OF THE SYSTEM

For a long time, each centralised or federal state has devised regional policies to assist its less-developed areas and has organised budgetary transfers to this end. Nevertheless, it must be emphasised that, in the Community, this movement has assumed three related and specific characteristics.

First, there is a solemn declaration in Article 23 of the Single Act that the Community will develop its action towards the reinforcement of 'economic and social cohesion', that is, to reduce the gap between the various regions of the Community. This cohesion is often presented as a basic condition of the economic development of the Community alongside the achievement of the internal market. Efforts at producing cohesion are therefore a Treaty obligation.

Second, due to the fact that member states retain their national autonomy, this represents a clear political decision. Since various states were fearful of being left behind in the expansion process triggered by the achievement of the internal market or anticipated negative results from it for some of their weaker areas, they asked for compensatory interventions, which they were able to request as member states through the Community political decision-making mechanism. Redistribution is therefore not linked to some parliamentary rule with all its biases but to a political agreement between the states themselves as a condition for taking part in the new developments engendered by the Single Act.

Finally, while redistribution generally occurs through some general legislation or through budgetary transfers, the system of intervention has been harnessed in the Community through Community Support Frameworks and Operational Programmes where the lines of action are precisely defined and which are based on the principles of partnership and additionality as explained in the contribution to this volume by Landaburu.

At the constitutional, political and organisational levels, the reform of the Structural Funds therefore presents specific features that give it its importance and originality.

We must analyse in this chapter industrialised areas in decline which are covered by Objective 2: converting the regions, frontier regions or parts of regions seriously affected by industrial decline.

Before the beginning of the procedure itself, member states had to propose regions or parts of regions responding to the Commission's criteria: some 900 areas were presented by the member states. After examination and after consultation with the Committee on the Development and Conversion of Regions, the Commission finally selected sixty eligible areas. These areas were mostly defined at the NUTS level III or were even smaller. The list of the regions to which they belong is given in Annex I. They cover a population of some 53.2 million inhabitants, that is, some 16.4 per cent of the Community's population.

The list of eligible areas is valid for three years only: this is the reason why the member states programmed their proposals for a three-year period. In accordance with their general planning systems, France and Spain nevertheless presented their proposals for their traditional five-year planning periods.

In the first stage of the procedure, 'regional plans' were established by the regions and sent via the governments of the member states to the Commission between March and October 1990. At the second stage, the Commission engaged in partnership negotiations with the central and regional authorities to define the contents of the 'Community Support Frameworks'. These CSFs were approved on 21 December 1989, except in the case of Spain, whose CSF was approved on 14 March 1990. While the CSFs were in principle drawn up for each area individually, Spain wanted a single CSF for its seven areas: there are therefore fifty-four CSFs for sixty areas.

In its guidelines, the Commission insisted on the promotion of productive investment. Even infrastructure investment should be linked to this by regenerating decayed cores of industrialised areas or modernising their capacities.

THE ANALYSIS OF INDUSTRIAL DECLINE IN THE REGIONAL PLANS

Old industrialised areas suffering from industrial decline display a certain number of symptoms that are documented in the regional plans. Three of them appear dominant.

First the decline of traditional heavy industries with accompanying dereliction has contributed to the poor image of these areas and has made the system of access to and within the areas obsolete. This is an important obstacle to the development process because it entails huge economic costs but more so because it makes the area unattractive to outside investment. The physical upgrading of these areas is a prime condition for their renovation.

The second symptom is linked to population trends. These areas generally have a decreasing population which goes hand in hand with three other characteristics which are interrelated:

- migrants tend to be the younger and better skilled residents who know that they have better job opportunities in more expansive and modern areas;
- there is a mismatch in the skills available. The restructuring of traditional industries has reduced the demand for traditional skills. Conversely, evidence is emerging of shortages in those skills most closely linked to new activities in the industrial and service sectors;
- basic unemployment statistics point to the lengthy duration of unemployment and to the high population of young people involved.

The third characteristic is the concentration of employment in industry, mainly in basic sectors (metallurgical and chemical for example) and in big establishments which are often branch plants of enterprises whose headquarters are located elsewhere. On the other hand, small and medium-sized enterprises (SMEs) are badly represented and often lack dynamism. Similarly, these conditions are not conducive to the growth of self-employment or to the creation of new enterprises.

This description is well known but it gains a sense of urgency when it is repeated in most of the regional plans and is documented with the same sort of statistics. Recent developments also make the problem urgent in another sense: as there is presently a new structural wave of industrial expansion, these areas have a unique opportunity to benefit from these trends and to modernise their structures: not to seize this opportunity could have grave detrimental consequences for the old industrialised areas in the future.

These were the main challenges to which the Community Support Programmes had to respond. Let us add that, at the time, eligible areas could benefit from some ongoing programmes from the European Regional Development Fund or the European Social Fund: the programmes to be included were then identified and the share of assistance for Objective 2 was increased.

Table 6.1 Structural Funds assistance for Objective 2 allocations (Million ECUs): 1989–91

Country	ERDF	ESF	Total
Belgium	145.0	50.0	195.0
Denmark	22.4	7.6	30.0
Germany	249.4	105.6	355.0
Spain	576.0	159.0	735.0
France	514.0	186.0	700.0
Italy	179.0	86.0	265.0
Luxembourg	15.0	–	15.0
Netherlands	56.8	38.2	95.0
United Kingdom	1,158.6	351.4	1,510.0
TOTAL	2,916.5	983.8	3,900.3

Source: EC Commission.

The breakdown of total assistance from the Structural Funds for Objective 2 between the ERDF and the ESF is given in Table 6.1. Out of a total appropriation of ECU 3,900 million for Objective 2, the ESF represents some 25.2 per cent of the amount available: this is the best indication of the importance given by the member states to initiatives such as vocational training, employment aid schemes and SME support.

The way in which Structural Funds assistance is subdivided between various functional headings gives a first clue to the understanding by the Commission of various sub-objectives and their quantitative importance. The following categories are used in the annual report on the implementation of the reform of the Structural Funds (COM (90) 516 Final):

A Ongoing operations and Community programmes.
B Increasing business competitiveness through measures such as aids to productive investment, research, innovation, training.
C Supporting infrastructures directly relevant for economic activities, such as aids to rehabilitation of sites, business service centres, waste disposal.
D Developing indigenous amenities, mainly tourism.
E Upgrading basic infrastructures, such as communications, roads.
F Obtaining technical assistance.

The breakdown by categories and for the two Funds is presented in Table 6.2.

Table 6.2 Structural Funds assistance by Category (Financial envelopes, 1989–91 Million ECU, 1989 prices)

Category	ERDF	ESF	Total
A. Ongoing operations	952.0	137.3	1,089.3
B. Business competitiveness	770.2	485.4	1,255.6
C. Support infrastructures	627.6	57.5	685.1
D. Indigenous amenities	157.8	46.2	204.0
E. Basic infrastructures	293.1	5.4	298.5
F. Technical assistance	4.1	13.3	17.4
TOTAL	2,804.8	745.1	3,549.9

Source: EC Commission.

Attention must be drawn to the fact that the Commission did not select a special heading for the development of human resources. It appeared more pertinent to include the related initiatives in the other objectives of economic conversion and valorisation of which they are a main ingredient. More particularly, the financial envelope for promoting business competitiveness falls under the ESF for some 40 per cent. Another clear result, in accordance with the Commission's policy, is the small part taken in the total envelope by the basic infrastructures.

The overall reactions of the member states look very similar according to Table 6.3 if we do not take into account the ongoing operations. Indigenous amenities, basic infrastructures and technical assistance account only for a very low percentage, except for a few special cases. Business competitiveness and support infrastructure take the lion's share but the relation is very different between countries. Extreme cases are the United Kingdom, where the percentage is about the same, and the Netherlands or Luxembourg, where the financial envelopes for support infrastructure are less than 10 per cent of those for business competitiveness.

After looking at the general conditions in which the reform of the Structural Funds has been applied to the old industrialised areas, we may begin to examine how it may influence the situation in these areas and what difficulties may be encountered in the process.

THE WAY OUT OF INDUSTRIAL DECLINE

A diagnosis is not an adequate basis on which to devise a sensible policy. It is also necessary to know what sort of new situation has to be

Table 6.3 Structural Funds assistance to different countries by category (1989–91) (%)

Category	Bg	Dk	Gr	Sp	Fr	It	Lu	Nl	UK
A. Ongoing operations	36	9	9	27	24	5	53	31	45
B. Business competitiveness	53	72	52	36	43	62	47	50	19
C. Support infrastructures	7	18	39	13	26	20	–	4	18
D. Indigenous amenities	3	–	–	–	–	–	–	13	9
E. Basic infrastructures	2	–	–	24	6	11	–	–	9
F. Technical assistance	–	1	1	–	1	2	–	2	–
TOTAL (Million ECUs)	179	30	335	724	606	221	15	77	1,364

Note: Bg: Belgium; Dk: Denmark; Gr: Greece; Sp: Spain; Fr: France; It: Italy; Lu: Luxembourg; Nl: Netherlands; UK: United Kingdom.

Source: EC Commission.

created and by which processes the transformation is possible. Most studies offer many hindsights on the diagnosis and list numerous factors of development, but few of them show how they can be integrated in a new and endogenous development process.

The problem is to make these areas pass from a process of relative decline to a process of expansion and modernisation. The present conditions of industrial modernisation must therefore be studied to know what elements they are made up of and how they can be reached. This is the reason why the problem of industrial decline, although an old problem, is presently being looked at in completely new terms.

Recent scientific literature concentrates on three aspects of industrial regeneration:

* increase in the rate of creation of new firms, even in the industrial sector;
* adaptation of managerial strategies to new international forms of development and competition;
* transformation of the service sector.

It can be shown that, for all three points, traditional areas of industrial decline are not doing well. If we look again at the regional plans, they show the same old picture: the rate of creation of new firms is very low; managerial strategies are old-fashioned, mainly in small and medium-sized enterprises; the share of services in total employment is low and this is particularly true for the high-level services. Let us look at each of these points in turn.

Creation of new firms

The increase in the number of new firms is well documented (Keeble and Wever 1986) and this increase seems to appear in specific areas where:

- the diversity of the industrial sector is the greatest;
- the basic industrial structure is dominated by small and medium-sized firms;
- the environment is pleasant.

As these conditions are not generally met in old industrialised areas, policy measures will have to compensate for the disadvantages.

Let us recognise that we cannot expect miracles in this field. The same studies show that new firms are highly vulnerable in the first years and generally stabilise their employment level at around fifteen people after 10–15 years.

Two criticisms may be levelled at these conclusions. It may well be enough for a few of these firms to reach a respectable dimension to change the local industrial structure and outlook. There is another element. Although our own studies indicate compatible results for the Hainaut area in Belgium until 1980, two new characteristics seem to appear between 1980 and 1988 (Hannequart 1989):

- the number of new firms created by entrepreneurs with a university degree increased in relation to the total number of new firms;
- the employment given by these firms grew rapidly to around 40–50 people.

This empirical result coincides with modern research on industrial dynamism. If the number of small firms tends to increase to serve growing local needs due to general economic expansion and the diversification of the product structure, only those enterprises with a 'firm advantage' can develop at the competitive edge of the market.

Revision of managerial strategies

Managerial strategies have to adapt to the new international industrial system (Ergas 1984). The main requirement in this respect is for firms to reach a high degree of excellence for their products or services and for their production processes. This necessitates a good technological or commercial position but, when we look at the performance of the most successful firms, it is also often interrelated with three other elements, mainly in the medium-sized firms:

- recourse to services delivered by firms in the vicinity because a small or medium-sized enterprise (SME) cannot build into its own organisational system the necessary service infrastructure without having problems at the level of economies of scale for each of the managerial functions (Perry 1990);
- the recourse to interfirm co-operation to be able to get an efficient production structure while remaining highly specialised and to gain access more easily to export markets (Hannequart 1987);
- structural internationalisation because the increasing specialisation of production and the reduction in the costs of human and information flows make traditional exports a poor platform for expansion (Hannequart 1987).

The main conclusion to be drawn from these remarks is that renovation is a global strategy for the firms which must simultaneously take into account these various factors.

Here again we must not start with false hopes. Most firms in an area will remain traditional local firms serving regional needs, but it is absolutely necessary that a few of them reach the high level of performance without which the area will be left behind in international industrial competition.

A point often discussed in this respect is the role of major enterprises in stimulating the local environment, especially through subcontracting. But the qualitative results of our studies show that this process only occurs in specific circumstances: the most favourable case is when the major firm has independent headquarters in the area, produces the whole of the product (and not only standardised parts) and when the product is divisible into high technology components.

Development of service industries

Service industries help regional development by creating employment: it is well known that the biggest share of employment creation occurs in this sector. But services are also increasingly integrated in the production process and in the qualities of the products: they have become a main ingredient of performance. It is therefore necessary to distinguish two types of services.

'Current services' are those linked with the usual needs of the population: they include, for example, retailing, banking and personal services. These services are strongly linked to population size. A study of retailing for a sample of Belgian cities shows no systematic difference according to the general degree of development in the area. But the structure of retailing is different: specialised and independent retailing enterprises are more prevalent in areas of high development than in areas of industrial decline.

'High level services', such as marketing, advertising and consultancy, present another picture. They are well represented and have a high rate of increase in the fastest-growing areas but are underrepresented in areas of industrial decline. These areas must therefore be equipped with an appropriate service structure if we wish them to develop (Goe 1990).

THE ROLE OF THE COMMISSION

The success of the reform of the Structural Funds will depend on the degree to which regional policies will be focused on the three trends described in the second section. As was stated briefly at the beginning of this chapter, the reform process has proceeded in three stages:

1 regional plans presented by eligible areas to the Commission through the member states;
2 'Community Support Frameworks' established by the Commission in partnership with the relevant authorities;
3 'Operational Programmes' submitted by eligible areas for the approval of the Commission, which include the main actions to be implemented with the designation of a specific operator in charge of each of them.

The regional plans for each area were 'classic' in their diagnosis and analysis. They first presented a general description of the area's problems, then listed a certain number of objectives and finally proposed the most significant types of measures to be implemented. It should be underlined that they generally focused upon industrial excellence, innovation, endogenous development, enterprise centres, small and medium-sized enterprises and creation of a skilled workforce; these are the same features which have been highlighted in our general overview above and on which the Commission has long insisted in its various communications and programmes.

Two remarks must nevertheless be made in relation to the contents of the regional conversion plans:

• some of the strategies alluded to above are rarely considered. This is mainly the case for interfirm co-operation and for structural internationalisation;

- the references to the Community action instruments are relatively vague. The policy proposals are much more inspired by national traditions and instruments than by the new developments indicated by the Commission.

These two remarks possibly point to the same problem. For various reasons, the focus of modern industrial policy has in fact shifted from the national states to the Community. Most structural industrial initiatives have originated from the Commission, for example, Esprit or Brite among a number of scientific programmes, the Sprint programme, Europartenariat, Euro-info centres, the new scheme for management retraining. National programmes have retained a more traditional outlook.

We consider that the 'Community Support Frameworks' which were drawn up for each eligible area might have been able to modify some of these traditional policies. The 'Frameworks' indeed define the main priorities of action that the Commission recognises and therefore define joint Community and national instruments of action. It is at this stage that the principles of partnership and additionality take on their meaning:

- under the principle of partnership, regional, national and Community authorities determine the main priorities for development and, among them, those on which Community action must be concentrated to give a greater leverage to the development process. Such priorities are, for example, the provision of business centres, assistance for co-financing innovation or consultancy, ESF support for accelerating and easing the introduction of new technologies in small and medium-sized firms;
- under the principle of additionality, Community funds must be matched by a similar effort from the national and regional authorities. The Community Support Frameworks indeed include the financial allocation by broad types of measure and sources of funding together with an estimate of private expenditures linked to the measures.

We would estimate that, in general, the additionality principle advanced by the Community together with regional political pressure have tended to increase the funds from national sources put at the disposal of the eligible areas; the increased contribution by the

Community seems not to have been generally translated into a decreased contribution at the national level. Furthermore, we would also estimate that, where political pressure is applied, the total amount of regional aid in the country will increase. Areas not eligible under the Community system will try to get some form of national compensation. It is nevertheless difficult to substantiate these hypotheses empirically.

There is still a puzzling point to be mentioned. The nature of these principles implies that Community intervention is in support of national intervention. This may lead to two shortcomings.

First, what is proposed by the national authorities will depend on the state of national legislation on industrial affairs. Neverthless, the state of this legislation seems relatively unified, probably because the pressures for industrial renovation are similar everywhere and because of political competition.

Second, and more importantly, the specific Community instruments have rarely been included in the discussion. This leads to a paradoxical result. These instruments have indeed been generally devised to activate the newest industrial strategies, for example, contacts with the universities through the Comett programme; technological research and innovations through many specific programmes such as Brite, Esprit; interfirm co-operation through the Sprint programme and so on. Many of these strategies are of prime importance for areas in industrial decline. Enterprises may apply for these programmes by themselves. But if industrial decline in the past has led to a lack of dynamism and to a narrowing of the innovative base, access to these programmes must be stressed and facilitated.

The Vade-Mecum of the Commission also provides for an efficient combination of grants and loans in financing the measures. Loans are mainly from the European Investment Bank and this combination requires a better co-ordination between the Commission and the EIB. As could be expected, it has been difficult to make this provision fully operational. Loan decisions are linked to the precise technical and financial nature of the project and the EIB must be consistent with its own rules in the field. What is important is that the national or private share of the programme may be helped by the EIB in case of need. Only at this stage will the problem of an efficient combination of grants, loans, seed capital and so on be posed.

CONDITIONS FOR SUCCESS

The test of success for the reform of the Structural Funds is the catching-up of the declining areas in relation to the Community average so that the gap becomes progressively more acceptable or even disappears.

At the quantitative level, the role of the Structural Funds is to reduce the cost of the physical or human investment that is called for if the area is to develop: this is the supply aspect of the equation. But there is also a demand aspect: projects of a suitable character have to be presented to meet the increased supply.

In an area that has suffered from industrial decline and continues to be in a difficult position the investment situation will normally have three characteristics:

- the rate of return will generally be lower than in the most advanced areas and the cost higher;
- the number of 'modern' projects will be lower;
- the investment or innovation decisions will be much less responsive to a cost decrease.

All these points may be subsumed under the general idea of an investment function that is highly inelastic. An improvement in the cost conditions, such as must result from the operation of the Structural Funds, may have a very low effect on the quantity of investment decisions if, at the same time, demand is not activated and made more elastic. There are three ways through which this activation of demand may be pursued (Hannequart 1990).

Information

First, firms must be informed of the new possibilities in an appropriate way. By that we mean that they must know that the system of intervention is linked to the development of their managerial functions, such as building a technological base, improving the management organisation, co-operating with firms of another country, engaging in specialised subcontracting, automating the production process.

It is not enough, as the Vade-Mecum does, to explain the principles and the structure which lie at the foundation of the reform of the Structural Funds. Such a presentation is only of theoretical interest for economic operators: what they need is to be able to relate managerial projects to the types of interventions most fitted to them. The information must therefore list various types of managerial decisions, an example of which has just been given, as well as the corresponding interventions on which economic operators can rely. Such a presentation will reinforce two tendencies:

- firms will have their attention drawn to these new managerial strategies which are not necessarily natural to them. It must be hoped that more firms will be attracted by these new ways of thinking;
- firms will know better in each case what kinds of interventions are available to them and how they can proceed to participate in the system.

Due to the fact that there are local organisational peculiarities and that Community interventions in principle complement national intervention, this information structure must be elaborated and activated by local partnership. It seems to us that this is the main point on which the partnership principle must be continued in the implementation phase of the reform with the impetus given by the Commission.

It must also be stressed that another major role of the Commission is to draw the attention of the local authorities to the programmes that are operated directly by the Commission in the field of industrial policy, such as Brite, Sprint, Europartenariat, Comett. The Commission rightly says that these programmes are tailored to the most modern forms of industrial restructuring: it would be paradoxical if these programmes were not publicised in the areas most in need of them.

Intermediation

Second, there is an interface problem. It is not enough that demand for, and supply of, public support exist: they must also meet. But it is well known today that, between the two, there are transaction costs that are multifarious. Among them we may cite being informed of the exact nature of the interventions, finding the place to which the demand should be made, taking the time to discuss the matter, complying with the rules.

These transaction costs are easily absorbed by large firms. In many cases, they are also absorbed by market-based forces. But interface through the market may only be profitable when there are many small standardised cases (general financial intermediation) or when the unitary value of the operation is very high (high technology transfer intermediation).

In most of the cases in our area of interest, these conditions do not obtain and no market develops. There is then a general tendency to entrust the task to an official organisation, but this may be a highly inefficient solution for at least two reasons:

- the 'privileged organisation' is limited by its own capacity and the cost of communication. The random process of information and activation will function the better the more economic operators there are interested in the system;
- the 'privileged organisation' may use its monopoly power to reinforce its position.

Even in this case, one way out of the dilemma is to encourage these institutions to build some sort of network of affiliates. Private operators who play an interface role may be so associated with the system.

In most cases, it must nevertheless be possible to have recourse to some kind of market system, involving, for example, banks or consultants. There is an excellent example of this for transnational co-operation between firms. The system was first operated by the 'Bureau de Rapprochement des Entreprises' which obtained some outstanding results but whose action was necessarily limited. Through the present Sprint programme, the Commission finances transnational meetings of consultants to arrange co-operation between the firms with which they are working.

Structural mixes

There is a third problem which is possibly even more difficult. When trying new forms of development, enterprises are usually confronted with various types of obstacle. For example, when they want to reinforce their technical bases, they may have to jump to a new technology, retrain their personnel or find partners in another country. It is indeed probable that the most interesting cases of industrial renovation imply action at various levels. If firms have to find solutions by themselves, the splitting up of projects into various parts will be maintained at the grass-roots level, despite a macro-regional co-ordination.

ANNEX I

Regions eligible under Objective 2

Belgium
> Turnhout
> Hainaut
> Liège province.
> Limburg
> Luxembourg

Denmark
> Storstrøm-Vestlolland
> Nordjyllands amt

France
> Picardie
> Champagne-Ardennes
> Haute-Normandie
> Basse-Normandie
> Bourgogne
> Nord-Pas-de-Calais
> Lorraine
> Franche-Comté
> Pays de la Loire
> Bretagne
> Poitou-Charentes
> Aquitaine
> Midi-Pyrénées
> Rhône-Alpes
> Auvergne
> Languedoc-Roussillon
> Provence-Alpes-Côte d'Azur

Germany
> Peine-Saltzgitter
> Emden
> Bremen
> Nordrhein – Westfalen
> Rheinhessen-Pfalz
> Saarland
> Berlin

Italy
   Piedmonte
   Valle d'Aosta
   Liguria
   Lombardia
   Veneto
   Toscana
   Umbria
   Marche
   Lazio

Luxembourg
   Luxembourg

Netherlands
   Groningen/Drenthe
   Twente
   Limburg

Spain
   Cantabria
   Pais Vasco
   Navarra
   Rioja
   Aragon
   Madrid
   Cataluna

United Kingdom
   North-East
   East
   Midlands
   North-West
   West Cumbria
   North Wales
   South Wales
   West Scotland
   East Scotland

REFERENCES

Ergas, H. (1984) 'Corporate strategies in transition', in A. Jacquemin (ed.) *European Industry: Public Policy and Corporate Strategy*, Oxford, Clarendon Press.

Goe, W.R. (1990) 'Producer services, trade and the social division of labour', *Regional Studies*, 24, 327–42.

Hannequart, A. (1987) 'Internationalisation des petites et moyennes entreprises et stratégies industrielles', Groupe d'Etudes Politiques Européennes, Brussels.

Hannequart, A. (1989) 'Le développement industriel du Hainaut', Unité de Recherche Systèmes Economiques, Régionaux et Publics, SERP, FUCAM, Mons.

Hannequart, A. (1990) 'Stratégies managérielles et coordination des Fonds Structurels dans les Régions de vieille industrialisation', Rapport pour la Commission des Communautés Européennes, Trans-European Policy Studies Association (TEPSA). Brussels.

Keeble, D. and Wever, E. (eds) (1986) *New Firms and Regional Development*, London, Croom Helm.

Perry, M. (1990) 'Business service specialisation and regional economic change', *Regional Studies*, 24, 163–71.

Chapter 7

The implementation of the reform of the Structural Funds in rural areas

Denis I. F. Lucey

Rural Development is a new policy area for the European Community
> (Ray MacSharry, Member of the Commission of the European Communities Responsible for Agriculture and Rural Development(1990a))

THE BACKGROUND

There are four features of the development of rural areas in the European Communities (EC) as well as in most Organisation for Economic Co-operation and Development (OECD) countries since the 1950s which deserve attention in order to understand the background to the issues involved in the current debates on rural development.

1 The objective of building the productive capacity of the farming sector during those decades was the subject of several public-support programmes directed towards the farming sector. Taken together, this set of programmes may be viewed as a highly successful example of the application of *several strands of activity over a protracted period of time* towards a single objective.

   A large number of policy instruments was, in fact, directed towards that objective. Production incentives were offered through product price supports; extension services were expanded to enhance the technical and managerial skills of individual farmers and to guide them in adopting various new technologies which were emerging from the agricultural research services; technical education was being enhanced for potential young farmers; input subsidies were offered in order to stimulate the adoption of new technologies and credit facilities were made available at attractive terms for farm business expansion. Meanwhile, university faculties of agriculture and food were expanded in order to provide the range and numbers of professional personnel required for the provision of these services either in public, private or mixed agencies.

The resulting development, diffusion and adoption of technical progress at farm level was quite impressive. Improved mechanisation, new plant and animal breeding techniques, mineral fertilisers, crop protection chemicals and compound animal feeding stuffs have all been associated with spectacular increases in yields per hectare or per livestock unit. The favourable output-input price ratios led to rapid intensification of farm production in the Community.

In general, throughout the Community, the volume of agricultural production has been steadily increasing at about 2 per cent *per annum* since the mid-1970s. Internal demand for food within the Community has only been growing at about 0.5 per cent *per annum* during the same period so these trends invariably led steadily, at first towards self-sufficiency and, then, to surpluses of a persistent nature, the disposal of which became increasingly costly. Certain policy changes designed to curb production (production quotas, reduced market intervention, and so on) have been either implemented or proposed for the Community's main agricultural products. The increased farm production levels which resulted from the application of these various output-increasing measures in several countries for the past decades, as well as their policy, trade and public finance implications have been the subject of several studies and of considerable public debate at national, European Community and international levels (General Agreement on Tariffs and Trade – GATT, and so on).

Agricultural policy reform has now become a significant political agenda item for all the major food producing areas of the world. The present Uruguay round of GATT negotiations underlines the international character of these production-consumption imbalances which have resulted from decades of sustained application of consistent sets of policy instruments aimed at a target which has by now been well achieved!

2 The second background feature of rural areas is that these developments have been accompanied by a persistent decline in the number of farm production units and in the number of people employed in production agriculture throughout the Community. By 1985, the number of people working in agriculture in the Community was almost half of what it had been twenty years earlier, in 1965.[4] Moreover, the relative economic role of farming has declined in the

Community as a whole, its share of employment falling from 13.8 per cent in 1970 to 8.7 per cent in 1985 and 7.4 per cent in 1988 (EC Commission 1989a, 1990). During the 1950s and 1960s and the first half of the 1970s, when economic expansion was heavily concentrated in large urban areas, many of the rural people who left farming also left rural areas, not only shrinking the human resource base for future growth in those communities, but also shrinking the demand for existing private services (shops, hairdressers, tradesmen, and so on) and causing a gradual withdrawal of public service provision (schools, medical clinics, police stations, post offices, and so on), thus limiting further economic opportunities in those areas.

3 The third feature is that a fundamental change in farming patterns has been occurring in recent decades in the Community as well as in other OECD countries. On the one hand, there is and will continue to be a trend towards fewness and largeness among commercial farms which will produce an increasing share of farm output if current policies continue. On the other hand, there is also an increasing number of families residing in rural areas, some of whose members are engaged in farming on smaller holdings (too small to generate a satisfactory family income) in conjunction with other gainful activity being pursued either by themselves, their spouses or other family members, such that their family income arises from a number of sources, each of which alone might be deemed to be inadequate if it were to be the sole source of family income (Lucey 1987).

In 1985, only 32 per cent of farms in the Community of Ten occupied one person on a full-time basis. In that year also, 30 per cent of farmers in the Community of Ten supplemented their farming with other gainful activity either on their own premises (farm tourism, processing and retailing of farm products, crafts, and so on) or by off-farm employment on a part-time or full-time basis (EC Commission 1989a).

The combination of part-time farming with various forms of employment in other sectors of activity has been enabled to become important mainly in regions or areas where the regional or local economy had become sufficiently diversified to be able to provide a range of sources of other gainful activity for the rural population. Many other regions or areas are less-developed economically and opportunities for combining farm work with other gainful employment are much less available.

Research in Ireland (Lucey and Kaldor 1969, Lucey et al. 1987) and in other countries demonstrates that complex flow patterns exist and will continue to exist in rural labour markets. These flows will be influenced particularly by the specific kinds of industrial and service employment opportunities which emerge in rural areas, by the willingness of various kinds of local residents to seek those employments, by their training to undertake those employments or to generate other opportunities and by the complex interactions between farm employment and other income-earning activities undertaken by pluri-active rural households.

4 The fourth background feature of analysis of rural development issues arises from increased Community concern with the environment. The process of economic development is, in some places, threatening the basic character of rural communities. Peri-urban pressure, arising not only from industrial processes but also from growing demands for recreation and leisure on the part of city dwellers is causing damage to green spaces. Intensive farming practices arising from the rapid technological changes in farming have also been associated with water pollution, soil contamination and loss of fauna and flora in areas of advanced farming development. In the more remote rural areas, economic decline and outmigration may cause settlements to fall below thresholds of ecological viability, with risks of forest fires, soil erosion, large-scale abandonment of land and 'desertification', thus reducing further their potential for developments in agri-tourism or forestry or even endangering the preservation of their cultural/architectural heritage.

An understanding of these four features facilitates an acceptance of the variety and complexity of rural conditions throughout the Community, an appreciation of the wide differences in locational endowments of rural areas and their competitive advantages/disadvantages and a realisation that diversification of local rural economies on the basis of their specific endogenous potential requires that each area's rural development strategy and package of instruments must be based on actual local circumstances. This is no small challenge!

Faced with the wide diversity of rural society in Europe and the range of specific problems experienced in each region or rural area, the EC Commission, in *The Future of Rural Society* in 1988, proposed a general typology of three standard problems, the solution of which – or the failure to solve which – could well prove crucial for the future of rural society. The three standard types of rural problem are based on *Twenty Years Work for Rural Development*, Council of Europe, 1987:

The *first* problem can be described as the pressure of modern life.

This type of problem appears in rural regions situated near to or within easy access of large urban areas. These regions have a fairly high population density and have enjoyed a fairly favourable economic environment during the past few decades.

These are the regions in which the drive towards more modern and intensive forms of agriculture, in some cases making heavy demands on the natural environment (pollution, damage to and destruction of parts of the countryside), has been strongest.

It is also in these regions that the rural economy's diversification has been most marked and the modern back to nature movement most evident: building of first and second homes (sometimes in unsightly speckling of the landscape), setting up of numerous tourist and leisure amenities (in some cases excessive and environmentally damaging), the decentralisation of the industrial and service sectors and the establishment of new industries at local level (resulting in some cases in industrial pollution). It is in those regions that the various combinations of agricultural and non-agricultural work have developed most successfully.

This type of problem is found mainly in:

1 Rural regions close to built-up areas and main roads, for example, south-east England and the Paris–Brussels–Bonn triangle.
2 Lowlands situated close to towns and cities, for example, East Anglia and the Po Valley, and many regions in the Community's northern mainland, in particular in the Netherlands, Flanders and northern Germany.
3 Coastal regions, in particular on the Mediterranean coast of Spain, France, Italy and Greece, and in the Algarve, the Azores, the Balearic Islands and southern England.

These areas are undergoing major changes, with rival interests competing for the use of land, transforming some of the landscape and conserving other parts, placing the ecological balance in increasing jeopardy, despoiling the countryside by splinter development (*Zersiedlung*) and the seasonal overload of tourism.

The *second* standard type of problem is that of rural decline, which is steadily altering the appearance of many rural regions. With this, there is a persistent drift from the land, which takes place either:

(a) in its traditional form, as a net migration from the region: people leave their region because there is no work, and try their luck in the large towns; this is what has occurred in several regions of Greece, the Mezzogiorno, inland Spain and Portugal, Ireland and Northern Ireland;

(b) as a process of migration within the same region, from rural to urban areas: people stay in the same region but not necessarily in the countryside.

In both cases, one of the main characteristics of the rural areas as such is the relative importance of agriculture, despite major natural and structural handicaps. There are many micro-farms, much too small to provide full-time employment for even one person. Additional or alternative employment/income is either insufficient or not available at all, resulting in a fairly high proportion of concealed and almost permanent underemployment and, by the same token, fairly low family incomes. Faced with these structural blockages, the 15–45 age group, in particular women and the young, leave the countryside and thus help to speed up the ageing of the population. The reduction in the population usually leads to a decline in public and private services (reduction in the number and quality of the services on offer) and an increase in the prices of those services and also of imported goods (problems of distance, transportation and fixed costs).

The most marginal land gradually tends to be abandoned, leading to greater damage by erosion. The failure to maintain woodlands, in particular in the Community's southern regions, even contributes to the destruction of the vegetation cover by fires. At the same time, the rapid and, in some cases, ill-planned concentration of the rural population in regional or supra-regional centres is engendering growing problems of urbanisation, pollution and environmental damage.

This type of problem is commonest in:

(a) certain outlying areas of western Europe, for example, north-west Spain, the west of Ireland, Northern Ireland and the west of Scotland;

(b) the Community's southern outlying areas (Greece, Portugal, central and southern Spain and southern Italy).

The *third* type of standard problem occurs chiefly in very marginal areas, which are often more difficult to reach. The symptoms are fairly similar to those of the second type of problem, except as regards the following two aspects:

1 Rural decline and depopulation are more marked.
2 The potential for economic diversification is much more limited

and the basic (infrastructural) development needed for such diversification is particularly costly.

This type of problem occurs above all in mountain areas, for example, in parts of the Alps and the Pyrenees, in the Massif Central, in southern mountain areas in Greece, Italy, Spain and Portugal, in the Highlands of Scotland and on many islands.

(Council of Europe 1987)

THE POLICY RESPONSES

Governments typically have responded to these issues in the past by means of policies based on a single sector. They have often attempted to redress rural income distribution problems by means of agricultural policy. Farming organisations have often cited the plight of low income farm households in their quest for higher farm product prices – the benefits of which, of course, would accrue in the main to the larger commercial farmers and only to a much lesser extent to small farmers.

Similarly, industrial policy has often been pursued on a single sector basis with the promotion of schemes to attract into rural areas branches of large firms, often multinationals, whose linkages with the rest of the local economy tend to be slight, so that the effects, welcome though they are, tend to be confined to the direct employment effects.

In like vein, tourist promotion, say hotel development, or fishing or other mechanisms, has often been promoted on a single-sector basis – almost as if each of these single-sector developments – or some infrastructural project on its own – would be a magic wand which would unleash the local rural development process.

The results of such single-sector interactions have been generally disappointing. Gradually, governments, development agencies, political decision-makers and their professionals came to realise that action on a broader front was needed so that rural development could be focused more on the territorial area involved and on the changing nature of the rural labour market through the transfer of organisation, technology and enterprise in a manner which genuinely spanned a number of local sectors or, in other words, which was genuinely integrated rural development.

The 1984 European Community Regulation on the European Regional Development Fund had already specifically cited endogenous develop-ment as a goal (EEC Reg. 1984). In the next year, 1985, the Commission of the European Communities, in its Green Paper *Perspectives for the Common Agricultural Policy* (EC Commission 1985), sought to promote:

the fuller integration of agriculture into the general economy, particularly by means of regional development plans for the rural zones of the Community.

and went on to state that:

it is not so much a question of agriculture, but rather of developing the regional economy as a whole.

A major review of rural policy-making, published in 1988 by the OECD (*New Trends in Rural Policy-making*) concluded that:

Traditionally, rural policies that are defined in sectoral terms only have not generally been successful. This is largely because an overall view of the rural economy was lacking and a piecemeal approach was politically unsatisfactory. This ad hoc approach is closely linked with the fact that these strategies have often been the public response to actions launched at the initiative of private protagonists calling on different parts of the governmental structure. Vice-versa, the governments' problem-by-problem approach, and their fragmented administrative structures catering to different clientele have, in turn, strengthened and perpetuated a situation where governments have the greatest difficulty in obtaining an overall view of the future economic development of rural areas. Nevertheless, sectoral policies have sometimes been allotted vast sums of money. Budget transfers have often been made to one sector without considering what effect this might have on other sectors or on broader rural issues such as the structure of the labour market and the quality of the environment.

(OECD 1988)

The Commission, in *The Future of Rural Society* (EC Commission 1989a),[4] suggested three basic strategies to match the three standard problems facing rural society. For rural areas subject to the pressures of modern development (first standard problem), strengthened protection of the rural environment is the key, with improved town and country planning to enable those regions to make the most of the growing demand from urban dwellers for access to the countryside. When addressing the problem of areas experiencing rural decline, the Commission's views were clear cut:

As for the problem of rural decline (second standard problem), what is needed, if new life is to be breathed into the rural areas faced with this kind of problem, to achieve proper integration, is not only action regarding agriculture itself but also a policy for creating lasting, economically justified jobs, outside the farming sector (economic diversification). A rural development policy of this kind must reflect very fully local needs and initiatives, particularly in respect of small and medium-sized firms, and lay heaviest emphasis on maximising indigenous potential.

In this connection, there are three aspects of particular importance:

(i)   the stimulation and the diversification of the supply of services for firms (feasibility studies, market surveys, management counselling, access to venture capital, dissemination of knowledge concerning innovation, and so on);

(ii) social and economic stimulation, the aim being more active management of public subsidy schemes for the prospecting of potential beneficiaries and the strengthening of links between the operators and the socio-economic environment;

(iii) acceptance, to some extent, of grouping of activities, while equilibrium in the geographical distribution of economic activity is maintained; one line of action could be that of encouraging the emergence of a number of development sub-poles in the regions and at the same time a strengthening of links between these intermediate centres and the surrounding countryside.

All the schemes must dovetail into an overall development logic. Thus, it is here that the integrated rural development programmes launched in connection with the reform of the Funds will need to ensure that the initiatives taken are properly related to each other. These programmes must be framed on the basis of close concerted discussion with the national, regional and local authorities. Based on joint preparation, follow-up and evaluation, they must form the basis of a genuine partnership.

When discussing strategies for the very marginal areas (third standard problem), the Commission emphasised that development processes 'are bound to be slow and, without unremitting effort, will fail'. Emphasis would need to be placed on extensive quality farming to maintain rural population, special support for one-person and very small businesses, and the conservation of environmental/cultural assets with a view to the gradual development of tourism.

The Commission also took care to stress that:

the diversification of the rural economies, on the basis of their indigenous potential, means that action as regards rural development must be based and devised on actual local circumstances. The basic strategies must therefore, in each case, be tailored to the particular economic and social circumstances of the relevant regions.

The spirit of those views can be said to have been woven through the June 1988 provisions of EEC Regulation no. 2052/88 with its emphasis on integration and its exhortations regarding partnerships at various levels of planning and decision-making (EEC Reg. 1988a). The same spirit can be read through the four Regulations of December 1988 on the co-ordination of the activities of the three Structural Funds and the provisions relating, in turn, to each of them (EEC Reg. 1988b, c, d, e).

The provisions governing the tasks of the Structural Funds span two regional objectives relating to rural areas (lagging regions – Objective 1 – and rural development areas – Objective 5(b)). In addition, the horizontal Objective 5(a) – speeding up the adjustment of agricultural structures in the context of the reform of the CAP – affects the whole of the Community.

The rural areas selected in respect of Objectives 1 and 5(b) are shown in Figure 7.1, while Table 7.1 provides data regarding the area and population of the regions selected (EC Commission 1990). It will be seen that both sets of regions together account for more than half of the surface area of the Community and slightly over one-quarter of the Community's population. The Community has committed itself to a 1989–93 contribution of ECU36,200 million in respect of Community Support Frameworks (CSFs) for Objective 1 regions and ECU2,607 million in respect of CSFs for Objective 5(b) regions.

COMMUNITY ACTION — THE INSTRUMENTS OF RURAL DEVELOPMENT

Community support frameworks (CSFs) and operational programmes

After detailed negotiations following the submission of plans for 1989–93 by the member states concerned with Objective 1 regions, the CSFs for those regions were adopted by the Commission on 31 October 1989, except for Greece, whose CSF was adopted on 30 March 1990. Negotiations on a series of operational programmes were conducted during 1990 and several have been approved. A few, in fact, (some for Greece and for Ireland) were even adopted by the Community prior to the CSFs!

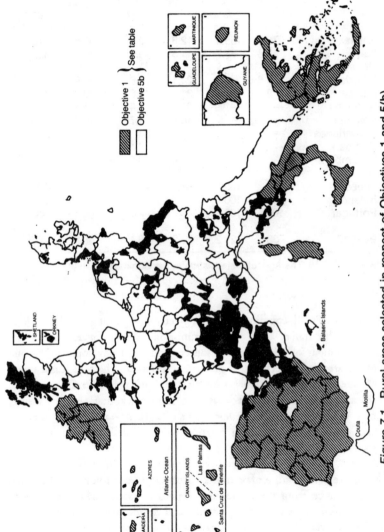

Figure 7.1 Rural areas selected in respect of Objectives 1 and 5(b).

Table 7.1 Area and population of the regions selected for Objectives 1 and 5(b) (Regulation (EEC) no. 2052/88) (%)

	Objective 1		Objective 5(b)		Objectives 1 + 5(b)	
	Area	Popu-lation	Area	Popu-lation	Area	Popu-lation
Spain	76.0	55.4	12.6	2.5	88.6	57.9
Italy	40.8	37.7	11.3	5.0	52.1	42.7
United Kingdom	5.8	2.8	24.1	2.6	29.9	5.4
France	9.1	2.6	31.0	10.0	40.1	12.6
Germany	—	—	21.4	7.4	21.4	7.4
Belgium	—	—	10.6	2.7	10.6	2.7
Netherlands	—	—	7.1	3.0	7.1	3.0
Denmark	—	—	4.0	2.1	4.0	2.1
Luxembourg	—	—	6.4	0.9	6.4	0.9
Greece	100	100	—	—	100	100
Ireland	100	100	—	—	100	100
Portugal	100	100	—	—	100	100
EUR 12	38	21.2	17.3	5.1	55.3	26.3

Source: DG VI 'The Agricultural situation in the Community'

The CSFs all contain laudable objectives regarding rural development. The Italian CSF (EC Commission 1989c), for example, lists 'development of agricultural resources and rural development' as one of six areas of concentration of Structural Funds. The text lists a range of measures related to rationalisation of agricultural structures, research and development related to food marketing and processing, new crop development, development of agricultural advisory services and rural development. In relation to rural development, the CSF states:

In regions with unfavourable production conditions, coordinated assistance from the Community Funds is particularly important to establish the basis for a genuine rural development process through appropriate measures and strategies which help to:

- create a variety of non-agricultural activities, full-time or part-time, which have future potential and provide alternative income;

- improve the service infrastructure needed to stem rural depopulation and achieve living standards similar to those in other regions;
- conserve the environment and countryside in rural areas;
- exploit indigenous potential specific to each region;
- maintain minimum levels of population in rural areas.

Measures specifically concerned with rural development are detailed in the regional sections of the CSF 'in order to take account of the problems and features peculiar to each of the regions concerned'.

For example, in relation to Campania, the Italian CSF provides:

Another priority area of activity in the agricultural sector is that concerned with bolstering and supplementing the incomes of rural communities to enable them to improve their standards of living and to make them comparable with those offered by other economic activities. It has been decided under the partnership arrangements that the EAGGF's key priority should be to develop agri-tourism, to promote farm-gate sales of typical products and to provide support for new types of product in strong demand, such as honey.

The ESF could finance the relevant training measures.

The Italian CSF provision in relation to Puglia includes:

Activities supplementing farm incomes: these activities concern, firstly, rural tourism, which will be supported through the improvement and optimum use of typical rural buildings (*masserie*, *trulli*), in areas of natural beauty. Other measures will be aimed at supporting rural crafts and developing bee-keeping. Tourism measures will also have a contribution to make.

The rural development measures will be taken under the priorities mentioned above and with contributions from the other Structural Funds, notably with a view to:

- creating activities outside farming in the rural areas, thereby providing alternative incomes;
- encouraging, notably through infrastructure improvement, a minimum number of people to stay in the rural areas, especially the most deprived ones;
- protecting the environment (for example by combating erosion) and exploiting the region's indigenous potential.

The CSF for Spain (EC Commission 1989e) also lists agriculture and rural development as one of the six priority areas:

Support for agriculture and rural development is implemented in accordance with the above subheadings, whose specific contribution varies from one region to another. There will be obvious synergy between the EAGGF Guidance Section, the ERDF and the ESF in the measures aimed at rural development (strengthening of the economic and social fabric, integration into economic activity of rural areas which are to benefit from ERDF support) and at the development of human resources (which are to benefit from ESF support) with a view to improving vocational training for farmers and facilitating the reallocation of surplus labour to other economic activities.

In the Spanish CSF, another priority relates to 'Industry, crafts sector and business services'. The CSF in this area refers to 'local development, which can usefully contribute to job-creation in small-scale activities'. Another section relates to tourism, which also includes references to rural tourism.

At the regional level in Spain, the activities agreed under 'agricultural and rural development' tend to focus on conventional agricultural policy measures. For example, in the case of Galicia, the focus is on 'improvement of the natural, infrastructure and structural conditions of production', 'protection of the environment and conservation of natural resources' and on 'redirection of production and improvements in quality'. It is under the heading 'Industry, crafts sector and business services' that one finds the following provision:

Given the importance of the rural economy in the region and the dispersal of the population already referred to on several occasions, local development measures have a certain role to play. These will of course be affected by the measures planned under the other priorities, which is why particular importance will be attached here to those smaller-scale measures, principally representing local initiatives, which are difficult to programme, cover various fields of assistance and are generally designed to encourage and develop the exploitation of indigenous potential in the different parts of the region.

Similarly, the CSF for Portugal (EC Commission 1989d) lists 'Improving the competitiveness of agricultural and rural development' as one of six priorities and goes on to elaborate that:

This priority can be divided into the following five sub-priorities:

- improvement of the production, processing and marketing conditions for agricultural products;
- development of human resources in a rural context;
- improvement in the efficiency of agricultural holdings and enhancement of the value of agricultural products;
- direction of production, including ancillary activities and quality improvements;
- promotion of rural development.

Support for agricultural and rural development will be provided under these sub-priorities and will take account of the need to strengthen the economic and social fabric.

The aforementioned rural development measures and those which, alongside assistance from the other Funds, form part of the programmes under Priority 6 are intended:

- to create non-agricultural activities, thereby providing alternative sources of income;
- to adapt vocational training to the needs of the new activities introduced into the regions concerned.

Priority No. 6 refers to 'Exploiting the growth potential of regions and local development'. Operational programmes for this priority are to be developed during 1990 and 1991 to replace the existing regional policy programmes.

The CSF for Northern Ireland (EC Commission 1989f) states that:

The CSF gives a high priority to the stimulation of the rural economy based upon a thriving and prosperous agricultural sector but also including development of rural firms, alternatives to agriculture and off-farm employment.

and

Measures in favour of job creation outside agriculture in the rural parts of Northern Ireland are contained under other specific priorities of the CSF, for example, tourism, industrial development, human resource development. Part of the remit of the current Rural Action Project funded by the ESF is to examine alternatives to traditional agriculture.

The CSF for Ireland (EC Commission 1989b) lists four specific priorities, one of which is 'Agriculture, fisheries, forestry, tourism and rural development, under which are stated as follows:

The Commission's paper on the Future of Rural Society pointed to the need to widen the base of activities in the rural areas of the Community. Many of the activities supported by the CSF will take place in rural areas and will have the effect of increasing the employment opportunities outside agriculture. In addition, it will be necessary to encourage initiatives in rural development not covered by other parts of the Community Support Frameworks.

A principal objective under 'Agriculture and Rural Development' is stated as:

- rural development, including alternative land uses and non-traditional enterprises for farmers. In the rural areas of Ireland policies will seek to encourage the development of off-farm employment and enterprises.

When dealing with individual forms of assistance, the Irish CSF states that:

Many of the other aspects of the Support Framework provide for activities which will take place in rural areas and which will contribute to rural development, for example, the agricultural measures mentioned above, the promotion of industrial development.

A multifund operational programme including the EAGGF, the ERDF and the ESF will provide complementary support.

EAGGF will fund activities (in addition to those core measures mentioned above) to develop alternative enterprises on farms (for example, farm tourism, farm services, aquaculture, recreational activities, and so on).

The contribution from the ERDF to the programme will be for the development of fishery ports, concentrated on a limited number of ports in compliance with the Community's fisheries policy. Not less than ECU5 million will be available for roads of importance for rural development. Other supporting infrastructure projects including research and development facilities may also be assisted. The rate of aid will be 50 per cent.

ESF support will take the form of an autonomous sub-programme combined with training for fisheries.

Approval of Community activities in relation to Objective 5(b) regions occurred subsequent to that for Objective 1 regions. The list of fifty-seven regions in the various countries was adopted in May 1989 (Commission Decision 89/426/EC), following which, plans were submitted and CSFs negotiated. The CSFs were approved in the summer of 1990 (twenty-five of them, for example, on 6 June 1990 and eighteen more on 27 June 1990) and the operational programmes are being elaborated. Typically, these CSFs identify priorities in the following areas for structural fund support:

1 development of farming, forestry and fishing, especially focusing on measures aimed at diversifying agricultural production and promoting new forms of activity on farms to enhance incomes of farm families;
2 development of other sectors of local rural economies especially through the promotion of small and medium enterprises;
3 development of tourism and recreation facilities, especially accommodation and the development and promotion of rural leisure and sporting facilities;
4 development of light infrastructure which may be necessary in connection with the other developments; and
5 development of human resources through training schemes related to the developments proposed for farming, fisheries, forestry, small and medium enterprises, tourism and recreation management.

The development plans submitted in respect of the Objective 5(b) areas of Italy contain a number of proposed measures in respect of various priority development lines as shown in Table 7.2, prepared by Canata, which contains a breakdown of each of the relevant regions of Italy. It will be seen that, in addition to the more traditional agricultural development activities, such as plant and animal production, a significant role is assigned to activities like small-scale industry, tourism and various kinds of professional training (Canata 1990).

For Germany, a total of 525 million ECU of Community funds has been allocated for Objective 5(b) areas. The objectives of the development plans have been summarised by Heitman:

In the majority of the cases development plans stipulate the following partial objectives: (a) creation of jobs in the non-farming sector; (b) improvement of the quality of existing jobs and additional occupational qualifications for the workforce; (c) improvement of the agricultural infrastructure (for example, land consolidation, the construction of roads) as well as the strengthening of local infrastructures (for example, village renewal, leisure-time facilities); (d) the establishment and improvement of semi-industrial infrastructures (for example, the development of industrial sites);

Table 7.2 Actions in the development plans for Objective 5(b) areas in Italy

Development Guidelines	Number of measures in plans for Objective 5(b) areas							
	BZ	Lazio	Marche	Piedmonte	Toscana	Trento	Umbria	Veneto
Improvement of environment resources	—	4	5	2	11	2	4	3
Improvement of vegetable production	1	9	—	—	—	—	6	4
Improvement of animal production	—	7	6	3	30	6	1	3
Improvement of forest resources	1	8	—	—	—	—	5	—
Infrastructure and activities ⎫ Integrating agricultural incomes ⎭	—	6	—	—	—	4	4	2
Handicraft and small industry development	2	8	2	2	14	3	3	4
Services	—	8	3	2	—	—	—	—
Tourist improvements	1	7	4	2	26	—	2	10
Professional training	1	3	5	2	11	—	3	4
Fishing	—	—	—	—	—	—	—	3
Improvement of cultural resources	—	—	—	—	4	—	—	—
Other activities: promotion	—	—	—	—	—	—	2	—
Other activities: implementation	—	1	—	—	3	—	1	1

Source: Canata 1990.

(e) the conservation and improvement of the natural environment and the cultural heritage as a basis for advancing the development of tourism; (f) the improvement of production, processing and marketing in the still-important farming sector by means of an increased adjustment to market developments and the creation of combined incomes (for example, in tourism and in landscape management).

(Heitman 1990)

In France, 950 million ECU of Community funds have been earmarked for Objective 5(b) areas. Six priority objectives have been identified for those areas, according to Grammont (1990):

 (i) developing a young active population, that is, young entrepreneurs in order to help the existing companies to carry on business, whether agricultural, craft industries or other small-scale companies;
 (ii) adaptation and modernisation of public services;
(iii) increasing the potential value of tourism in rural zones;
(iv) adaptation and improvement of agricultural and forestry production systems;
 (v) helping rural areas to break out of their isolation;
(vi) to prevent major natural disasters – floods, avalanches, and so on.

'Horizontal' instruments

For several years, the Community has operated a series of measures in the agricultural structures area. These measures, adapted to the new funding co-ordination mechanisms, continue to be the basis of the set of 'horizontal' measures, applicable throughout the Community, which are directed towards Objective 5(a) – speeding up the adjustment of agricultural structures.

For example, investment in processing and marketing facilities has generally received about one-fourth of the agricultural structural fund expenditure. The relevant scheme was enacted under EEC Regulation no. 355/77 (EEC Reg. 1977). In April 1990, the *Council adopted EEC Regulation no. 886/90* 'on improving the processing and marketing conditions for agricultural produce' (EEC Reg. 1990) as a common measure and under Objective 5(a), with the added statement:

This measure shall also help to achieve Objectives 1 and 5(b).

In fact, Article 16 of this Regulation provides that the maximum rate of aid from the Fund in relation to the eligible costs of the selected investments will be 50 per cent in the Objective 1 regions and 30 per cent in other regions.

Title I of the Regulation deals with Sectoral Plans, Community Support Frameworks and selection criteria and provides that:

> the financing of investments must take place within the framework of plans designed to improve the structures relating to the various products in question (hereinafter referred to as 'sectoral plans') to be drawn up by the Member States, and on the basis of corresponding Community support frameworks, drawn up with due regard for the criteria of selection of investments eligible for Community financing (hereinafter referred to as 'selection criteria') to be laid down by the Commission.

Title II deals with forms of assistance by means of contributions to operational programmes or the provision of global grants while Title III covers a range of financial and general provisions.

At farm level, several schemes have been operated under the terms of Regulation no. 797/85. These include the highly popular scheme of compensatory allowances for natural handicaps in mountainous and other less-favoured or disadvantaged areas, which was first implemented in 1975. These 'headage payments' and crop payments also absorb about 25 per cent of agricultural structural funds. Another scheme which has been used extensively throughout the Community provides a range of investment aids on farms, also under Regulation no. 797/85. This scheme provides assistance for improving production quality, reducing pollution costs, saving energy, improving farm working conditions, protecting the environment, and so on. About 15 per cent of agricultural structural expenditure has been devoted to this scheme.

Other schemes involve special assistance to young farmers, vocational training, aids for establishing producer groups and associations, early retirement, accounting services, set-aside and extensification measures. These latter schemes, in general, have not been widely used throughout the Community, partly, it seems, due to the complex processes involved in designing and implementing national schemes which would qualify for Community support and partly because the Community objectives and national priorities might not have coincided on these topics. In addition, it would appear that provisions in some schemes for support for farm diversification into non-farm activities, tourism, environment, craft, and so on, were not particularly popular with Ministries of Agriculture, so that the new method of operation of the Structural Funds may simplify access to these latter provisions, via operational programmes developed under the CSFs. Various changes along these lines in the operation of these measures have been made in Regulation no. 3809/89, adopted in December 1989.

That Regulation also contained a provision of great significance to the process of rural development based on farm households being engaged in a combination of various farm and non-farm activities. Previously, full eligibility for some forms of agricultural structural assistance had been confined to operators of full-time farms or potentially viable farms. Regulation no. 3809/89 extended eligibility to include part-time farmers.

Other Community measures

In addition to the measures specifically directed towards the 'regional' Objectives 1 and 5(b) and the 'horizontal' Objective 5(a), there is a variety of other Community programmes which can influence rural areas and their development – some of which, admittedly, can be linked with operational programmes under the CSFs for Objective 1 and 5(b) regions.

Conceptually close to agriculture, of course, would be measures aimed at forestry, fishing and the environment. There are schemes, for example, for the protection of the Community's forests against atmospheric pollution and fire. Similarly, there are schemes of assistance for the afforestation of farming land and for investment in woodland improvement including forest roads, which are being implemented in some Community member states.

Community initiatives in relation to small and medium-sized enterprises (SMEs) may also have effects on rural areas, especially if they cover SMEs located in smaller population centres. These initiatives relate mainly to actions supporting subcontracting by SMEs and to the establishment of information/consultancy centres (Euro-Info Centres) and mechanisms enabling SMEs to identify other firms in the Community with whom they might develop business relationships (BC-Net).

In the education and training areas, projects under several programmes can have a rural area dimension, for example, PETRA, EUROTECNET, Comett, FORCE, while assistance from the European Social Fund in relation to combating long-term unemployment and the occupational integration of young people can also be applied to rural area projects.

Specific Community initiatives for rural development

In 1989 and 1990, the Community undertook a modulation of the expenditure pattern under the Guarantee Section of the Agricultural Fund, designed to adapt the price mechanism so as to channel additional current resources towards smaller farm producers and/or those located in less-developed areas. In 1989/90, for example, the milk co-responsibility levy was abolished in less-favoured areas.

In the 1990/91 farm price package, this approach was continued with the extension of the suckler cow premium to beef cows in mixed herds belonging to farmers holding a small milk quota; the introduction of a supplementary ewe premium in hill and less-favoured areas (on top of the normal ewe premium); a limited milk quota redistribution in favour of small-scale producers; aid per hectare for small-scale producers of arable crops; and aid per hectare for the production of minor traditional cereals (buckwheat, canary seed, millet) and aid for small-scale producers of cotton (Webb 1990). Speaking in Galway, Ireland, in June 1990, Commissioner MacSharry said:

> It is my intention to continue this approach of using the Guarantee Fund so as to help ensure a more stable rural economy.
>
> (MacSharry 1990b)

In addition to the foregoing, the Commission has proposed two initiatives directly related to rural development and a reinforcement of the environmental dimension of the Common Agricultural Policy. The Community initiatives comprise a programme to promote integrated rural development at local level and a proposal to establish a network of information centres in rural areas.

The initiative to promote local rural development – 'LEADER' – is designed to help groups based in local communities who develop plans for integrated local development in their particular areas. The groups are to be selected by the Commission and the member states from lists proposed by the member states. They are to cover areas with a population between 5,000 and 100,000 in Objective 1 and 5(b) regions. Initially, the Commission aims to support about 100 such groups. The Community has allocated some 400 million ECU to this project for the period 1990–93, through the provision of global grants to national intermediary bodies. Co-financing will be required.

The Commission is anxious to use this initiative to encourage a locally-based approach to rural development. Among the sets of local proposals, the following are expected to feature: organisation of rural development in the area concerned, feasibility studies for new activities, proposals for rural tourism, small enterprises, crafts, local services and the encouragement of higher value added on-farm activities. Information technology centres will also be provided to each chosen area, both for exchanging experiences among the groups chosen and for supporting the new economic activities in the rural areas. The proposed 100 groups are to act as a model, first for other groups to study and benefit from their experience and, second, to pave the way for future structural fund actions in rural areas when the current regulations expire in 1993.

The second Community initiative programme – 'MIRIAM' – concerns the establishment of a network of information centres on rural development initiatives and agricultural markets. The aim is to choose organisations which have good contacts in the rural development field and to provide them with an extra role as a channel of information on Community measures in favour of rural areas, including CAP and other decisions of relevance to rural areas, agricultural prices and quality norms and the possibilities of agricultural diversification.

The centres will be chosen throughout the Community, although Objective 1 and 5(b) regions will have priority. Commission assistance will consist of access to Community data banks, staff training and a three-year financial contribution on a declining scale. Seven such centres have already been established in different member states on a pilot basis.

It is expected that both the LEADER and MIRIAM proposals will be adopted towards the end of 1990 or at the beginning of 1991.

EVALUATION OF THE INSTRUMENTS OF RURAL DEVELOPMENT

Quality and scope of the instruments relative to the scale of the problem

Reform of the Common Agricultural Policy and the development of the Single Market have assisted the process of encouraging policy-makers, administrators and the public to place a greater emphasis on rural development in a manner which focuses increasingly on the links between non-agricultural and agricultural sources of development of rural areas. Policies are changing but, to quote Conway (June 1990).

it should be recognised that policy change is gradual and tends to lag behind the trend of change in economic circumstances. . . . The decline in support for agriculture has been happening for a decade and seems likely to continue. Therefore, rural areas are faced with a real immediate problem as agricultural support declines, affecting not only agriculture but also related activities in rural areas. Meanwhile, new measures which are being developed are not very well in place. Relative to the substantial changes in agricultural support the changes in structural measures have at this point developed more rhetoric than substance.

(Conway 1990)

Conway points out that the combined Structural Funds were 0.17 per cent of Community GDP in 1987, so that, if they double, they will amount to 0.34 per cent and, if matched by funds from member states, will amount to 0.68 per cent of GDP. 'There does seem', he says, 'to be an imbalance between rhetoric and financial commitment'.

However, when one analyses the agreed breakdown of the use of Community funds on various programmes, real concern must emerge regarding the quality of the instruments proposed in relation to the nature of the various development issues confronting rural areas. It will be recalled that the various CSFs all contain 'objectives' and 'priorities' for 'rural development', sometimes linked with agriculture and sometimes accompanied by 'local development' under an industry priority, with a range of policy instruments cited, as on pages 124–133 above. Serious concern must, however, be expressed at the relatively low use of Community funds for 'rural development' or 'local development' subheadings.

In Spain, for example, out of a total Community contribution of 9,393 million ECU, 'Agriculture and Rural Development' is to receive 2,304 million ECU. The bulk of this (1,500 million ECU) is earmarked for 'improvement of the conditions of production', with a further 477 million ECU for Objective 5(a) measures. 'Local Development', it will be recalled, featured as a subheading under 'Industry, Crafts Sector and Business Services'. 'Local Development' is alloted 132 million ECU of Community funds.[9]

Similarly, in Italy, 'Agriculture and Rural Development' is to receive 735 million ECU out of a total Community contribution of 7,583 million ECU. Objective 5(a) measures, however, account for 359 million ECU, while 'Activities Supplementing Income' receives 46 million ECU. 'Local Development' features under 'Industry, Crafts and Services' with 88 million ECU of the 1,319 million ECU allocated to that priority area (EC Commission 1989c).

From the total of 7,368 million ECU allocated to Portugal, 'Rural Development' is to receive 46 million ECU as part of the 558 million

ECU to be devoted to 'Agricultural and Rural Development'. It is not possible, of course, to disentangle the rural area component of the 1,161 million ECU devoted to Portugal's Priority 6 – 'Development of the region's growth potential and local development' (EC Commission 1989d).

Of the 3,672 million ECU allocated to Ireland, 'Rural Development, including alternatives to agriculture, infrastructure and human resources' is to receive 75.3 million ECU, compared with 396 million ECU for Objective 5(a) activities (EC Commission 1989b).

It would appear, therefore, that the vast bulk of the use of Community Funds will be spent on traditional single-sector instruments, rather than on integrative programmes. While the traditional agricultural measures, the industrial, training, infrastructural and tourist measures will, of course, have significant impacts on rural areas, a real question still remains regarding their choice, compatibility and co-ordination in any rural area.

Organisation/co-ordination issues

It is increasingly evident that, at a policy-making level in the EC, there is a new positive attitude to rural development based on a holistic approach across sectors of activity and specifically providing for pluri-activity among sectors as one norm for many rural households. Articulating meaningful programmes for 'rural development' or 'local development' at national level in the member states is quite difficult, however, as the bulk of the activities of member state administrations are organised through government ministries or departments with sectoral jurisdictions. Problems of co-ordinating the activities of government ministries are well-known in all member states. The problems relate, not only to harmonising the implementation of sectoral programmes but, often more seriously, to the lack of mechanisms to design, develop and propose to governments a range of integrated programmes directed towards specific issues or problems and genuinely conceived as such rather than merely resulting from the assembly of sectoral programmes under an umbrella of convenience!

It is generally understood that one of the features which contributed to lengthening the period of time which elapsed between the submission of development plans by member states and the approval of CSFs was the dialogue between the Commission and the member states regarding the grouping of sectoral proposals into more cohesively-focused packages. In this regard, an illuminating exchange took place at a Conference organised in February 1990 by the Chamber of Commerce in Galway, Ireland.

Mr Esben Poulsen of the Commission told the Conference that the Commission desired to have clear priorities for Community intervention (Poulson 1990). He instanced the priority which had been agreed with the Irish Government in relation to supporting measures which would set off the effects of peripherality, under which expenditure on national primary routes and other projects which facilitate transport links between Ireland and the rest of the world would be supported. He contrasted this approach with the sets of activities which had been proposed in separate programmes for the departments involved. Mr Michael Tutty, Assistant Secretary of the Irish Department of Finance, when he was explaining the priority groupings in the CSF, told the same Conference: 'This grouping covers all the sectors for which Community assistance was sought under the Plan. The CSF simply rearranges things into a different format.' (Tutty 1990)

It is unlikely that the *modus vivendi* of government ministries of member states will be reorganised fundamentally as a response to the co-ordination requirements of rural development! Irrespective of the existence of coherent national programmes for rural development or the existence of national co-ordinating mechanisms across sectoral programmes, it is essential to focus also on the quality of the co-ordination of sectoral measures at the level of implementation, that is, in the individual rural areas themselves. Rural development or local development in rural areas is not facilitated by the existence in many member states of local branches of government ministries and their subsidiary agencies who are charged solely with the local administration of the nationally-determined programmes relating to their own individual sectors. The lack at regional or local level of credible regional or local bodies with the competence to plan, budget, mobilise resources and ensure the implementation of integrated programmes is a problem in several member states.

Specific attention to the development of various forms of 'Partnerships for Rural Development' was advocated by the OECD in a publication of the same name (OECD 1990) which focused on the challenges of rural policy and programme implementation through partnership arrangements involving public and private sector actions. Such partnerships could be considered:

1 among government ministries;
2 between central and local public bodies;

3 among local public, private business, co-operative organisations and voluntary bodies.

The Irish Government, with Community assistance, has promoted the development of twelve pilot projects in rural development during 1989 and 1990. It is intended that the experience gained will be evaluated and used as an input in developing the future Irish programmes for rural development. Co-ordination issues have been widely acknowledged to be in need of resolution – to achieve synergy among the various approaches, to ensure an integrated approach, and to combine official and voluntary effort. In the view of Mr Bart Brady, Assistant Secretary of the Irish department of Agriculture.

> The immediate challenge ahead, therefore, is one of organisation. When we get the organisation right, we can be reasonably sure that we have the means to make a significant contribution to rural development.
>
> (Brady 1990)

Market imperfections

There is increasing evidence that the markets for transfer of organisation, technology and enterprise to peripheral/rural areas are not efficient. In particular, the transaction costs are high and there is often a dearth of personnel/agencies available to perform market intermediation roles, especially across less-developed regions. Hannequart et al. (1988) have demonstrated an interest in the development of transnational contacts by operators of small and medium enterprises in Greece and Ireland coupled with a lack of knowledge of where, if anywhere, one could look for help and a fear of high marginal costs to be incurred in seeking partners and effecting business arrangements. These features would militate against the commonly-held view supporting a trickle-down development effect spreading out from major metropolitan concentrations to rural areas.

A similar view was expressed by Cuddy and Ó Cinneide[14] when they referred to:

> a cumulative process of self-reinforcing trends towards increased concentration of economic activity and population in urban areas. Concentrated demand, capital availability, entrepreneurship skills, technology, services, all of which are essential to economic development, are associated with 'urban' and 'agglomeration'. A downward spiral of economic activity is occasioned by the absence or weakness

of these factors in rural areas. The presence (strength) and absence (weakness) of the economic and social infrastructure in the areas of concentration and depopulation, respectively, again reinforce the trends in opposite directions.

Finally, recent work on the distribution of economic activity emphasises access to information as being more important than economies of scale. Since this access is greater in core areas than in peripheral areas, the reinforcing process of divergence continues. Thus, the traditional theory, that there is a self-adjusting mechanism which eliminates disparities between regions, is not tenable. Rather, the principle of cumulative causation where disparities are self-reinforcing, in this instance between urban centres and declining rural areas, is clearly more apt.

(Cuddy and ÓCinneide)

Access to information, however, must be coupled with development of the ability to evaluate information and use it in improved decision-making – in other words, education and training are needed to convert information into knowledge! The rapporteur of a workshop on German rural development issues concluded:

> Our problem is that there is such a large amount of information being given to people in the area, they do not know how to use it or how to link up the separate pieces. It is important to ensure that people do not just get the information, but that they know how to use it efficiently for themselves.

(Owens 1990)

A FUTURE FOR RURAL DEVELOPMENT?

In this chapter I have endeavoured to demonstrate that the development and application of conventional agricultural development policies involved a multi-strand set of activities involving product and input price policies, capital grants, farm restructuring, comprehensive advisory services, substantial research, training programmes and the development of university courses to provide the range of professional personnel needed for intermediation among those involved in scientific advances, on-farm applications and the range of transactions linking consumer demand to farmers' decisions. Those programmes, sustained over decades, enabled the goals of increased productive capacity to be achieved.

Rural development is at least as large a problem! It too will require sustained effort over a couple of decades to achieve success. The effort will have to cross sectors, so imaginative and real partnership procedures will be essential. The range of situations in different areas will necessitate tailor-making the chosen local strategies to suit the various situations. Education and training to see the development issues, to choose strategies wisely, to implement them and to intermediate between local, member state and Community levels, especially when it comes to reconciling local programme flexibility with procedures for accountability of public funds, will be essential to the success of rural development initiatives.

The long time-scale required has been seen clearly by Lowe, who refers to the practice of rural development as a 'hard grind' and who stresses the importance:

> that the towns and cities within a short driving distance from rural areas provide an adequate range of educational and training facilities as well as cultural and social amenities.
>
> (Lowe 1990)

The political realisation of the rural development issue exists. A modest beginning has been made in the commitment of Community funds towards rural development. The good intentions must be further transformed into real and sustained commitment if general rural development is to become more than rhetoric accompanied by minor modifications of conventional sectoral policies.

It was encouraging to read the October 1990 statement by Commissioner MacSharry to the European Parliament's Committee on Agriculture, Fisheries and Rural Development:

> Mr Chairman, the Commission is now firmly committed to a policy which ensures that the needs of rural areas are taken into account across the board in Community policies. Over the past two years, starting with agriculture, but going much wider than that one sector alone, we have adopted an integrated approach and are targeting assistance on areas of greatest need.
>
> (MacSharry 1990c)

The Commissioner is obviously aware of the nature of the rural development challenge. 'We must', he said in June 1990, 'overcome the compartmentalised approach we have followed in the past in favour of one which encourages Integrated Rural Development' (MacSharry 1990b).

Finally, the Commission, the Council, the member states and the various interested parties need to reflect on the budgetary framework which will take the Community beyond 1993 and enable us to learn from the experience of the first reform of the Structural Funds and give appropriate priority to rural development issues. Commissioner Mac-Sharry has already expressed some views on the magnitude of the response which may be needed at various levels:

> I would hope that as rural development policy comes into focus, as the Structural Fund plans are implemented on the ground and bear fruit and as the debate begins in the Parliament and the Council on how to carry forward this new policy, the necessary resources will be mobilised at local, national and Community level.

> (MacSharry 1990c)

REFERENCES

Brady, B. (1990) 'The Case of Objective 1 Regions: Ireland', in Cuddy *et al.* (eds) *Revitalising the Rural Economy.* Galway, Ireland, Centre for Development Studies, University College Galway.

Canata, G. (1990) 'The case of Objective 5(b) Regions in Italy', in M. Cuddy, M. Ó. Cinneide and M. Owens (eds) *Revitalising the Rural Economy*, Galway, Ireland, Centre for Development Studies, University College Galway.

Commission Decision 89/426/EC. OJ no. L 198, 12.7.1989, p.1; Commission Decisions 90/557–600/EC, OJ no. L 322, 21.11.1990, pp.1–88.

Conway, A. (1990) 'Concluding reflections', M. Cuddy, M. Ó. Cinneide and M. Owens (eds) *Revitalising the Rural Economy*, Galway, Ireland, Centre for Development Studies, University College Galway.

Council of Europe (1987) *Twenty Years Work for Rural Development*, Strasbourg.

Cuddy, M. and Ó. Cinneide, M. (1990) 'Critical issues in rural development', in M. Cuddy, M. Ó. Cinneide and M. Owens (eds) *Revitalising the Rural Economy*, Galway, Ireland, Centre for Development Studies, University College Galway.

EC Commission (1985) *Perspectives for the Common Agricultural Policy*, Brussels.

EC Commission (1989a) *The Future of Rural Society*, Commission Communication transmitted to the Council and to the European Parliament on 29 July 1989 (COM(88) 371 final), Brussels, Bulletin of the European Communities Supplement 4/88.

EC Commission (1989b) *Community Support Framework 1989–93 – Ireland*, Luxembourg.

EC Commission (1989c) *Community Support Framework 1989–93 – Italy*, Luxembourg.

EC Commission (1989d) *Community Support Framework 1989–93 – Portugal*, Luxembourg.

EC Commission (1989e) *Community Support Framework 1989–93 – Spain*. Luxembourg.

EC Commission (1989f) *Community Support Framework 1989–93 – United Kingdom (Northern Ireland)*, Luxembourg.

EC Commission (1990) *The Agricultural Situation in the Community. 1989 Report*, Brussels.

EEC Reg. (1977) Regulation (EEC) no. 355/77. OJ no. L 51, 23.2.1977, p. 1.
EEC Reg. (1984) Regulation (EEC) no. 1787/84. OJ no. L 169, 28.6.1984, p. 1.
EEC Reg. (1988a) Regulation (EEC) no. 2052/88. OJ no. L 185, 15.7.1988, p. 9.
EEC Reg. (1988b) Regulation (EEC) no. 4253/88. OJ no. L 374, 31.12.1988, p. 1.
EEC Reg. (1988c) Regulation (EEC) no. 4254/88. OJ no. L 374, 31.12.1988, p. 15.
EEC Reg. (1988d) Regulation (EEC) no. 4255/88. OJ no. L 374, 31.12.1988, p. 21.
EEC Reg. (1988e) Regulation (EEC) no. 4256/88. OJ no. L 374, 31.12.1988, p. 25.
EEC Reg. (1990) Regulation (EEC) no. 886/90. OJ no. L 51, 6.4.1990, p. 1.
Grammont, A. (1990) 'Rural development policy in France', in M. Cuddy, M Ó Cinneide and M. Owens (eds) *Revitalising the Rural Economy*, Galway, Ireland, Centre for Development Studies, University College Galway.
Hannequart, A., Demathas, Z. and Lucey, D. I. F. (1988) *Coopération Internationale entre Petites et Moyennes Entreprises et Développement Endogne Régional*, Trans-European Policy Studies Association for DG XVI, EC Commission. Brussels.
Heitman, J. H. (1990) 'Rural development policy in the Federal Republic of Germany after the reform of the Structural Funds', in M. Cuddy, M Ó Cinneide and M. Owens (eds) *Revitalising the Rural Economy*, Galway, Ireland, Centre for Development Studies, University College Galway.
Lowe, P. (1990) 'The role of rural development in community regional policies', in M. Cuddy, M. Ó. Cinneide and M. Owens (eds) *Revitalising the Rural Economy*, Galway, Ireland, Centre for Development Studies, University College Galway.
Lucey, D. I. F. (1987) 'Higher education in agriculture under the impact of changes in society and rural areas', Paper to 8th OECD Working Conference of Representatives of Higher Education in Agriculture. OECD AGR/REE (87) 33, Paris.
Lucey, D. I. F. and Kaldor, D. R. (1969) *Rural Industrialisation – the Impact of Industrial Development on two Rural Communities in Western Ireland*, London, Geoffrey Chapman LD.
Lucey, D. I. F., Walker, S. *et al.* (1987) *New Jobs in Mayo – A Study of Recent Major Employment Developments*, Castlebar, Mayo, Mayo County Development Team.
MacSharry, R. (1990a) 'Rural Development: the Challenge of the 1990s', the Bass Ireland lecture, Belfast, 26 February.
MacSharry, R. (1990b) 'Rural development', in M. Cuddy, M. Ó. Cinneide and M. Owens (eds) *Revitalising the Rural Economy*, Galway, Ireland, Centre for Development Studies, University College Galway.
MacSharry, R. (1990c) Opening statement to hearing on 'The use of rural areas', European Parliament Committee on Agriculture, Forestry and Rural Development, Brussels, 30 October.
OECD (1988) *New Trends in Rural Policy-making*, Paris.
OECD (1990) *Partnerships for Rural Development*, Paris.
Owens, M. (1990) 'Some issues emerging from workshop discussions', in M. Cuddy, M. Ó. Cinneide and M. Owens (eds) *Revitalising the Rural Economy*, Galway, Ireland, Centre for Development Studies, University College Galway.
Poulsen, E. (1990) 'European Regional Development Fund and regional policies', in *The Implementation of the Structural Funds*, Conference Proceedings, Chamber of Commerce, Galway, Ireland, February.

Tutty, M. G. (1990) 'Overview of Ireland's use of the Structural Funds', in *The Implementation of the Structural Funds*. Conference Proceedings, Chamber of Commerce, Galway, Ireland, February.

Webb, M. (1990) 'Rural development: the contribution of the Commission's Directorate-General for Agriculture', in M. Cuddy, M Ó Cinneide and M. Owens (eds) *Revitalising the Rural Economy*, Galway, Ireland, Centre for Development Studies, University College Galway.

Appendix: Legislation

Council Regulation (EEC) No. 2052/88

of 24 June 1988 on the tasks of the Structural Funds and their effectiveness and on coordination of their activities between themselves and with the operations of the European Investment Bank and the other existing financial instruments

THE COUNCIL OF THE EUROPEAN COMMUNITIES

Having regard to the Treaty establishing the European Economic Community, and in particular Article 130d thereof.

Having regard to the proposal from the Commission.[1]

Having regard to the opinion of the European Parliament.[2]

Having regard to the opinion of the Economic and Social Committee.[3]

Whereas Article 130a of the Treaty provides for the Community to develop and pursue its actions leading to the strengthening of its economic and social cohesion and in particular for it to aim at reducing disparities between the various regions and the backwardness of the least-favoured regions;

Whereas Article 130c states that the European Regional Development Fund (ERDF) is intended to help redress the principal regional imbalances in the Community through participating in the development and structural adjustment of regions whose development is lagging behind and in the conversion of declining industrial regions;

Whereas, to that end, Article 130d of the Treaty provides for a comprehensive proposal the purpose of which will be to make such amendments to the structure and operational rules of the European Agricultural Guidance and Guarantee Fund, Guidance Section (EAGGF Guidance Section), the European Social Fund (ESF) and the

ERDF as are necessary to clarify and rationalize their tasks in order to contribute to the achievement of the objectives set out in Articles 130a and 130c of the Treaty, to increase their efficiency and to coordinate their activities between themselves and with the operations of the existing financial instruments;

Whereas Community action through the Structural Funds, the European Investment Bank (EIB) and the other existing financial instruments must be in support of the objectives set out in Articles 130a and 130c;

Whereas the action taken through the Structural Funds, the EIB and the other existing financial instruments, the coordination of Member States' economic and social policies, the coordination of national regional policies, the coordination of national schemes of assistance and other measures taken with a view to implementing the common policies and the internal market form, in accordance with Article 130b of the Treaty, part of a series of policies and measures aimed at strengthening economic and social cohesion, and whereas the Commission is called upon to make appropriate proposals in this regard;

Whereas it is necessary in order to achieve the aim set by Article 130d of the Treaty to direct all Community activity in this field towards the attainment of priority objectives which are clearly defined in the light of that aim;

Whereas on 11 and 12 February 1988 the European Council with a view to strengthening the impact of Community structural measures, agreed to double in real terms commitment appropriations for the Structural Funds by 1993 as compared with the 1987 level; whereas at the same time it fixed the increases to be made up to 1992; whereas within this context the Structural Fund contributions for regions coming under Objective 1, (see Article 1 below) are to be doubled in real terms by 1992; whereas in so doing the Commission is to ensure that, in the framework of the additional funds for the regions falling within Objective 1, a particular effort is made to assist the least-prosperous regions;

Whereas it is necessary to specify which Funds are to contribute – and to what extent and under what conditions they are to do so – to the achievement of each of the priority objectives and to determine the conditions under which the EIB and other existing Community financial instruments can make their contributions, particularly in conjunction with operations of the Funds;

Whereas, of the three Structural Funds, the ERDF is the main instrument for achieving the objective of ensuring the development and structural adjustment of regions whose development is lagging behind, whereas it plays a central role in the conversion of regions, frontier regions and parts of regions (including employment areas and urban communities) seriously affected by industrial decline;

Whereas the essential tasks of the ESF are combating long-term unemployment and the occupational integration of young people; whereas it helps to support economic and social cohesion; whereas it is also an instrument of decisive importance in the promotion of consistent employment policies in the Member States and in the Community;

Whereas the Guidance Section of the EAGGF is, within the context of support for economic and social cohesion, the main instrument for financing the adjustment of agricultural structures and the development of rural areas with a view to reform of the common agricultural policy;

Whereas action by the Funds, the EIB and the other financial instruments must *inter alia* underpin implementation of a policy of rural development;

Whereas the tasks of the Funds must be defined so as to specify the broad categories of tasks assigned to each of them respectively for the purpose of achieving the priority objectives; whereas Fund operations must be consistent with Community policies, *inter alia* as regards rules of competition, the award of public contracts and environmental protection;

Whereas achievement of the priority objective of ensuring the structural adjustment of the regions whose development is lagging behind necessitates a significant concentration of the resources of the Community's Structural Funds on that objective;

Whereas provisions on the indicative allocation of commitment appropriations between Member States are laid down under the ERDF so as to make it easier for the Member States to programme the measures which come within the ERDF framework;

Whereas the regions, areas and individuals in the Community eligible for Community structural assistance in connection with the various priority objectives should be determined;

Whereas a list should be drawn up of the regions whose development is lagging behind; whereas this list should comprise adminstrative level NUTS II[4] regions where per capita GDP measured in terms of purchasing power parity is less that 75 per cent of the Community average, and other regions whose per capita GDP is close to that of regions under 75 per cent and whose inclusion is justified by special circumstances;

Whereas it is necessary to draw up criteria for defining declining industrial areas; whereas, moreover, Community action could, in order to ensure effective concentration of assistance cover up to 15 per cent of the Community population living outside the regions whose development is lagging behind;

Whereas criteria must be laid down for the selection of rural areas;

Whereas Community action is intended to be complementary to action by the Member States or to back up national measures; whereas, in order to impart added value to their own initiatives at the appropriate territorial level, close consultations should be instituted between the Commission and the Member State concerned at the competent authorities designated by the latter at national, regional, local or other level, with each party acting as a partner, within the framework of its responsibilities and powers, in the pursuit of a common goal;

Whereas it is necessary to specify the principal forms of structural assistance to be provided by the Community for the purposes of the objectives set out in Articles 130a and 130c of the Treaty; whereas those forms of assistance must enhance the effectiveness of the measures taken by it and at the same time, account being taken of the proportionality principle, satisfy the needs of the different situations that may arise;

Whereas the main emphasis must be placed on assistance in the form of multiannual operational programmes;

Whereas, in order to secure joint action between one or more funds, the EIB and one or more of the other existing financial instruments, those programmes may be drawn up and implemented on the basis of an integrated approach to the measures involved;

Whereas mechanisms should be established for varying Community assistance in line with the particular features of the measures to be supported and in the light of the context in which they are to be carried out and the financing capacity of the Member State concerned, having regard in particular to its relative prosperity;

Whereas, in implementing this Regulation, it is necessary to establish procedures for ensuring close association between the Commission and the Member States as well as, where appropriate, national, regional and local authorities designated by them;

Whereas it is necessary to establish effective methods of monitoring, assessing and carrying out checks in respect of Community structural operations, based on objective criteria and to ensure that those methods are adapted to the tasks of the different Funds as specified in this Regulation;

Whereas the principles for the necessary transitional provisions as well as for the combining and overlapping of Community operations or measures must be laid down;

Whereas it is advisable to include a review clause;

Whereas it is necessary to lay down in subsequent implementing legislation the detailed rules governing the individual Funds, together with the arrangements for the coordination and joint deployment of the Community's various Structural Funds and instruments;

Whereas, while performing the tasks assigned to it by Articles 129 and 130 of the Treaty, the EIB is to cooperate in achieving the objectives set out in this Regulation in accordance with the procedures laid down in its Statute;

HAS ADOPTED THIS REGULATION

I. OBJECTIVES AND TASKS OF THE STRUCTURAL FUNDS

Article 1

Objectives

Community action through the Structural Funds, the EIB and other existing financial instruments shall support the achievement of the general objectives set out in Articles 130a and 130c of the Treaty by contributing to the attainment of the following five priority objectives:

1. promoting the development and structural adjustment of the regions whose development is lagging behind (hereinafter referred to as 'Objective 1');
2. converting the regions, frontier regions or part of regions (including employment areas and urban communities) seriously affected by industrial decline (hereinafter referred to as 'Objective 2');
3. combating long-term unemployment (hereinafter referred to as 'Objective 3');
4. facilitating the occupational integration of young people (hereinafter referred to as 'Objective 4');
5. with a view to reform of the common agricultural policy:
(a) speeding up the adjustment of agricultural structures, and

(b) promoting the development of rural areas
(hereinafter referred to as 'Objective 5 (a) and 5 (b)').

Article 2

Means

1. The Structural Funds, the 'EAGGF Guidance Section', the 'ESF' and the 'ERDF' shall contribute, each according to the specific provisions governing its operations, to the attainment of Objectives 1 to 5 on the basis of the breakdown given below:

- Objective 1: ERDF, ESF, EAGGF Guidance Section;
- Objective 2: ERDF, ESF;
- Objective 3: ESF;
- Objective 4: ESF;
- Objective 5 (a): EAGGF Guidance Section;
      5 (b): EAGGF Guidance Section, ESF, ERDF.

2. The EIB, while performing the tasks assigned to it by Articles 129 and 130 of the Treaty, shall cooperate in achieving the objectives set out in Article 1 of this Regulation in accordance with the procedures laid down in its Statute.

3. The other existing financial instruments may contribute, each according to the specific provisions governing its operations to any measure supported by one or more of the Structural Funds in connection with one of the abovementioned five objectives. Where appropriate, the Commission shall take measures to enable these instruments to make a better contribution to the objectives set out in Article 1.

Article 3

Tasks of the Funds

1. In accordance with Article 130c of the Treaty, the ERDF:

- shall have the essential task of providing support for Objectives 1 and 2 in the regions concerned;
- in addition, shall participate in the operations of Objective 5(b).

It shall in particular provide support for:

(a) productive investment;

(b) the creation or modernization of infrastructures which contribute to the development or conversion of the regions concerned;

(c) measures to exploit the potential for internally generated development of the regions concerned.

The ERDF shall also provide support for studies or pilot schemes concerning regional development at Community level, especially where frontier regions of Member States are involved.

2. In the framework of Article 123 of the Treaty and having regard to the Decisions adopted pursuant to Article 126 of the Treaty, the ESF shall:

– have as priority missions to provide support throughout the Community for vocational-training measures and aids for employment and for the creation of self-employed activities, in order to combat long-term unemployment (Objective 3) and integrate young people into working life (Objective 4);

– also support measures for Objectives 1, 2 and 5 (b).

The following categories of persons shall qualify for ESP support:

(a) the long-term unemployed (Objective 3);

(b) young people who have completed the compulsory full-time education period (Objective 4);

(c) in addition to the categories of persons referred to in (a) and (b), where the ESF helps to finance measures necessary to achieve Objectives 1, 2 or 5 (b), unemployed people or persons at risk of unemployment in particular shall qualify for vocational-training measures or aid for employment or for the creation of self-employed activities with the aim of providing them with the occupational qualifications required either to promote the stability of their employment or to develop new employment opportunities for them. Categories of persons other than unemployed people or people at risk of unemployment may be included in these measures in accordance with Article 3 (4).

In this respect, support shall take into account the requirements of the labour markets and the priorities laid down in employment policies within the Community.

3. In line with the priorities set out in Article 39 of the Treaty, assistance from the EAGGF Guidance Section shall be geared in particular to the following tasks:

(a) strengthening and reorganizing agricultural structures, including those for the marketing and processing of agricultural and fishery products, including forestry products, especially with a view to reform of the common agricultural policy;

(b) ensuring the conversion of agricultural production and fostering the development of supplementary activities for farmers;

(c) ensuring a fair standard of living for farmers;

(d) helping to develop the social fabric of rural areas, to safeguard the environment, to preserve the countryside (*inter alia* by securing the conservation of natural agricultural resources) and to offset the effects of natural handicaps on agriculture.

4. The specific provisions governing operations under each Structural Fund shall be laid down in the implementing Decisions adopted pursuant to Article 130e of the Treaty. They shall establish in particular the procedures for providing assistance in one of the forms defined in Article 5 (2), the conditions of eligibility and the rates of assistance. Without prejudice to paragraph 5 of this Article they shall also establish the arrangements for the monitoring, assessment, financial management and checking of measures and any transitional provisions necessary in relation to existing rules.

5. The Council, acting on the basis of Article 130e of the Treaty, shall adopt the provisions necessary for ensuring coordination between the different Funds, on the one hand, and between them and the EIB and the other existing financial instruments, on the other. The Commission and the EIB shall establish by mutual agreement the practical arrangements for coordinating the operations.

The implementing Decisions referred to in this Article shall also lay down the transitional provisions concerning the integrated approaches adopted under existing rules.

II ARRANGEMENTS FOR STRUCTURAL OPERATIONS

Article 4

Complementarity, partnership, technical assistance

1. Community operations shall be such as to complement or contribute to corresponding national operations. They shall be established through close consultations between the Commission, the Member State concerned and the competent authorities designated by the latter at national, regional, local or other level, with each party acting as a partner in pursuit of a common goal. These consultations are herein-

after referred to as the 'partnership'. The partnership shall cover the preparation, financing, monitoring and assessment of operations.

2. Acting in accordance with the provisions of this Regulation and with the provisions referred to in Article 3(4) and (5), the Commission shall take the steps and measures necessary to ensure that Community operations are in support of the objectives set out in Article 1 and impart to national initiatives an added value.

3. Within the framework of the partnership, the Commission may, in accordance with procedures laid down in the provisions referred to in Article 3 (4), contribute to the preparation, implementation and adjustment of operations by financing preparatory studies and technical assistance operations locally, in agreement with the Member State concerned and, where appropriate, with the authorities referred to in paragraph 1.

4. For each objective, tasks shall be shared between the Commission and the Member State during the preparation of operations in accordance with Articles 8 to 11.

Article 5

Forms of assistance

1. Financial assistance under the Structural Funds, the EIB and the other existing Community financial instruments shall be provided in a variety of forms that reflect the nature of the operation to be carried out.

2. In the case of the Structural Funds, financial assistance shall be provided in one of the following forms:

(a) part financing of operational programmes;
(b) part-financing of a national aid scheme including repayments;
(c) provision of global grants, as a general rule managed by an intermediary designated by the Member State in agreement with the Commission and allocated by the intermediary in the form of individual grants to final beneficiaries;
(d) part-financing of suitable projects including repayments;
(e) support for technical assistance and studies in preparation for operations.

Acting by a qualified majority on a proposal from the Commission and in cooperation with the European Parliament, the Council may introduce other forms of assistance of the same type.

3. In the case of the EIB and the other existing financial instruments, each observing its own specific rules, financial assistance shall be provided in one of the following forms:

- loans or other forms of part-financing specific investment projects;
- global loans;
- part-financing of technical assistance or of studies in preparation for operations;
- guarantees.

4. Community assistance shall combine in an appropriate way assistance in the form of grants and loans referred to in paragraphs 2 and 3 in order to maximize the stimulus provided by the budgetary resources deployed, making use of existing financial engineering techniques.

5. An operational programme within the meaning of paragraph 2 (a) shall comprise a series of consistent multiannual measures which may be implemented through recourse to one or more Funds, to one or more of the other existing financial instruments, and to the EIB.

Where an operational programme involves operations under more than one Fund and/or more than one other financial instrument, it may be implemented in the form of an integrated approach, the details of which shall be determined by the provisions referred to in Article 3 (5).

Operational programmes shall be undertaken on the initiative of the Member States or of the Commission in agreement with the Member State concerned.

Article 6

Monitoring and assessment

1. Community operations shall be constantly monitored to ensure that the commitments entered into as part of the objectives set out in Articles 130a and 130c of the Treaty are effectively honoured. Such monitoring shall, where necessary, make it possible to adjust operations in line with requirements arising during implementation.

The Commission shall periodically submit reports on the implementation of operations to the Committees referred to in Article 17.

2. In order to gauge their effectiveness, Community structural operations shall be the subject of an *ex-ante* and an *ex-post* assessment designed to highlight their impact with respect to the objectives set out in Article 1 and to analyse their effects on specific structural problems.

3. The procedures for monitoring and assessing Community operations

shall be established by the provisions referred to in Article 3 (4) and (5) and, in the case of the EIB, in the manner provided for in its Statute.

Article 7

Compatibility and checks

1. Measures financed by the Structural Funds or receiving assistance from the EIB or from another existing financial instrument shall be in keeping with the provisions of the Treaties, with the instruments adopted pursuant thereto and with Community policies, including those concerning the rules on competition, the award of public contracts and environmental protection.

2. Without prejudice to the Financial Regulation, the provisions referred to in Article 3 (4) and (5) shall lay down harmonized rules for strengthening checks on structural operations. They shall be adjusted to reflect the special nature of the financial operations concerned. The procedures for carrying out checks on operations undertaken by the EIB shall be as set out in its Statute.

PROVISIONS RELATING TO THE SPECIFIC OBJECTIVES

Article 8

Objective 1

1. The regions concerned by Objective 1 shall be regions at NUTS level II whose per capita GDP, on the basis of the figures for the last three years, is less than 75 per cent of the Community average.
They shall also include Northern Ireland, the French overseas departments and other regions whose per capita GDP is close to that of the regions referred to in the first subparagraph and which have to be included within the scope of Objective 1 for special reasons.

2. The list of regions concerned by Objective 1 is given in the Annex.

3. The list of regions shall be applicable for five years from the entry into force of this Regulation. The Commission shall review the list in good time before the five years have elapsed in order for the Council, acting by a qualified majority on a proposal from the Commission and after consulting the European Parliament, to establish a new list to apply for the period after the five years have elapsed.

4. The Member States shall submit to the Commission their regional development plans. Those plans shall include in particular:

- a description of the regional developments priorities selected and of the corresponding operations;
- an indication of the use to be made of assistance available under the Funds, the EIB and the other financial instruments in implementing the plans.

The Member States may submit overall regional development plans for all their regions included in the list referred to in paragraph 2, provided that such plans comprise the features listed in the first subparagraph.

Member States shall also submit the plans referred to in Article 10 (2) and the operations referred to in Article 11 (1) for the regions concerned, including the data relating to the operations under Article 11 (1), which under Community rules constitute rights for the beneficiaries.

In order to expedite the examination of applications and the implementation of action, the Member States may include with their plans applications for operational programmes that they cover.

5. The Commission shall examine the proposed plans and operations and the other information referred to in paragraph 4 to determine whether they are consistent with the objectives of this Regulation and with the provisions and policies referred to in Articles 6 and 7. On the basis of all the plans and operations referred to in paragraph 4, it shall establish, through the partnership referred to in Article 4 (1) and in agreement with the Member State concerned, the Community support framework for Community structural operations, in accordance with the procedures referred to in Article 17.

The Community support framework shall cover in particular:

- the priorities adopted for Community assistance;
- the forms of assistance;
- the indicative financing plan, with details of the amount of assistance and its source;
- the duration of the assistance.

The Community support framework shall provide coordination of Community structural assistance towards those of the objectives referred to in Article 1 which may be pursued in a particular region.

The Community support framework may, if necessary, be revised and adjusted, on the initiative of the Member State or of the Commission in agreement with the Member State, in the light of relevant new information and of the results obtained during implementation of the operations concerned.

At the duly substantiated request of the Member State concerned, the

Commission shall adopt the distinct Community support frameworks for one or more of the plans referred to in paragraph 4.

6. Assistance in respect of Objective 1 shall be predominantly in the form of operational programmes.

7. The provisions for implementation of this Article shall be specified in the provisions referred to in Article 3 (4) and (5).

Article 9

Objective 2

1. The declining industrial areas concerned by Objective 2 shall comprise regions, frontier regions or parts of regions (including employment areas and urban communities).

2. The areas referred to in paragraph 1 must represent or belong to a NUTS level III territorial unit which satisfies all the following criteria:

(a) the average rate of unemployment recorded over the last three years must have been above the Community average;

(b) the percentage share of industrial employment in total employment must have equalled or exceeded the Community average in any reference year from 1975 onwards;

(c) there must have been an observable fall in industrial employment compared with the reference year chosen in accordance with point (b).

Community assistance may, subject to the provisions of paragraph 4 below, also extend to:

– adjacent areas satisfying criteria (a) to (c) above;

– urban communities with an unemployment rate at least 50 per cent above the Community average which have recorded a substantial fall in industrial employment;

– other areas which have recorded substantial job losses over the last three years or are experiencing or are threatened with such losses in industrial sectors which are vital to their economic development, with a consequent serious worsening of unemployment in those areas.

3. As soon as this Regulation has entered into force, the Commission shall, in accordance with the procedure laid down in Article 17 and on the basis of paragraph 2 above, establish an initial list of the areas referred to in paragraph 1.

4. In establishing the list and in defining the Community support

framework referred to in paragraph 9 below, the Commission shall seek to ensure that assistance is genuinely concentrated on the areas most seriously affected, at the most appropriate geographical level, taking into account the particular situation of the areas concerned. Member States shall supply to the Commission all information which might be of assistance to it in this task.

5. Berlin shall be eligible for aid under this objective.

6. The list of areas shall be reviewed by the Commission periodically. However, the assistance granted by the Community in respect of Objective 2 in the various areas listed shall be planned and implemented on a three-yearly basis.

7. Three years after this Regulation enters into force, the criteria laid down in paragraph 2 may be altered by the Council, acting by a qualified majority on a proposal from the Commission and after consulting the European Parliament.

8. The Member States shall submit their regional and social conversion plans to the Commission. Those plans shall include in particular:

– a description of the conversion priorities selected for the areas concerned and of the corresponding operations;

– an indication of the use to be made of assistance available under the Funds, the EIB and the other financial instruments in implementing the plans.

In order to expedite the examination of applications and the implementation of action, the Member States may include with their plans applications for operational programmes that they cover.

9. The Commission shall examine the proposed plans to determine whether they are consistent with the objectives of this Regulation and with the provisions and policies referred to in Articles 6 and 7. It shall establish, through the partnership defined in Article 4 (1) in agreement with the Member State concerned and in accordance with the procedures referred to in Article 17, the Community conversion support framework for Community structural operations.

The Community support framework shall cover in particular:

– the priorities adopted for Community assistance;
– the forms of assistance;
– the indicative financing plan, with details of the amount of assistance and its source;
– the duration of the assistance.

The Community support framework may, if necessary, be revised and adjusted, on the initiative of the Member State or of the Commission and in agreement with the Member State in the light of relevant new information and of the results obtained during implementation of the operations concerned.

10. Assistance in respect of Objective 2 shall be predominantly in the form of operational programmes.

11. The arrangements for implementation of this Article shall be specified in the provisions referred to in Article 3 (4) and (5).

Article 10

Objectives 3 and 4

1. In accordance with the procedure laid down in Article 17, on the basis of this Regulation and the provisions implementing this Regulation, the Commission shall establish for a period covering a number of years general guidelines that set out and clarify the Community choices and criteria concerning action to combat long-term unemployment (Objective 3) and to facilitate the occupational integration of young people (Objective 4).

2. The Member Sates concerned shall submit to the Commission plans for operations to combat long-term unemployment (Objective 3) and to facilitate the occupational integration of young people (Objective 4) for which they are applying for Community support. Those plans shall include in particular:

- information on the employment and labour market policy implemented at national level;
- an indication of the priority operations for which Community support is sought, planned in principle for a specific number of years to help those sections of the population concerned by Objectives 3 and 4, and coherent with the general guidelines laid down by the Commission;
- an indication of the use to be made of assistance available under the ESF – where appropriate, in conjunction with assistance from the EIB or other existing Community financial instruments – in implementing the plans.

In order to expedite the examination of applications and the implementation of action, the Member States may include with their plans applications for operational programmes that they cover.

3. The Commission shall examine the proposed plans to determine whether they are consistent with the objectives of this Regulation, with

the general guidelines laid down by it and with the provisions and policies referred to in Articles 6 and 7. It shall establish for each Member State and for the individual plans submitted to it through the partnership referred to in Article 4 (1), in agreement with the Member State concerned and in accordance with the procedures referred to in Article 17, the Community support framework for the attainment of Objectives 3 and 4.

The Community support framework shall cover in particular:

- the specific priorities adopted for Community assistance in respect of the persons concerned by Objectives 3 and 4;
- the forms of assistance;
- the indicative financing plan, with details of the amount of assistance and its source;
- the duration of the assistance.

The Community support framework may, if necessary, be revised and adjusted on the initiative of the Member State in the light of relevant new information and of the results obtained during implementation of the operations concerned.

4. Assistance in respect of Objectives 3 and 4 shall be predominantly in the form of operational programmes.

5. The arrangements for implementation of the Article shall be specified in the provisions referred to in Article 3 (4) and (5).

Article 11

Objective 5

1. The arrangements for implementation of operations connected with the accelerated adaptation of agricultural structures (Objective 5 (a)) shall be determined in the provisions referred to in Article 3 (4) and (5).

2. Areas eligible under Objective 5 (b) shall be selected in accordance with the procedure referred to in Article 17, taking into account in particular the degree to which they are rural in nature, the number of persons occupied in agriculture, their level of economic and agricultural development, the extent to which they are peripheral and their sensitivity to changes in the agricultural sector, especially in the context of reform of the common agricultural policy.

These criteria shall be specified in the provisions adopted pursuant to Article 3 (4) and (5).

3. The Member States shall submit their development plans for rural areas to the Commission. Those plans shall include in particular:

- a description of the rural development priorities and the corresponding measures;
- an indication of the use to be made of assistance available under the different Funds, the EIB and the other financial instruments in implementing the plans;
- any link with the consequences of reform of the common agricultural policy.

To expedite the examination of applications and implementation of assistance, Member States may attach to their plans applications for operational programmes covered by the latter.

The Commission shall examine the proposed plans to determine whether they are consistent with the objectives of this Regulation and with the provisions and policies referred to in Articles 6 and 7. It shall establish, through the partnership referred to in Article 4 (1), in agreement with the Member State concerned and in accordance with the procedures referred to in Article 17, the Community support framework for rural development.

The Community support framework shall cover in particular:

- the rural development priorities adopted for Community assistance;
- the forms of assistance;
- the indicative financing plan, with details of the amount of assistance and its source;
- the duration of the assistance.

The Community support framework may, if necessary, be revised and adjusted on the initiative of the Member State concerned or of the Commission in agreement with the Member State in the light of relevant new information and of the results obtained during implementation of the operations concerned.

The arrangements for implementation of this paragraph shall be specified in the provisions referred to in Article 3 (4) and (5).

4. The part-financing of national aids and of operational programmes shall be the predominant form of assistance.

5. Operations eligible for assistance under the different Funds in respect of Objective 5 shall be specified in the provision referred to in Article 3 (4) and (5). In the case of the EAGGF Guidance Section, those provisions shall distinguish between operations to be financed in

connection with the adaptation of agricultural structures (Objective 5 (a)) and operations to be financed in connection with rural development (Objective 5 (b)).

IV. FINANCIAL PROVISIONS

Article 12

Fund resources and concentration

1. Within the framework of the multiannual budget forecasts, the Commission shall present each year a five-year projection of the appropriations needed for the three Structural Funds taken together. The projection shall be accompanied by an indicative breakdown of the commitment appropriations to be assigned to each objective. In drawing up each preliminary draft budget, the Commission shall, where the allocation for the Structural Funds is concerned, take account of the indicative breakdown by objective.

2. Commitment appropriations for the Structural Funds shall be doubled in real terms in 1993 by comparison with 1987. In addition to the resources earmarked for 1988 (7,700 million ECU), the amounts of annual increase in commitment appropriations for this purpose shall be 1,300 million ECU each year from 1989 to 1992, resulting in 1992 in a figure of 12,900 million ECU (1988 prices). The effort shall be continued in 1993 to achieve doubling.

To these amounts shall be added those required to aid for farm incomes and the set-aside scheme up to a maximum of 300 million ECU and 150 million ECU respectively in 1992 (1988 prices).

3. A considerable proportion of budgetary resources shall be concentrated on the less-developed regions covered by Objective 1.

The contributions of the Structural Funds (commitment appropriations) to these regions shall be doubled in real terms between now and 1992. All operations under Objectives 1 to 5 to assist the regions covered by Objective 1 shall be taken into account for that purpose.

4. The Commission shall ensure that, in the framework of the additional resources for the regions covered by Objective 1, a special effort is undertaken for the least prosperous regions.

5. The ERDF may devote approximately 80 per cent of its appropriations to Objective 1.

6. To facilitate the planning of assistance in the regions concerned, the Commission shall, for a period of five years and as a guide, establish the

allocation per Member State of 85 per cent of the commitment appropriations of the ERDF.

This allocation shall be based on the socio-economic criteria determining the eligibility of regions and areas for ERDF assistance under Objectives 1, 2 and 5 (b), while ensuring that the objective of doubling appropriations for the regions covered by Objective 1 takes the form of a substantial increase in assistance in those regions, particularly in the least prosperous regions.

Article 13

Differentiation of rates of assistance

1. The Community contributions to the financing of operations shall be differentiated in the light of the following:

- the seriousness of the specific, notably regional or social problems to be tackled;
- the financial capacity of the Member State concerned, taking into account in particular the relative prosperity of that State;
- the special importance attaching to measures from a Community viewpoint;
- the special importance attaching to measures from a regional viewpoint;
- the particular characteristics of the types of measure proposed.

2. Such differentiation shall take account of the planned link between grants and loans, as referred to in Article 5 (4).

3. The rates of Community assistance granted by the Funds in respect of the various objectives listed in Article 1 shall be subject to the following ceilings:

- a maximum of 75 per cent of the total cost and, as a general rule, at least 50 per cent of public expenditure in the case of measures carried out in the regions eligible for assistance under Objective 1;
- a maximum of 50 per cent of the total cost and, as a general rule, at least 25 per cent of public expenditure in the case of measures carried out in the other regions.

The minimum rates of assistance laid down in the first indent shall not apply to revenue-bearing investment.

4. Preparatory studies and technical assistance measures undertaken on the initiative of the Commission may be financed at 100 per cent of total cost in exceptional cases.

5. The arrangements for implementation of this Article, including those concerning public funding of the operations concerned, and the rates applied to investment generating revenue, shall be laid down in the provisions referred to in Article 3 (4) and (5).

V. OTHER PROVISIONS

Article 14

Combination and overlapping of assistance

1. For any given period, an individual measure or operation may benefit from assistance from only one Fund at a time.

2. An individual measure or operation may benefit from assistance from a Fund or other financial instrument in respect of only one of the objectives set out in Article 1 at a time.

3. The arrangements governing the combination and overlapping of assistance shall be laid down in the provisions referred to in Article 3 (4) and (5).

Article 15

Transitional provisions

1. This Regulation shall not affect multiannual operations approved by the Council or by the Commission on the basis of the existing rules governing the Funds before adoption of this Regulation.

2. Applications for assistance from the Funds towards a multiannual operation which are submitted before this Regulation is adopted shall be considered and approved by the Commission on the basis of the rules governing the Funds before the adoption of this Regulation.

3. New applications for assistance from the Funds for a multiannual operation, submitted after the adoption of this Regulation and before the entry into force of the provisions referred to in Article 3 (4) and (5) shall be examined in the light of the provisions of this Regulation. Approval for Community assistance, if given, shall be in accordance with the forms and procedures laid down by the rules in force at the time of the approval of the application.

4. Applications for aid for assistance for non-multiannual operations which are submitted before the entry into force of the provisions referred to in Article 3 (4) and (5) of this Regulation shall be examined

and approved on the basis of the rules governing the Funds in force before the entry into force of this Regulation.

5. The provisions in this Regulation which require the Member States to draw up plans and operational programmes shall be implemented progressively as laid down in the transitional provisions referred to in Article 3 (4) and (5), in accordance with rules applied without discrimination to all the Member States. The Commission shall help with implementation in particular by means of the technical assistance measures referred to in Article 4 (3).

6. The provisions referred to in Article 3 (4) and (5) shall, where appropriate lay down specific transitional provisions relating to the implementation of this Article, including provisions to ensure that aid to Member States is not interrupted pending the establishment of the plans and operational programmes in accordance with the new system and that the higher rates of assistance can apply to all forms of assistance as from 1 January 1989.

Article 16

Reports

Within the framework of Articles 130a and 130b of the Treaty before 1 November of each year, the Commission shall submit to the European Parliament, to the Council and to the Economic and Social Committee a report on the implementation of this Regulation during the preceding year.

In this report, the Commission shall in particular indicate what progress has been made towards achieving the objectives set out in Article 1 and in concentrating assistance as required by Article12.

Article 17

Committees

1. In implementing this Regulation, the Commission shall be assisted by three Committees dealing respectively with:

- Objectives 1 and 2
  - Advisory Committee composed of representatives of the Member States;
- Objectives 3 and 4
  - Committee under Article 124 of the Treaty;

- Objective 5 (a) and 5 (b)
  - Management Committee composed of representatives of the Member States.

2. Provisions setting out the arrangements for the operation of the Committees referred to in paragraph 1 and measures concerning the tasks of those Committees in the framework of management of the Funds shall be adopted in accordance with Article 3 (4) and (5).

VI. FINAL PROVISIONS

Article 18

Implementation

The Commission shall be reponsible for the implementation of this Regulation.

Article 19

Review clause

On a proposal from the Commission, the Council shall re-examine this Regulation five years after its entry into force. It shall act on the proposal in accordance with the procedure laid down in Article 130d of the Treaty.

Article 20

Entry into force

This Regulation shall enter into force on 1 January 1989.
Subject to the transitional provisions laid down in Article 15 (2) and (3), it shall be applicable as from that date.

The date of entry into force may be deferred by the Council, acting by a qualified majority on a proposal from the Commission, to allow for the entry into force of the provisions referred to in Article 3 (4) and (5).

This Regulation shall be binding in its entirety and directly applicable in all Member States.

Done at Luxembourg, 24 June 1988.

For the Council
The President
M. BANGEMANN

ANNEX

Regions concerned by Objective 1

SPAIN:	Andalusia, Asturias, Castilla y Léon, Castilla-La Mancha, Ceuta-Melilla, Valencia, Estremadura, Galicia, Canary Islands, Murcia
FRANCE:	French overseas departments, Corsica
GREECE:	the entire country
IRELAND:	the entire country
ITALY:	Abruzzi, Basilicata, Calabria, Campania, Molise, Apulia, Sardinia, Sicily
PORTUGAL:	the entire country
UNITED KINGDOM:	Northern Ireland

NOTES

* Appeared in the *Official Journal of the European Communities* 15 July 1988, pp. L185/9–20.
1 OJ No C 151, 9. 6. 1988, p. 4
2 OJ No C 167, 27. 6. 1988
3 OJ No C 175, 4. 7. 1988
4 Nomenclature of territorial units for statistical purposes (NUTS). See Eurostat 'Statistiques rapides des régions' of 25 August 1986.

I
COUNCIL REGULATION (EEC) No 4253/88

of 19 December 1988 laying down provisions for implementing Regulation (EEC) No 2052/88 are regards coordination of the activities of the different Structural Funds between themselves and with the operations of the European Investment Bank and the other existing financial instruments

THE COUNCIL OF THE EUROPEAN COMMUNITIES

Having regard to the Treaty establishing the European Economic Community, and in particular Articles 130e and 153 thereof,

Having regard to the proposal from the Commission,[1]

In cooperation with the European Parliament,[2]

Having regard to the opinion of the Economic and Social Committee,[3]

Whereas the Council adopted Regulation (EEC) No 2052/88 of 24 June 1988 on the tasks of the Structural Funds and their effectiveness and on the coordination of their activities between themselves and with the operations of the European Investment Bank and the other existing financial instruments;[4]

Whereas the doubling of the Structural Funds between 1987 and 1993 is covered by the Interinstitutional Agreement of 29 June 1988, whereas provisions for the implementation of Regulation (EEC) No 2052/88 should be laid down so that the new financial means allocated to the Funds are used in compliance with the new rules laid down in the Regulation and in accordance with the guidelines of the European Council;

Whereas Article 3 (5) of Regulation (EEC) No 2052/88 provides that the Council, acting on the basis of Article 130e of the Treaty, shall adopt the provisions necessary for ensuring coordination between the different Structural Funds, on the one hand, and between them and the European Investment Bank (EIB) and the other existing financial instruments, on the other;

Whereas it is necessary to ensure and strengthen, in a manner consistent with the partnership, the coordination between the Structural Funds and between these Funds, the EIB and the Community's other existing financial instruments, in order to enhance the effectiveness of their contributions to the attainment of the objectives set out in Article 1 of Regulation (EEC) No 2052/88; whereas the Commission has an important role to play in this respect;

Whereas, to this end, the Commission must, where necessary, associate the EIB with the preparation of its decisions; whereas the EIB is prepared to cooperate in the implementation of this Regulation, in keeping with its own powers and responsibilities;

Whereas Articles 8 to 11 of the said Regulation provide for measures relating to their implementation to be laid down in the implementing decisions referred to in Article 130e of the Treaty; whereas it is necessary to determine the criteria which the Commission should use to select those rural areas outside the regions designated for assistance from the Funds under Objective 1 which may receive assistance under Objective 5 (b) as defined in Article 1 of Regulation (EEC) No 2052/88; whereas these criteria must ensure that there is effective concentration on those areas suffering from the most serious problems of development, while account is taken of difficulties in other rural areas, in the regions of Member States with socio-economic imbalances such as would threaten their development;

Whereas it is necessary to specify the scope, content and duration of the plans to be submitted by the Member States and the time limits for their submission;

Whereas, with a view to helping Member States in the preparation of plans, the Commission should be in a position to supply the necessary technical assistance;

Whereas it is necessary to give guidelines on the content and duration of the Community support frameworks to be established by the Commission in agreement with the Member State concerned and on the time limit for their establishment;

Whereas, when the Community support frameworks are being worked out and implemented, care should be taken to see that any increase in appropriations from the Funds has a genuine additional economic impact in the regions concerned;

Whereas the Commission should be able to adapt, in agreement with the Member State concerned, Community support frameworks to take account of measures not provided for in the plans submitted by the Member States, including measures resulting from new Community initiatives;

Whereas assistance from the Funds envisaged in the Community support frameworks should be provided mainly in the form of part-financing of operational programmes;

Whereas it is necessary to specify the conditions for the implementation of operational programmes under the integrated approach;

Whereas it is necessary to specify the general conditions governing the processing of applications for financial assistance from the Structural Funds;

Whereas financial assistance from the Structural Funds Objectives 1 to 4 and 5 (b) should normally be provided only for measures indicated in the Community support frameworks and for expenditure incurred after presentation of an application for assistance from the structural Funds; whereas it is, however, necessary to provide that expenditure incurred before that date for the part-financing of projects and aid systems should be eligible;

Whereas it is necessary to define the conditions under which the Structural Funds may provide global grants and part-finance projects;

Whereas provision should be made for the conditions under which studies and technical assistance linked to the joint or coordinated use of the Structural Funds, the EIB and the other financial instruments may be financed;

Whereas care must be taken to ensure that the technical and administrative difficulties which might hinder implementation of the reform of the Funds, particularly in regions whose development is lagging behind, do not result in inadequate take-up of the budgetary resources nor in the effective doubling of those resources being called into question;

Whereas, in order to ensure a measure of flexibility in the implementation of the reform of the Funds, it is appropriate that the rates of assistance from the funds be fixed, on the basis of Article 13 of Regulation (EEC) No 2052/88 and under the conditions laid down in this Regulation, in the framework of the partnership, for Objectives 1 to 4 and 5 (b), on the one hand, and by subsequent decisions taken by the Council for Objective 5 (a), on the other;

Whereas, to promote efficient and coordinated management of the Funds' financial resources, it is necessary to lay down common rules and procedures on commitments, payments and controls;

Whereas, in the interests of the wider use of the ecu in financial transactions in the Community and, in particular, in the implementation of the Community budget, it is important that the Community's financial entitlements and obligations with respect to the Structural Funds should also be expressed in ecus, in keeping with the Financial Regulation;

Whereas it is necessary to specify the arrangements for the monitoring and assessment of Community structural action in order to strengthen the effectiveness of assistance methods in achieving the objectives and to assess the impact of assistance;

Whereas it is necessary to determine the arrangements for the working of the committees called upon to assist the Commission in the implementation of Regulation (EEC) No 2052/88;

Whereas there is a need to specify the content of the report referred to in Article 16 of the said Regulation;

Whereas provision should be made to give adequate publicity to Community assistance provided towards specific schemes;

Whereas it is necessary to determine more specifically the transitional arrangements for assistance from the Funds which was approved or applied for before the entry into force of the implementing decisions referred to in Article 130e of the Treaty and whereas it may also prove necessary, with a view to ensuring continuity in the operations of the Funds, to provide for approval of certain measures before the Commission has decided the relevant Community support frameworks.

HAS ADOPTED THIS REGULATION

TITLE I
COORDINATION

Article 1

General provisions

Pursuant to Regulation (EEC) No 2052/88, the Commission shall, in a manner consistent with partnership, ensure coordination of the activities of the different Funds as between themselves and with the operations of the EIB and the other existing financial instruments.

Article 2

Coordination between the Funds

Coordination between the activities of the various Funds shall be carried out in particular through:

- Community support frameworks,
- multiannual budget forecasts,
- where advisable, the implementation of integrated operational programmes,
- monitoring and assessment of operations under the Funds carried out in connection with a single objective and of those carried out in connection with a number of objectives in the same territory.

Article 3

Coordination between the Funds, the EIB and the other existing financial instruments

1. In implementing the objectives referred to in Article 1 of Regulation

(EEC) No 2052/88, the Commission shall ensure, within the framework of the partnership, coordination and consistency between assistance from the funds and assistance provided:

- by the European Coal and Steel Community in the form of re-adaptation aids, loans, interest subsidies or guarantees,
- by the EIB, the New Community Instrument and Euratom in the form of loans and guarantees,
- from resources from the Community budget allocated to other action for structural purposes,
- from the resources of the Community research budget.

Such coordination shall be carried out in keeping with the EIB's own powers and responsibilities and with the objectives of the other instruments concerned.

2. The Commission shall associate the EIB in the use of the Funds or the other existing financial instruments with a view to the part-financing of investments that are eligible for financing by the EIB in accordance with its Statute.

Article 4

Selection of rural areas outside the regions in Objective 1 (Objective 5 (b))

1. In accordance with Article 11 (2) of Regulation (EEC) No 2052/88, the rural areas that may receive Community assistance under Objective 5 (b) shall meet each of the following criteria:

(a) high share of agricultural employment in total employment;
(b) low level of agricultural income, notably as expressed in terms of agricultural value added by agricultural work unit (AWU);
(c) low level of socio-economic development assessed on the basis of gross domestic product per inhabitant.

Assessment of the eligibility of areas according to the above three criteria shall take into account socio-economic parameters which indicate the seriousness of the general situation in the areas concerned, and how it is developing.

2. In addition, on receipt of a reasoned request from a Member State, Community assistance may also be extended to other rural areas with a low level of socio-economic development, if they meet one or more of the following critera:

- low population density and/or a significant depopulation trend in the areas concerned,
- the peripheral nature of areas or islands in relation to major centres of economic and commercial activity in the Community,
- the sensitivity of the area to developments in agriculture, especially in the context of reform of the common agricultural policy, assessed on the basis of the trend in agricultural incomes and the size of the agricultural labour force,
- the structure of agricultural holdings and the age structure of the agricultural labour force,
- the pressures exerted on the environment and on the countryside,
- the situation of areas within mountain or less-favoured areas classified pursuant to Article 3 of Directive 75/268/EEC,[5] as last amended by Regulation (EEC) No 797/85.[6]

3. Member States shall, in respect of the areas which in their view should benefit from assistance under Objective 5 (b), provide the Commission with such information as may help it to determine which areas are eligible. On the basis of that information and of its overall assessment of the proposals submitted, the Commission shall determine which areas are eligible by following the procedures set out in Title VIII and shall invite the Member States to forward the necessary plans to it.

4. In selecting rural areas and in defining the Community support frameworks referred to in Article 11 (3) of Regulation (EEC) No 2052/88, the Commission, in the context of reform of the common agricultural policy, shall take care to ensure that assistance is effectively concentrated on areas suffering from the most serious problems of rural development.

TITLE II
PLANS

Article 5

Scope and content

1. Subject to the guidelines laid down in this Article, plans submitted in connection with Objectives 1 to 4 and 5 (b) shall be drawn up at the geographical level deemed to be most appropriate. They shall be

prepared by the competent national, regional or other authorities designated by the Member State and shall be submitted by the Member State to the Commission.

Plans submitted in connection with Objective 1 shall, as a general rule, cover one region at NUTS level II. However, in implementation of the second subparagraph of Article 8 (4) of Regulation (EEC) No 2052/88, Member States may submit a plan for more than one of their regions included in the list referred to in paragraph 2 of that Article, provided that such plans comprise the features listed in the first subparagraph of the said paragraph 4.

Plans submitted in connection with Objectives 2 and 5 (b) shall normally cover one or more regions at NUTS level III.

Member States may submit plans covering a wider territory than that of eligible regions or areas, provided they distinguish between operations in eligible regions or areas and operations elsewhere.

2. For regions concerned by Objective 1, the regional development plans shall include measures relating to the conversion of declining industrial areas and the development of rural areas, together with employment and vocational training measures other than those covered by plans submitted in connection with objectives 3 and 4.

Regional and social conversion plans submitted in connection with Objective 2 and rural development plans submitted in connection with Objective 5 (b) shall also include employment and vocational training measures other than those covered by plans submitted in connection with objectives 3 and 4.

Plans submitted in connection with Objectives 3 and 4 shall distinguish between expenditure in respect of the regions covered by Objectives 1, 2 and 5 (b) and expenditure in respect of other regions.

Data concerning the operations carried out under Objective 5 (a) will be indicated, as appropriate, in the plans in connection with Objectives 1 and 5 (b).

In the plans, Member States shall indicate the particulars relating to each Fund, including the volumes of assistance requested. In accordance with Articles 8, 9, 10 and 11 of Regulation (EEC) No 2052/88, in order to expedite the examination of applications and the implementation of action, they may include in their plans applications for assistance for operational programmes.

3. Member States shall ensure, when the plans are drawn up, that plans relating to the same objective within a Member State and plans relating to different objectives in the same geographical area are mutually consistent.

4. Member States shall ensure that the plans take full account of Community policies.

Article 6

Duration and timetable

Each plan shall cover a period of between three and five years. As a general rule, the plans may be revised on an annual basis and in the event of significant changes in the socio-economic situation and the labour market.

Four regions are areas defined before 31 January 1989, the first relating to objectives 1, 2 and 5 (b) shall cover a period which shall commence on 1 January 1989 and shall be submitted not later than 31 March 1989. Plans relating to Objectives 3 and 4 shall be submitted not later than four months after the Commission has published the guidelines referred to in Article 4 (1) of Regulation (EEC) No 4255/88 of 19 December 1988 laying down provisions for inplementing Regulation (EEC) No 2052/88 as regards the European Social Fund.[7]

The dates relating to the Submission of subsequent plans will be fixed by the Commission in cooperation with the Member State concerned.

Article 7

Preparation

1. The Commission may provide Member States at their request with any technical assistance necessary in the preparation of plans.
2. The plans shall contain information making it possible to assess the link between structural action and the Member State's economic and social policies.

TITLE III
COMMUNITY SUPPORT FRAMEWORKS

Article 8

Preparation, scope and content

1. The Community support frameworks relating to Objectives 1 to 4 and 5 (b) shall be drawn up at the appropriate geographical level in agreement with the Member State concerned within the framework of

the partnership and shall be established by decision of the Commission in accordance with the procedures laid down in Title VIII. The EIB shall also be involved in the preparation of the Community support frameworks.

Without prejudice to the first subparagraph of Article 8 (5) of Regulation (EEC) No 2052/88, the Commission shall, if appropriate, in drawing up Community support frameworks for Objectives 1 and 5 (b), take account of information regarding the impact of the measures taken under Objective 5 (a) which contribute to the development of the regions or areas concerned.

2. A Community support framework may cover a period of three to five years.

3. Each Community support framework shall include:

- a statement of the priorities for joint Community and national action in relation to the objecives set out in Article 1 of Regulation (EEC) No 2052/88, together with information on their consistency with the economic and social policies of the Member State concerned,
- an outline of the forms of assistance to be provided including, for operational programmes, their specific objectives and the main types of measure involved,
- an indicative financing plan specifying the financial allocations envisaged for the various forms of assistance and the duration thereof, including those of the Funds, the EIB and the other existing financial instruments provided for in Article 3 (1), where they contribute directly to the financing plan concerned,
- where appropriate, information on the means available for any studies or technical assistance operations relating to the preparation, implementation or adaptation of the measures concerned.

Article 9

Impact of measures

In establishing and implementing the Community support frameworks, the Commission and the Member States shall ensure that the increase in the appropriations for the Funds provided for in Article 12 (2) of Regulation (EEC) No 2052/88 has a genuine additional economic impact in the regions concerned and results in at least an equivalent increase in the total volume of official or similar (Community and national) structural aid in the Member State concerned, taking into account the macro-economic circumstances in which the funding takes place.

Article 10

Approval and implementation

1. Unless otherwise agreed between the Commission and the Member State concerned, the Commission shall take a decision approving the Community support framework not later than six months after receiving the relevant plan or plans.

In order to expedite implementation of the measures provided for in a Community support framework, Member States may submit applications for assistance in good time for the Commission to approve them at the same time as it takes its decision on the Community support framework. In this case, the operational programmes may be implemented immediately.

2. The Commission decision on the Community support framework shall be sent as a declaration of intent to the Member State. The declaration shall be published in the *Official Journal of the European Communities*.

The Commission and the Member States shall ensure that measures accounting for at least two-thirds of assistance from the funds during the first year of the Community support framework are approved by the Commission within two months of adoption of its decision on the Community support framework.

Article 11

Community initiatives

In accordance with Article 5 (5) of Regulation (EEC) 2052/88, the Commission may, on its own initiative and in accordance with the procedures provided for in Title VIII, decide to propose to the Member States that they submit applications for assistance in respect of measures of significant interest to the Community not covered by the plans referred to in Title II. Any assistance approved pursuant to this provision shall be reflected in the establishment or revision of the relevant Community support framework.

Article 12

Forms of assistance

Assistance covered by a Community support framework shall be provided predominantly in the form of operational programmes which may be implemented in the form of an integrated approach if the conditions laid down in Article 13 are met.

Article 13

Integrated approach

1. At the initiative of a Member State or of the Commission pursuant to Article 11, in agreement with the Member State concerned, an operational programme may be implemented in the form of an integrated approach if:

(a) the programme involves financing by more than one Fund or at least one Fund and one financial instrument other than a loan instrument;

(b) the measures to be financed by different Funds or financial instruments are mutually reinforcing and significant benefits are likely to accrue from close coordination between all the parties involved;

(c) the appropriate administrative structures are provided at national, regional and local level in the interests of integrated implementation of the programme.

2. The desirability of implementing measures on the basis of an integrated approach shall be considered when establishing or revising a Community support framework.

3. In the implementation of integrated approaches the Commission shall ensure that Community assistance is provided in the most effective manner, taking into account the special coordination effort required.

TITLE IV
ASSISTANCE FROM THE FUNDS

Article 14

Processing of applications

1. Applications for assistance from the Structural Funds shall be

prepared by the competent national, regional, local or other authorities designated by the Member States and shall be submitted to the Commission by the Member State or by any body it may designate to do so. Each application shall relate to one of the forms of assistance provided for in Article 5 of Regulation (EEC) No 2052/88.

2. Applications shall contain the information the Commission needs in order to assess them, including a description of the operation proposed, its scope, including geographical coverage, and specific objectives, the bodies responsible for implementation, the proposed beneficiaries and the proposed limitable and financing plan, together with any other information necessary to verify that the operation concerned is compatible with Community legislation and policies.

3. The Commission shall examine applications with a view in particular:

- to assessing the conformity of the proposed operations and measures with the relevant Community legislation and, where appropriate, with the relevant Community support framework,
- to assessing the contribution of the proposed operation to the achievement of its specific objectives and, in the case of an operational programme, the consistency of the constituent measures,
- to checking that the administrative and financial mechanisms are adequate to ensure effective implementation,
- to determining the precise arrangements for providing assistance from the Fund or Funds concerned on the basis, where appropriate, of the information already given in any relevant Community support framework.

The Commission shall decide on assistance from the Funds, provided the requirements of the article are fulfilled, as a general rule within six months of receipt of the application. A single Commission decision shall be taken in respect of assistance from all the Funds and other existing financial instruments contributing to the financing of an operational programme, including operational programmes in the form of an integrated approach. This provision does not preclude the possible application of shorter time limits pursuant to Article 7 of Regulation (EEC) No 4255/88 (ESF Regulation).

4. The respective commitments of the partners, in the framework of an agreement within the partnership, shall be reflected in the Commission's decisions to grant assistance.

Article 15

Eligibility

1. Subject to Article 33, expenditure in respect of measures covered by Objectives 1 to 4 and 5 (b) shall be eligible for financial assistance from the Structural Funds only if the measures in question come within the relevant Community support framework.

2. Except as provided for in Article 33 of this Regulation, in Article 9 of Regulation (EEC) No 4255/88 and in Article 2 (1) of Council Regulation (EEC) No 4256/88 of 19 December 1988 laying down provisions for implementing Regulation (EEC) No 2052/88 as regards the EAGGF Guidance Section,[8] expenditure may not be considered eligible for assistance from the Funds if incurred before the date on which the corresponding application reaches the Commission.

However, for the part-financing of projects and aid schemes, expenditure may be deemed to be eligible for assistance from the Funds if incurred during the six months preceding the date on which the Commission received the corresponding application.

Article 16

Specific provisions

1. In the case of global grants, the intermediaries who shall be designated by the Member State concerned in agreement with the Commission must provide appropriate guarantees of solvency and have the necessary administrative capability to manage the operations envisaged by the Commission. The intermediaries shall also be selected in the light of the particular situation in the Member States or areas concerned. Without prejudice to Article 23, the management of global grants shall be subject to control by the competent authorities designated by the Member States.

2. The Funds may provide financial assistance towards expenditure in respect of major projects if the total cost taken into account in determining the amount of Community assistance is, as a general rule, greater than ECU15 million for infrastructure investments or greater than ECU10 million for productive investments.

However, projects costing less than this in the fisheries sector may be financed if they are covered by a multiannual guidance programme approved by the Commission under Regulation (EEC) No 4028/86.[9]

3. In addition to similar assistance connected with the operations of the

various Funds, the Commission may, for up to 0.3 per cent of the Funds' total allocation, finance studies and technical assistance linked to the joint or coordinated deployment of the Structural Funds, the EIB and the other financial instruments:

- in preparation for the establishment of plans,
- with a view to assessing the impact and effectiveness of assistance provided under the relevant Community support frameworks,
- in relation to integrated operational programmes.

4. For the regions designated under objective 1, the total cost of an operational programme to which the ERDF is contributing must, as a general rule, reach ECU100 million, with the proviso that the average annual cost of the programme may not be less than ECU15 million.

TITLE V
DIFFERENTIATION OF COMMUNITY ASSISTANCE

Article 17

Financial contribution from the Funds

1. Pursuant to Article 13 (5) of Regulation (EEC) No 2052/88, the rate of contribution by the Funds to the financing of measures covered by Objectives 1 to 4 and 5 (b) shall be laid down by the Commission, within the framework of the partnership, on the basis of Article 13 (1) of Regulation (EEC) No 2052/88, within the limits laid down by Article 13(3) of the said Regulation and in accordance with the procedures provided for in that Article.

The rates applicable under Objective 5 (a) shall be laid down pursuant to the procedure provided for by Article 1 (3) of Regulation (EEC) No 4256/88.

2. The financial contribution from the Funds shall be fixed as a percentage and shall be calculated in relation to either the total eligible cost of, or the total public or similar expenditure (national, regional or local, and Community) on, each measure (operational programme, aid scheme, global grant, project, technical assistance, study).

3. Where the measure concerned entails the financing of revenue-generating investments, the Commission shall determine, within the framework of the partnership, the rate of contribution from the Funds for these investments, in compliance with the provisions of Article 13 (3) of Regulation (EEC) No 2052/88 and on the basis of the criteria referred to in paragraph 1 of that Article, taking account, amongst

their intrinsic characteristics, of the size of the gross self-financing margin which would normally be expected for the class of investments concerned in the light of the macro-economic circumstances in which the investments are to be implemented, and without there being any increase in the national budget effort as a result of contribution by the Fund.

In any event, in connection with the development effort in the regions concerned, the contribution from the Funds to investments in firms may not exceed 50 per cent of the total cost in the regions covered by Objective 1 and 30 per cent of the total cost in the other regions.

4. The rates of contribution for individual measures forming part of operational programmes may be differentiated in accordance with agreements to be concluded within the framework of the partnership.

Article 18

Combination of grants and loans

The combination of loans and grants referred to in Article 5 (4) of Regulation (EEC) No 2052/88 shall be determined in conjunction with the EIB when the Community support framework is being established. It shall take account of the balance in the proposed financing plan, the rates of contribution from the Funds established in accordance with Article 17 and the development objectives pursued.

TITLE VI
FINANCIAL PROVISIONS

Article 19

General provisions

1. Financial assistance from the Structural Funds shall be subject to the relevant rules applicable to the Funds under the Financial Regulation.
2. The financial assistance to be granted in respect of specific measures undertaken in implementing a Community support framework shall be consistent with the financing plan laid down in that support framework.
3. In order to avoid administrative delays at the end of the year, Member States shall ensure that request for payments are, as far as possible, submitted in accordance with a balanced schedule throughout the year.

Article 20

Commitments

1. Budgetary commitments shall be made on the basis of the Commission decisions approving the operations concerned. They shall be valid for a period, depending on the nature of the operations and on the specific conditions for their implementation.

2. Commitments in respect of operations to be carried out over a period of two or more years shall, as a general rule, be effected in annual instalments. The commitments in connection with the first annual instalment shall be made when the decision approving the operation is adopted by the Commission.

Commitments in connection with subsequent annual instalments shall be based on the financing plan for the operation concerned and on the progress made in implementing it.

3. For operations to be carried out over a period of less than two years, the total amount of Community assistance shall be committed when the Commission adopts the decision approving the operation.

Article 21

Payments

1. Payments of financial assistance shall be made in accordance with the corresponding budgetary commitments to the authority designated for the purpose in the application submitted through the Member State concerned. They may take the form either of advances or of final payments in respect of expenditure actually incurred. For operations to be carried out over a period of two or more years payments shall relate to the annual instalments of commitment referred to in Article 20 (2).

2. The advance made following each commitment may be up to 50 per cent of the amount committed, taking into account the nature of the operation concerned.

3. A second advance such that the sum of the two advances does not exceed 80 per cent of the commitment shall be made after the responsible body has certified that at least half of the first advance has been used up and that the operation is progressing at a satisfactory rate and in accordance with the objectives laid down.

4. Payment of the balance in respect of each commitment shall be conditional on:

– submission to the Commission by the designated authority referred

to in paragraph 1 of a request for payment within six months of the end of the year concerned or of completion in practice of the operation concerned,
- submission to the Commission of the relevant reports referred to in Article 25 (4),
- transmission by the Member State to the Commission of a certificate confirming the information contained in the request for payment and the reports.

5. Member States shall designate the authorities empowered to issue the certificates referred to in paragraphs 3 and 4 and shall ensure that the beneficiaries receive the advances and payments as soon as possible.

6. In the case of measures that are designed to support agricultural incomes, such as compensation for natural handicaps in less-favoured or mountain areas, and that are governed by the provisions referred to in Article 11 (1) of Regulation (EEC) No 2052/88, the condition and procedures applicable in respect of advances or final payments shall be laid down in the corresponding Commission decisions, due regard being had to the specific nature of those measures.

7. In the case of studies and innovation schemes, the Commission shall determine the appropriate payment procedures.

Article 22

Use of the ECU

Commission decisions, commitments and payments shall be denominated and carried out in ecus. In compliance with the provisions of the Financial Regulation and in accordance with the arrangements to be drawn up by the Commission pursuant to the procedures referred to in Title VIII hereof.

This Article shall be applicable as soon as the Commission decision referred to in the first subparagraph has been adopted.

Article 23

Financial control

1. In order to guarantee successful completion of operations carried out by public or private promoters. Member States shall take the necessary measures:

- to verify on a regular basis that operations financed by the Community have been properly carried out,
- to prevent and to take action against irregularities,
- to recover any amounts lost as a result of an irregularity or negligence. Except where the Member State and/or the intermediary and/or the promoter provide proof that they were not responsible for the irregularity or negligence, the Member State shall be liable in the alternative for reimbursement of any sums unduly paid.

Member States shall inform the Commission of the measures taken for those purposes and, in particular, of the progress of administrative and judicial proceedings.

When submitting requests for payment, Member States shall make available to the Commission any appropriate national control reports on the measures included in the programmes or other operations concerned.

2. Without prejudice to checks carried out by Member States, in accordance with national laws, regulations and administrative provisions and without prejudice to the provisions of Article 206 of the Treaty or to any inspection arranged on the basis of Article 209 (c) of the Treaty, Commission officials may carry out on-the-spot checks, including sample checks, in respect of operations financed by the Structural Funds.

Before carrying out an on-the-spot check, the Commission shall give notice to the Member State concerned with a view to obtaining all the assistance necessary. If the Commission carries out on-the-spot checks without giving notice, it shall be subject to agreements reached in accordance with the provisions of the Financial Regulation within the framework of the partnership. Officials of the Member State concerned may take part in such checks.

The Commission may require the Member State concerned to carry out an on-the-spot check to verify the regularity of payment requests. Commission officials may take part in such checks and must do so if the Member State concerned so requests.

The Commission shall ensure that any checks that it carries out are performed in a coordinated manner so as to avoid repeating checks in respect of the same subject matter during the same period. The Member State concerned and the Commission shall immediately exchange any relevant information concerning the results of the checks carried out.

3. For a period of three years following the last payment in respect of

any operation, the responsible body and authorities shall keep available for the Commission all the supporting documents regarding expenditure on the operation.

Article 24

Reduction, suspension and cancellation of assistance

1. If an operation or measure appears to justify only part of the assistance allocated, the Commission shall conduct a suitable examination of the case in the framework of the partnership, in particular requesting that the Member State or other authorities designated by it to implement the operation submit their comments within a specified period of time.

2. Following this examination, the Commission may reduce or suspend assistance in respect of the operation or measure concerned if the examination reveals an irregularity and in particular a significant change affecting the nature or conditions of the operation or measure for which the Commission's approval has not been sought.

3. Any sum received unduly and to be recovered shall be repaid to the Commission. Interest on account of late payment may be charged on sums not repaid in compliance with the provisions of the Financial Regulation and in accordance with the arrangements to be drawn up by the Commission pursuant to the procedures referred to in Title VIII hereof.

TITLE VII
MONITORING AND ASSESSMENT

Article 25

Monitoring

1. Within the framework of the partnership, the Commission and the Member States shall ensure effective monitoring of implementation of assistance from the Funds, geared to the Community support framework and specific operations (programmes, etc.). Such monitoring shall be carried out by way of jointly agreed reporting procedures, sample checks and the establishment of monitoring committees.

The Commission shall report each year to the committees referred to in Title VIII on the progress made in implementing assistance operations under the Funds, including the use made of appropriations in relation to the particulars given in the Community support frameworks. The findings of this report and the opinions of the Committee shall be forwarded to the European Parliament for information.

2. Monitoring shall be carried out by reference to physical and financial indicators specified in the Commission decision approving the operation concerned. The indicators shall relate to the specific character of the operation, its objectives and the form of assistance provided, and to the structural and socio-economic situation in the countries in which the assistance is to be provided. They shall be arranged in such a way as to show, for the operations in question:

- the stage reached in the operation,
- the progress achieved on the management side and any related problems.

3. Monitoring Committees shall be set up, within the framework of the partnership, by agreement between the Member State concerned and the Commission.

The Commission and, where appropriate, the EIB may delegate representatives to those Committees.

4. For each multiannual operation, the authority designated for the purpose by the Member State shall submit progress reports to the Commission within six months of the end of each full year of implementation. A final report shall be submitted to the Commission within six months of completion of the operation.

For each operation to be implemented over a period of less than two years, the authority designated for the purpose by the Member State shall submit a report to the Commission within six months of completion of the operation.

5. After the Monitoring Committee has delivered its opinion, the Commission shall, in cooperation with the Member State, make any necessary adjustments to the volume or conditions of assistance as initially approved and to the schedule of payments envisaged.

6. For the greater effectiveness of the Funds, the Commission shall ensure that particular attention is paid to transparency of management in its administration of them.

7. Whereas this Regulation or Regulations (EEC) No 4254/88 of 19 December 1988 laying down provisions for implementing Regulation (EEC) No 2052/88 as regards the European Regional Development Fund,[10] (EEC) No 4255/88 and (EEC) No 4256/88 provide for the Commission to determine detailed arrangements for implementation,

the precise details which are adopted shall be notified to the Member States and published in the *Official Journal of the European Communities*.

Article 26

Assessment

1. Assessment shall be carried out within the framework of the partnership. The competent authorities in the Member States shall, where appropriate, contribute in such a way as to ensure that assessment can be carried out in the most effective manner. In this connection, assessment shall make use of the various particulars that the monitoring arrangements can yield in order to gauge the socio-economic impact of the operations, where appropriate in close association with the monitoring committees.

2. *Ex ante* and *ex post* assessment of operations undertaken for structural purposes by the Community shall be concerned with their effectiveness at three levels:

– their overall impact on the objectives set out in Article 130a of the Treaty, and in particular the strengthening of the economic and social cohesion of the Community,

– the impact of operations under each Community support framework,
– the impact of individual operations (programmes, etc.).

Assessment shall, according to the circumstances, be carried out by reference to macroeconomic indicators based on regional or national statistics, to information yielded by descriptive and analytical studies and to qualitative analyses.

3. In drawing up Community support frameworks and in getting individual applications for assistance, the Commission shall take into account the findings of assessments made in accordance with this Article.

4. The assessment principle and procedures shall be laid down in the Community support frameworks.

5. The results of the assessments shall be submitted to the European Parliament and the Economic and Social Committee within the framework of the annual report pursuant to Article 16 of Regulation (EEC) No 2052/88.

TITLE VIII
COMMITTEES

Article 27

Advisory Committee on the Development and Conversion of Regions

In accordance with Article 17 of Regulation (EEC) No 2052/88, an Advisory Committee on the Development and Conversion of Regions, made up of Member States' representatives and chaired by the Commission representative, is hereby set up under the auspices of the Commission. The EIB shall appoint a non-voting representative. The European Parliament shall receive regular information on the outcome of the proceedings of this Committee.

The Commission representative shall submit to the Committee a draft of the measures to be taken. The Committee shall deliver its opinion on the draft within a time limit which the chairman may lay down according to the urgency of the matter, where appropriate by taking a vote.

The opinion shall be recorded in the minutes. In addition, each Member State shall have the right to request that its position be recorded in those minutes.

The Commission shall take the utmost account of the opinion delivered by the Committee. It shall inform the Committee of the manner in which it took account of the opinion.

The Committee shall deliver opinions on draft Commission decisions concerning the Community support frameworks as provided for in Articles 8(5) and 9 (9) of Regulation (EEC) No 2052/88, on the regular reports provided for in Article 8 of Council Regulation (EEC) No 4254/88 and on the drawing-up and revision of the list of areas eligible in connection with Objective 2. The matter referred to in Article 10 of Regulation (EEC) No 4254/88 may also be referred to it by the Commission.

The Committees referred to in Articles 28 and 29 shall be informed of the Committee's opinions.

The Committee shall draw up its rules of procedure.

Article 28

Committee referred to in Article 124 of the Treaty

In accordance with Article 17 of Regulation (EEC) No 2052/88, the Committee referred to in Article 124 of the Treaty shall be composed of two government representatives, two representatives of the workers' organizations and two representatives of the employers' organizations from each Member State. The member of the Commission responsible for chairing the Committee may delegate that responsibility to a senior Commission official.

For each Member State, an alternat [sic] shall be appointed for each category of representative mentioned above. In the absence of one or both members, the alternat [sic] shall be automatically entitled to take part in the proceedings.

The members and alternates [sic] shall be appointed by the Council, acting on a proposal from the Commission, for a period of three years. They may be re-appointed. The Council shall, as regards the composition of the Committee, endeavour to ensure fair representation of the different groups concerned. For the items on the agenda affecting it, the EIB shall appoint a non-voting representative.

The Committee shall deliver opinions on the draft Commission decisions relating to the guidelines for action in connection with Objectives 3 and 4, on the Community support frameworks relating to those objectives and, in the case of support from the European Social Fund, on the Community support frameworks relating to Objectives 1, 2 and 5 (b).

For their adoption, the opinions of the Committee shall require an absolute majority of the votes validly cast. The Commission shall inform the Committee of the manner in which it took account of those opinions.

The Committees referred to in Articles 27 and 29 shall be informed of the Commitee's opinions.

The Committees shall draw up its rules of procedure.

Article 29

Committee on Agricultural Structures and Rural Development

In accordance with Article 17 of Regulation (EEC) No 2052/88, a Committee on Agricultural Structures and Rural Development, made up of Member States, representatives and chaired by the Commission representative, is hereby set up under the auspices of the Commission. The EIB shall appoint a non-voting representative.

The Commission representative shall submit to the Committee a draft of the measures to be taken. The Committee shall deliver an opinion on the draft within a time limit which the chairman may lay down according to the urgency of the matter under consideration. The opinion shall be delivered by the majority stipulated in Article 148 (2) of the Treaty in the case of decisions which the Council is requested to adopt on a proposal from the Commission; when a matter is put to the vote within the Committee, the votes of the Member States', representatives shall be weighted as provided for in the aforementioned Article. The chairman shall not vote.

The Commission shall adopt measures which shall apply immediately. However, if they are not in accordance with the opinion delivered by the Committee, they shall be communicated forthwith by the Commission to the Council. In that event, the Commission may defer application of the measures which it has decided for a period of not more than one month from the date of such communication.

The Council, acting by a qualified majority, may take a different decision within the period provided for in the third subparagraph.

The Committee shall deliver opinions on draft Commission decisions:

- relating to common measures in connection with Objective 5 (a),
- relating to Community support frameworks in connection with Objective 5 (b).

The Committee provided for in this Article shall replace the Standing Committee on Agricultural Structures, set up by Article 1 of the Council Decision of 4 December 1962,[11] in respect of all the functions assigned to it under that Decision or under Article 6 of Regulation (EEC) No 727/70,[12] as last amended by Regulation (EEC) No 2048/88.[13]

The Committees referred to in Articles 27 and 28 shall be informed of the Committee's opinions.

The Committee shall draw up its rules of procedure.

Article 30

Other provisions

1. The Commission shall periodically refer to the Committees provided for in Articles 27, 28 and 29 the reports referred to in Article 16 of Regulation (EEC) No 2052/88. It may seek the opinion of those Committees on any matter relating to assistance operations under the Funds, other than those provided for in this Title, notably in connection with its power of initiative referred to in Article 5 (5) of Regulation (EEC) No 2052/88.

Moreover, all the specific cases laid down in Regulation (EEC) No 2052/88 and by all the implementing Regulations referred to in Article 130e of the Treaty shall be referred to the Committees.

2. Decisions 75/185/EEC[14] and Decision 83/517/EEC[15] shall be repealed and, as regards the EAGGF, Guidance Section, the provisions of Articles 11 to 15 of Regulation (EEC) No 729/70 concerning the EAGGF Committee shall no longer apply.

TITLE IX
REPORTS AND PUBLICITY

Article 31

Reports

1. The annual reports referred to in Article 16 of Regulation (EEC) No 2052/88 shall review *inter alia*:

- the efforts deployed under all the Funds, the EIB and the other existing financial instruments in support of the priority objectives referred to in Article 1 of the aforementioned Regulation,
- the activities of each Fund, the utilization of their budgetary resources and the concentration of assistance within the meaning of Article 12 of Regulation (EEC) No 2052/88, the deployment of the other financial instruments for which the Commission has responsibility and where their resources have been concentrated,
- the coordination of assistance provided by the Funds between themselves and with the assistance granted by the EIB and the other existing financial instruments,
- the results of the assessment referred to in Article 26,
- the results of analysis of the impact of Community assistance and policies as compared with the objectives listed in Article 1 of Regulation (EEC) No 2052/88 and in particular their impact on the socio-economic development of the regions.

2. Each year, the Commission shall consult the social partners organized at European level on the structural policy of the Community.

3. In the annual report of the year preceding completion of the internal market, the Commission shall consider the extent to which the Community has become cohesive and the impact of the implementation of Community policies.

Article 32

Information and publicity

1. The body responsible for implementing an operation carried out with financial assistance from the Community shall ensure that adequate publicity is given to the operation with a view to:

- making potential beneficiaries and trade organizations aware of the opportunites afforded by the operation,
- making the general public aware of the role played by the Community in relation to the operation.

Member States shall consult the Commission on, and inform it about, the initiatives taken for these purposes.

TITLE X
FINAL PROVISIONS

Article 33

Transitional provisions

1. In accordance with Article 15 (3) of Regulation (EEC) No 2052/88, applications in respect of multiannual operations received after adoption of that Regulation but before the entry into force of the implementing decisions referred to in Article 130e of the Treaty must be in keeping with the objectives set out in Article 1 of that Regulation and involve one of the forms of assistance provided for in Article 5 of that Regulation.

2. In drawing up Community support frameworks, the Commission shall take account of any multiannual operation already approved by the Council or by the Commission before the entry into force of the implementing decisions referred to in Article 130e of the Treaty and having financial repercussions during the period covered by those support frameworks.

3. The Commission may propose that the Member State concerned apply the provisions set out in the Funds' rules which enter into force on 1 January 1989 to operations decided on before that date.

4. In order to guarantee continuity of the activities of the Funds in the period between 1 January and 1 October 1989, approval by the Commission of any new applications submitted during that period shall not be subject to compliance with Article 15. Such operations shall be

indicated in the subsequent decision on the relevant Community support framework.

5. In accordance with Article 15 (4) of Regulation (EEC) No 2052/88, any applications in respect of non-multiannual operations submitted before entry into force of this Regulation may be approved after that date on the basis of the rules in force at the time of submission of such applications.

Article 34

Entry into force

This Regulation shall enter into force 1 January 1989.

This Regulation shall be binding in its entirety and directly applicable in all Member States.

Done at Brussels, 19 December 1988.

For the Council
The President
Th. PANGALOS

NOTES

* Appeared in the *Official Journal of the European Communities* 31 December 1988 pp. 374/1–14.
 1 OJ No C 256, 3. 10. 1988, p. 1
 2 OJ No C 326, 19. 12. 1988 and decision of 14 December 1988 (not yet published in the Official Journal).
 3 OJ No C 337, 31. 12. 1988
 4 OJ No L 185, 15. 7. 1988, p. 9
 5 OJ No L 128, 19. 5. 1975, p. 1
 6 OJ No L 93, 30. 3. 1985, p. 1
 7 OJ No L374, 31.12.1988, p. 21 (p. 207 this volume)
 8 OJ No L374, 31.12.1988, p. 25 (p. 215 this volume)
 9 OJ No L 376, 31. 12. 1986, p. 7
10 OJ No L374, 31.12.1988, p. 15 (see below)
11 OJ No 136, 17. 12. 1962, p. 2892/62
12 OJ No L 94, 28. 4. 1970, p. 13
13 OJ No L 185, 15. 7. 1988, p. 1
14 OJ No L 73, 21. 3. 1975, p. 47
15 OJ No L 289, 22. 10. 1983, p. 42

COUNCIL REGULATION (EEC) No 4254/88

of 19 December 1988 laying down provisions for implementing
Regulation (EEC) No 2052/88 as regards the European Regional
Development Fund

THE COUNCIL OF THE EUROPEAN COMMUNITIES

Having regard to the Treaty establishing the European Economic
Community, and in particular Article 130e thereof,

Having regard to the proposal from the Commission,[1]

In cooperation with the European Parliament,[2]

Having regard to the opinion of the Economic and Social Committee,[3]

Whereas Article 130c of the Treaty states that the European Regional
Development Fund is intended to help redress the principal regional
imbalances in the Community through participating in the development
and structural adjustment of regions whose development is lagging behind
and in the conversion of declining industrial regions;

Whereas Council Regulation (EEC) No 2052/88 of 24 June 1988 on the
tasks of the Structural Funds and their effectiveness and on coordination of
their activities between themselves and with the operations of the
European Investment Bank and the other existing financial instruments[4]
states in Article 3 (1) that the European Regional Development Fund shall
have the essential task of providing support for Objectives 1 and 2
specified in Article 1 of the same Regulation, that it shall participate in the
operations of Objective 5 (b) and, in addition, shall provide support for
studies or pilot schemes concerning regional development at Community
level;

Whereas provisions common to the Community's Structural Funds
have been established by Council Regulation (EEC) No 4253/88 of
19 December 1988 laying down provisions implementing Regulation
(EEC) No 2052/88 as regards coordination of the activities of the different
Structural Funds as between themselves and with the operations of the
European Investment Bank and the other existing instruments,[5] together
with other provisions common to the activities of the Funds;

Whereas these common provisions must be supplemented, in accordance with Article 3 (4) of Regulation (EEC) No 2052/88, by specific
provisions concerning the activities of the European Regional Development Fund (ERDF); whereas the nature of the measures which may be
financed by the ERDF, the information to be included in the plans of
Member States under Objectives 1 and 2 and the types of activities which
will have a privileged place in ERDF assistance must be clarified;

Whereas, as part of the reform of the Funds, the Commission should lay down the regional policy guidelines to be applied in the various stages of planning, notably in establishing the Community support frameworks and in the activities of the European Regional Development Funds,

HAS ADOPTED THIS REGULATION:

TITLE 1
SCOPE AND FORMS OF ASSISTANCE

Article 1

Scope

Within the framework of the task entrusted to it by Article 130c of the Treaty the ERDF shall, in accordance with Article 3 (1) of Regulation (EEC) No 2052/88 participate in the financing of:

(a) productive investment to enable the creation or maintenance of permanent jobs;

(b) investment in infrastructure, namely:

- in the regions designated under Objective 1, investment contributing to increasing economic potential, development, structural adjustment of these regions; financing may also be provided, in areas where the need is demonstrated, for certain facilities contributing to the structural adjustment of these areas, particularly health and educational facilities;
- in the regions or areas designated under Objective 2, investment relating to the regeneration of areas suffering from industrial decline, including inner cities, and those whose modernization or laying out provides the basis for the creation or development of economic activity;
- in the areas designated under Objective 5 (b), investment directly linked to economic activity which creates jobs other than in agriculture, including communication infrastructure links and others on which the development of such activities depends;

(c) the development of indigenous potential in the regions by measures which encourage and support local development initiatives and the activities of small and medium-sized enterprises, involving in particular:

- assistance towards services for firms, in particular in the fields of management, study and research of markets and services common to several firms,

- financing the transfer of technology, including in particular the collection and dissemination of information and financing the introduction of innovation in firms,

. - improvement of access for firms to the capital market, particularly by the provision of guarantees and equity participation,

- direct aid to investment, where no aid scheme exists,
- the provision of small-scale infrastructure;

(d) operations planned in the context of regional development at Community level, in particular in the case of frontier regions of the Member States, in accordance with Article 3(1), last subparagraph, of Regulation (EEC) No 2052/88;

(e) the preparatory, accompanying and assessment measures referred to in Article 7;

(f) productive investment and investment in infrastructure aimed at environmental protection where such investment is linked to regional development.

Article 2

Regional plans

1. Apart from the general provisions laid down in Title II of Regulation (EEC) 4253/88, the following specific provisions shall apply to the regional plans referred to in Articles 8 (4) and 9 (8) of Regulation (EEC) No 2052/88.

2. The plans relating to the regions designated under Objective 1 shall, as a general rule, cover one region at NUTS level II. However, pursuant to the second subparagraph of Article 8 (4) of Regulation (EEC) No 2052/88, Member States may submit a plan for more than one of their regions included in the list referred to in paragraph 2 of that Article, provided that the plan comprises the features listed in the first subparagraph of the said paragraph 4.

These plans shall contain the following information:

(a) a succinct analysis of the socio-economic situation of the region, indicating, *inter alia*, the demographic outlook thereof,

(b) a description of the development strategy envisaged by the Member State, with an indication of the national and regional financial resources proposed;

(c) the Member State's priorities for action and the regional development measures for which it plans to request Community financial participation, together with the estimated sums involved in these requests for the various forms of Community assistance.

When submitting the plans, the Member States shall supply information on the national, regional, local or other authorities which are to be responsible for implementing the measures.

As a general rule, these plans shall be for a period of five years and may be updated annually. Data for the fourth and fifth years may be given as a guide.

3. The plans relating to the regions designated under Objective 2 shall normally cover one or more areas at NUTS level III.

These plans shall contain the following information:

(a) a description of the conversion strategy envisaged by the Member State, with an indication of the national or regional financial resources proposed;

(b) the Member State's priorities for action and the regional conversion measures for which it plans to request Community financial participation, together with the estimated sums involved in these requests for the various forms of Community assistance;

(c) information allowing an assessment to be made of the overall regional economic situation.

When submitting the plans, the Member States shall supply information on the national, regional, local or other authorities which are to be responsible for implementing the measures.

As a general rule, these plans shall be for a period of three years and may be updated annually.

4. The plans relating to the regions designated under Objective 5 (b) shall be drawn up in accordance with the procedure laid down in Article 7 of Council Regulation (EEC) No 4256 of 19 December 1988 laying down provisions for implementing Regulation (EEC) No 2052/ 88 as regards the EAGGF Guidance Section.[6]

5. While submitting applications to the ERDF, Member States shall ensure that a sufficient proportion is allocated to investment in industry, craft industry and services, particularly through part-financing of aid schemes.

Article 3

Regional operational programmes

1. For the regions designated under Objective 1, regional operational

programmes shall in principle cover one region of NUTS level II or, in specific cases, one area at NUTS level III or more than one region at NUTS level II. For regions and areas designated under Objectives 2 and 5 (b), and for frontier regions, they shall in general cover one or more areas at NUTS level III.

2., The programmes may be undertaken on the initiative of the Member States or of the Commission in agreement with the Member State concerned, in accordance with the last subparagraph of Article 5 (5) of Regulation (EEC) No 2052/88.

When they are undertaken on the initiative of a Member State, they shall be drawn up by the authorities designated by the Member State, in consultation with the Commission.

When they are undertaken on the initiative of the Commission, the Commission, after consulting the Committee referred to in Article 27 of Regulation (EEC) No 4253/88, shall lay down the guidelines and invite the Member States concerned to establish operational programmes. It shall order their publication in the *Official Journal of the European Communities*.

The Commission's initiative shall be designed, within the framework of the tasks entrusted to the ERDF by Article 3 (1) of Regulation (EEC) No 2052/88:

- to help resolve serious problems directly associated with the implementation of other Community policies and affecting the socio-economic situation of one or more regions, or
- to promote the application of Community policies at regional level, or
- to help resolve problems common to certain categories of region.

The Commission's initiatives shall normally be financed from that part of ERDF commitment appropriations which is not the subject of the indicative allocation provided for in Article 12 (6) of Regulation (EEC) No 2052/88.

Article 4

Part-financing of aid schemes

1. The grant of Community assistance to regional aid schemes shall constitute one of the main forms of incentive to investment in firms.
2. With a view to deciding the Community's financial participation,

the Commission shall examine, with the competent authorities designated by the Member State, the characteristics of the aid scheme concerned. It shall take account of the following:

- the rate of assistance to be tailored to the socio-economic situation of the regions concerned and the consequent locational disadvantages ·for firms,
- operating procedures and the types of aid, including rates, to be varied to meet the needs,
- priority to be given to small and medium-sized enterprises and to the encouragement of services supplied to them such as management advice and market surveys,
- the economic repercussions of the aid scheme on the region.
- the characteristics and impact of any other regional aid scheme in the same region.

Article 5

Projects

In addition to the information specified in Article 16 of Regulation (EEC) No 4253/88, applications for ERDF assistance for the projects referred to in Article 5 (2) (d) of Regulation (EEC) No 2052/88 submitted individually or within the framework of an operational programme shall provide the following details:

(a) for investment in infrastructures:

- analysis of the costs and socio-economic benefits of the project, including an indication of the excepted [sic] rate of use,
- the expected impact on the development or conversion of the region concerned,
- an indication of the consequences that Community participation will have on the completion of the project;

(b) for productive investment:

- an indication of the market outlook for the sector concerned,
- the effects on employment,
- an analysis of the excepted [sic] profitability of the project.

Article 6

Global grants

1. In accordance with Article 5 (2) (c) of Regulation (EEC) No 2052/88,

the Commission may entrust to appropriate intermediaries, including regional development organizations, designated by the Member State in agreement with the Commission, the management of global grants, which it shall use primarily to assist local development initiatives. These intermediaries must be present or represented in the regions concerned and must operate in the public interest and shall associate adequately the socio-economic interests directly concerned by the implementation of the measures planned.

2. The procedures for the use of global grants, shall be the subject of an agreement concluded, in agreement with the Member State concerned, between the Commission and the intermediary concerned.

These procedures shall detail in particular:

- the types of measure to be carried out,
- the criteria for choosing beneficiaries,
- the conditions and rates of ERDF assistance,
- the arrangements for monitoring use of the global grants.

Article 7

Preparatory, accompanying and assessment measures

1. The ERDF may finance, up to a limit of 0.5 per cent of its annual allocation, the preparatory, accompanying and assessment measures necessary for the implementation of this Regulation carried out by the Commission or by outside experts. They shall include studies, among them studies of a general nature concerning Community regional action, and technical assistance or information measures, including, in particular, measures to provide information for local and regional development agents.

2. Measures carried out on the Commission's initiative may, in exceptional circumstances, be financed by the ERDF at a rate of 100 per cent, it being understood that those carried out by the Commission itself are financed at a rate of 100 per cent. For other measures the rates laid down in Article 17 of Regulation (EEC) No 4253/88 shall apply.

TITLE II
GUIDELINES AND PARTNERSHIP

Article 8

Periodic report and guidelines

1. A periodic report on the social and economic situation and

development of the regions of the Community, which also indicates the macro-economic effects of the Community's regional action, shall be prepared by the Commission at three-yearly intervals in accordance with the procedures laid down in Title VIII of Regulation (EEC) No 4253/88. Member States shall provide the Commission with the relevant information enabling it to make an analysis of all the regions of the Community on the basis of statistics which are as comparable and as up to date as possible. The report must also make it possible to assess the regional impact of other Community policies.

The first periodic report shall be prepared by 31 December 1990 at the latest.

2. This report shall constitute a basis for the establishment of guidelines for Community regional policy. These shall be applied by the Commission in the various stages of planning, notably in establishing Community support frameworks and in the activities of the ERDF. These guidelines shall be forwarded to the Council and the European Parliament and shall be published for information in the *Official Journal of the European Communities*.

Article 9

Regional partnership

The Community's regional action shall be carried out in close consultation between the Commission, the Member State concerned and the competent authorities designated by the latter, in accordance with Article 4 (1) of Regulation (EEC) No 2052/88, for the implementation of measures at regional level.

TITLE III
REGIONAL DEVELOPMENT AT COMMUNITY LEVEL

Article 10

Definition of assistance

1. In accordance with the last subparagraph of Article 3 (1) of Regulation (EEC) No 2052/88, the ERDF may also contribute to the financing at Community level of:

(a) studies at the Commission's initiative aiming to identify:

- the spatial consequences of measures planned by the national authorities, particularly major infrastructures, when their effects go beyond national boundaries,
- measures aiming to correct specific problems of the border regions within and outside the Community,
- the elements necessary to establish a prospective outline of the utilization of Community territory.

(b) pilot schemes which:

- constitute incentives to the creation of infrastructure, investment in firms and other specific measures having a marked Community interest, in particular in the border regions within and outside the Community,
- encourage the pooling of experience and development co-operation between different Community regions, and innovative measures.

2. On the Commission's initiative, matters relating to regional development at Community level, coordination of national regional policies or any other problem connected with implementation of Community regional action may be referred to the Committee specified in Article 27 of Regulation (EEC) No 4253/88. The Committee may arrive at common conclusions on the basis of which the Commission shall, where appropriate, address recommendations to the Member State.

TITLE IV
GENERAL AND FINAL, PROVISIONS

Article 11

Monitoring of compatibility

Where appropriate and through procedures suitable to each policy, Member States shall supply the Commission with information concerning compliance with Article 7(1) of Regulation (EEC) No 2052/88.

Article 12

Information and publicity

The provisions on information and publicity referred to in Article 32 of Regulation (EEC) No 4253/88 concerning ERDF assistance shall be adopted by the Commission and published in the *Official Journal of the European Communities*.

Article 13

Indicative allocation of ERDF resources

In accordance with Article 12(6) of Regulation (EEC) No 2052/88, the Commission shall, before 1 January 1989, decide for a period of five years and as a guide, on the allocation per Member State of 85 per cent of the commitment appropriations of the ERDF.

Article 14

Final provisions

Regulation (EEC) No 1787/84[7] is hereby repealed, subject to the application of Article 15 of Regulation (EEC) No 2052/88 and of Article 33 of Regulation (EEC) No 4253/88 (coordinating Regulation).

Article 15

Entry into force

This regulation shall enter into force on 1 January 1989.

However, Article 14 shall apply with effect from the date of adoption of this Regulation.

This Regulation shall be binding in its entirety and directly applicable in all Member States.

Done at Brussels, 19 December 1988.

For the Council
The President
Th. PANGALOS

NOTES

* Appeared in the *Official Journal of the European Communities* 31 December 1988, pp. 374/15 – 20.
1 OJ No C. 256, 3. 10. 1988, p. 12.
2 OJ No C 326, 19.12. 1988 and decision of 14 December 1988.
3 OJ No C 337, 31. 12. 1988.
4 OJ No L 185, 15. 7. 1988, p. 9.
5 OJ No L 374, 31.12.88, p. 1 (p. 170 of this volume).

6 OJ No L 374, 31.12.88, p. 25 (see below).
7 OJ No L 169, 28. 6. 1984, p. 1

COUNCIL REGULATION (EEC) No 4255/88
of 19 December 1988 laying down provisions for implementing Regulation (EEC) No 2052/88 as regards the European Social Fund

THE COUNCIL OF THE EUROPEAN COMMUNITIES

Having regard to the Treaty establishing the European Economic Community, and in particular Articles 126 and 127 thereof,

Having regard to the proposal from the Commission,[1]

Having regard to the opinion of the European Parliament,[2]

Having regard to the opinion of the Economic and Social Committee,[3]

Whereas Article 3 (4) of Council Regulation (EEC) No 2052/88 of 24 June 1988 on the tasks of the Structural Funds and their effectiveness and on coordination of their activities between themselves and with the operations of the European Investment Bank and the other existing financial instruments[4] provides for the Council to adopt the specific provisions governing operations under each Structural Fund,

Whereas it is appropriate to define the various types of measures to be supported by the European Social Fund (hereinafter referred to as 'the Fund'), including those which represent new tasks, in context of the Fund's contribution to the attainment of the five objectives provided for in Article 1 of Regulation (EEC) No 2052/88,

Whereas objectives 3 and 4 are applicable to the whole of the Community's territory;

Whereas expenditure eligible for assistance from the Fund should be defined;

Whereas expenditure trends should not be allowed to diverge and average indicative amounts should be introduced by stages for contributions by the Fund towards operating costs in respect of training;

Whereas Article 10 (1) of Regulation (EEC) No 2052/88 requires the Commission to establish guidelines for the attainment of Objectives 3 and 4 laid down in that Regulation;

Whereas arrangements should be specified for the submission of the plans to be drawn up by Member States pursuant to Regulation (EEC) No 2052/88;

Whereas it is necessary to define the forms of assistance to be granted by the Fund and to specify the content of applications relating to operations to be carried out within the framework of Member States' labour market policies;

Whereas arrangements should be laid down for the submission and approval of applications for assistance from the Fund, as should details of the arrangements for monitoring;

Whereas the transitional provisions should be specified.

HAS ADOPTED THIS REGULATION:

Article 1

Eligible operations

1. Under the conditions laid down by Council Regulation (EEC) No 2052/88 and Regulation (EEC) No 4253/88 of 19 December 1988 laying down provisions for implementing Regulation (EEC) 2052/88 as regards coordination of the activities of the different Structural Funds between themselves and with the operations of the European Investment Bank and the other existing financial instruments[5] and those specified in this Regulation, the Fund shall contribute to the financing of the following:

(a) vocational training operations, accompanied where necessary by vocational guidance;

(b) subsidies towards recruitment into newly created stable jobs and towards the creation of self-employed activities.

2. In this connection, the Fund shall also contribute up to 5 per cent of its annual budget to the financing of the following:

(a) operations of an innovatory nature which are intended to test new approaches to the content, methods and organization of vocational training and more generally the development of employment, with a view to establishing a basis for subsequent Fund assistance in a number of Member States;

(b) preparatory, accompanying and management measures needed for the implementation of this Regulation; such measures shall include studies, technical assistance and the exchange of experience which has a multiplier effect, and follow-up to and detailed evaluation of, measures financed by the Fund;

(c) measures aimed, within the framework of social dialogue, at staff from undertakings in two or more Member States, concerning the transfer of special knowledge relating to the modernization of the production apparatus;

(d) guidance and advice for the reintegration of the long-term unemployed.

3. Vocational training within the meaning of paragraph 1 (a) means any measure aimed at providing the skills necessary to carry out one or more specific types of employment, with the exception of apprenticeship schemes, and any measure with the relevant technology content required by technological change and requirements and developments on the labour market.

4. By way of derogation from paragraph 3, vocational training, shall include, in the regions concerned by Objectives 1, 2 and 5 (b), any vocational training and further training measure required for the use of new production and/or management techniques in small and medium-sized enterprises.

5. By way of derogation from paragraph 3, vocational training shall include, in the regions concerned by Objective 1:

- the theoretical portion of apprenticeship training given outside the firm,
- in specific cases to be defined according to the particular needs of the countries and regions concerned, that part of national secondary, or corresponding education systems specifically devoted to vocational training following compulsory full-time schooling where that part meets the challenges posed by economic and technological changes.

6. In the regions concerned by Objective 1, and for a period of three years following the entry into force of this Regulation, recruitment subsidies shall be extended to non-productive projects which fulfil a public need involving the creation of additional jobs of at least six months' duration for the long-term unemployed aged over 25.

Article 2

Scope

In accordance with Article 3 (2) of Regulation (EEC) No 2052/88, Fund assistance shall be granted:

(a) as regards its priority Objectives (3) and (4), throughout the Community, to operations intended to:

- combat long-term unemployment by means of the occupational integration of persons aged over 25 who have been unemployed for more than 12 months; this period may be reduced in specific cases to be decided upon by the Commission,
- facilitate the occupational integration of persons under 25 from the age at which compulsory full-time schooling ends, however long or short the period during which they have been seeking employment;

(b) as regards Objectives 1, 2 and 5 (b) to measures intended to:

- encourage job stability and develop new employment possibilities, organized for persons:
  - who are unemployed,
  - who are threatened with unemployment particularly within the context of restructuring requiring technological modernization or substantial changes in the production or management system,
  - employed in small and medium-sized enterprises,
- facilitate vocational training for any working person involved in an operation which is essential to the achievement of the development and conversion objectives of an integrated programme.

(c) as regards Objective 1, operations for persons:

- training for persons under apprenticeship contracts qualifying under the first indent of Article 1 (5),
- trained under national secondary vocational education systems, in accordance with the second indent of Article 1 (5),
- employed within the framework of the operations referred to in Article 1 (6).

Article 3

Eligible expenditure

1. Fund assistance may be granted only towards expenditure to cover:

(a) the income of persons receiving vocational training;
(b) the cost;

- of preparing, operating, managing and assessing vocational training operations including vocational guidance, including the costs of training teaching staff,

– subsistance and travel costs of those covered by vocational training operations;

(c) the granting, for a maximum period of 12 months per person, of subsidies towards recruitment into newly created stable jobs and towards the creation of self-employed activities together with subsidies of at least six months' duration per person, for recruitment as referred to in Article 1 (6);

(d) the cost of operations which receive assistance from the Fund under Article 1 (2) (b) (c) and (d).

2. The Commission shall determine each year, within the framework of the partnership, the maximum eligible amount per person and per week granted under paragraph 1 (c). This amount shall be based on 30 per cent of the average gross earnings of industrial workers in each Member State, determined in accordance with the harmonized definition of the Statistical Office of the European Communities; it shall be published in the *Official Journal of the European Communities* in good time to be included in the applications submitted in accordance with Articles 7 (1) and 9 (3).

3. The Commission shall ensure that Fund expenditure for operations of the same type does not develop in different ways. To this end, after the Committee referred to in Article 28 of Regulation (EEC) No 4253/88 has delivered its opinion, it shall determine for each Member State, in cooperation with that State and progressively, the indicative average amounts for such expenditure to be borne by the Fund according to the type of training involved; it shall order their publication in the *Official Journal of the European Communities*. They shall be applicable during the following financial year.

Article 4

Guidelines

1. In accordance with Article 10 (1) of Regulation (EEC) No 2052/88, the Commission shall establish before 15 February 1989, for a period of a least three years, the guidelines concerning action under objectives 3 and 4 which it will follow in defining the Community support frameworks; it shall order their publication in the *Official Journal of European Communities*.

2. Any amendments necessitated by substantial changes on the labour market shall be made before 1 February of a financial year; they shall

apply to the new Community support frameworks or amended frameworks in respect of the following financial years.

3. The guidelines shall establish the training and employment policies covering measures that may be eligible for Fund assistance; apart from regions covered by Objectives 1, 2 and 5 (b), priority shall be given to Community financing for measures that meet the requirements and prospects of the labour market.

Article 5

Plans

The plans referred to in Articles 8 to 11 of Regulation (EEC) No 2052/88 shall, in particular, indicate in the part concerning the Fund, estimates with respect to:

- the disparity between job applications and vacancies, including, as far as possible, data concerning female employment,
- the nature and characteristics of unfilled vacancies,
- the occupational opportunities which appear on labour markets,
- the measures to be implemented or under way in regard to training and employment,
- the number of persons concerned per type of measure.

Article 6

Forms of assistance

1. In accordance with Article 5 of Regulation (EEC) No 2052/88, applications for Fund assistance shall be presented in the form of operational programmes, global grant schemes or action within the meaning of Article 1 (2) (b), (c) and (d). The operational programmes and global grant schemes may include associated preparatory, accompanying, management and assessment measures.

2. The Member States shall communicate the information necessary for the examination of measures, in particular the information specified in Article 14 (2) of Regulation (EEC) No 4253/88 and the information specifically related to the European Social Fund (location, number of persons, duration of the operation for each person, occupational level concerned), specifying as a general rule:

- in the case of unemployed persons and other without jobs, their occupational qualifications at the beginning of the operations,

- in the case of employed persons, the nature and scope of proposed occupational conversion operations,
- in the case of operations involving conversion or economic restructuring, the volume and type of investment planned and changes in products or production systems.

Article 7

Submission and approval of applications for assistance

1. Applications for assistance shall be submitted at least three months before the start of operations. They shall be accompanied by a form drawn up, within the framework of the partnership, using computerized means listing the particulars for each measure so that it can be monitored from budgetary commitment to final payment.
2. The Commission shall decide on these applications before the beginning of operations and shall inform the Member State concerned.

Article 8

Monitoring

In accordance with Article 23 (2) of Regulation (EEC) No 4253/88, the Commission may carry out on-the-spot checks. These checks may take the form of representative sample checks. In this case, after consultation with the Member State concerned, the Commission shall establish the proportion of samples taken in the light of the material and technical conditions of the operation concerned. If, after the results have been checked in the framework of the partnership, the sample reveals insufficient implementation, the Commission may make suitable reduction, which may be applied as a proportion of the total amount for which payment is requested, after the Member State has had an opportunity to submit its comments.

Article 9

Transitional provisions

1. In accordance with Article 15 (4) of Regulation (EEC) No 2052/88, applications for assistance for 1989 submitted before 21 October 1988 shall continue to be covered by Council Decision 83/516/EEC,[6] as

amended by Decision 85/568/EEC,[7] and the provisions implementing it.

2. The first plans shall cover a period beginning on 1 January 1990. Plans concerning Objectives 1, 2 and 5 (b) shall be presented not later than 31 March 1989. Plans concerning Objectives 3 and 4 shall be presented within four months of the publication in the *Official Journal of the European Communities* of the guidelines referred to in Article 4.

3. Applications for assistance for operations to be implemented in 1990 shall be submitted before 31 August 1989.

Article 10

Entry into force

1. This Regulation shall enter into force on 1 January 1989. Subject to the transitional provisions laid down in Article 9, it shall be applicable as from that date.

2. Subject to Article 15 of Regulation (EEC) No 2052/88 and Article 33 of Regulation (EEC) No 4253/88, Regulation (EEC) No 2950/83[8] is hereby repealed.

This Regulation shall be binding in its entirety and directly applicable in all Member States.

Done at Brussels, 19 December 1988.

For the Council
The President
Th. PANGALOS

NOTES

* Appeared in the *Official Journal of the European Communities* 31 December 1988, L374/21 – 4.
1 OJ No C 256, 3. 10. 1988, p. 16.
2 OJ No C 326, 19. 12. 1988.
3 OJ No C 337, 31. 12. 1988.
4 OJ No L 185, 15. 7. 1988, p. 9.
5 OJ No L 374, 31.12.1988, p. 1 (p. 170 of this volume).
6 OJ No L 289, 22. 10. 1983, p. 38.
7 OJ No L 370, 31. 12. 1985, P. 40.
8 OJ No L 289, 22. 10. 1983, P. 1.

COUNCIL REGULATION (EEC) No 4256/88
of 19 December 1988 laying down provisions for implementing Regulation (EEC) No 2052/88 as regards the EAGGF Guidance Section

THE COUNCIL OF THE EUROPEAN COMMUNITIES,

Having regard to the Treaty establishing the European Economic Community, and in particular Article 43 thereof,

Having regard to the proposal from the Commission.[1]

Having regard to the opinion of the European Parliament,[2]

Having regard to the opinion of the Economic and Social Committee,[3]

Whereas Article 3 (4) of Regulation (EEC) No 2052/88[4] provides for the Council to adopt the specific provisions governing operations under each structural Fund;

Whereas the tasks laid down for the Guidance Section of the European Agricultural Guidance and Guarantee Fund, (hereinafter called 'the Fund'), by Article 3 (3) of the above Regulation should be further specified in the light of the contribution it makes to achieving Objectives 1, 5(a) and 5 (b) as set out in Article 1 of that Regulation;

Whereas measures to speed up the adjustment of agricultural structures with a view to the reform of the agricultural Funds must include measures closely connected with the common agricultural policy and designed to meet its general requirements;

Whereas, however, some of those measures, which already exist at Community level, may require adjustment to allow for the differing structural situations in the different regions of the Community, by increased diversification, and specially by differentiation of the contribution in favour of the areas concerned by Objective 1;

Whereas measures designed to contribute to Objective 1 and to promoting the development of rural areas (Objective 5 (b)) should include action to respond to those areas' specific structural problems;

Whereas measures for the development and exploitation of woodland are of particular interest, not only as offering alternative activity and income for agriculture in those areas but also in order to increase woodland's contribution to improving the environment and to expand its protective function;

Whereas the forms of assistance by the Fund should be determined and whereas operational programmes, and where appropriate global grants, are the most appropriate forms, both for measures for the development of less-developed areas and of rural areas and for measures to improve strucures for marketing and processing agricultural products.

HAS ADOPTED THIS REGULATION:

Article 1

1. The Guidance Section of the European Agricultural Guidance and Guarantee Fund, (hereinafter called 'the Fund'), referred to in Article 1 (1) of Regulation (EEC) No 729/70,[5] as last amended by Regulation (EEC) No 2048/88,[6] may, in accordance with the criteria and objectives laid down in Titles I to IV of this Regulation, finance measures for performing the tasks referred to in Article 3 (3) of Regulation (EEC) No 2052/88 in order to attain Objectives 1 and 5 as set out in Article 1 of that Regulation.

2. The conditions and criteria laid down in Council Regulation (EEC) No 4253/88 of 19 December 1988 laying down provisions for implementing Regulation (EEC) No 2052/88 as regards coordination of the activities of the different Structural Funds between themselves and with the operations of the European Investment Bank and the other existing financial instruments[7] shall apply to measures financed under this Regulation, except if this Regulation or provisions adopted under Article 2 (1) thereof specify otherwise.

3. Without prejudice to Article 33 Regulation (EEC) No 4253/88 and Article 10 of this Regulation, the Council, acting on a proposal from the Commission in accordance with the procedure laid down in Article 43 of the Treaty, shall decide by 31 December 1989 on any alterations to the common measures introduced under Article 6 of Regulation (EEC) No 729/70 in order to achieve the objectives referred to in Regulation (EEC) No 2052/88, in conformity with the rules laid down by Regulation (EEC) No 4253/88 and with this Regulation.

TITLE I

Speeding up the adjustment of agricultural structures with a view to the reform of the common agricultural policy

Article 2

1. The Fund may finance common measures adopted by the Council in accordance with the procedure provided for in the third subparagraph

of Article 43 (2) of the Treaty, in order to speed up the adjustment of agricultural structures, with a view in particular to the reform of the common agricultural policy.

2. The common measures referred to in paragraph 1 may concern:

- , measures accompanying the market policy that help re-establish a balance between production and market capacity such as adjusting production potential and reorientating and converting production including measures to promote quality products,
- forestry measures to assist agricultural holdings and the afforestation of farmland in particular,
- measures to encourage early retirement from farming, in order to reduce the areas of land devoted to surplus farm production,
- measures to support farm incomes, and to maintain viable agricultural communities in mountain, hill or less-favoured areas by means of agricultural aid such as compensation for permanent natural handicaps,
- measures to protect the environment and safeguard the landscape by encouraging suitable agricultural production practices,
- measures to encourage the installation of young farmers,
- measures, including accompanying measures, to improve the efficiency of the structures of holdings, especially investments aimed at reducing production costs and improving the living and working conditions of farmers, and promoting the diversification of their activities, as well as preserving and improving the natural environment,
- measures to improve the marketing, including the marketing of produce at the farm, and processing of agricultural and forestry products (in accordance with the conditions and the criteria laid down in the provisions referred to Article 10 (1)) and to encourage the establishment of producers' associations,
- measures to improve the marketing and processing of fishery products.

3. The common measures which are applicable at present in the domain covered by this Title shall remain in force until they are adjusted pursuant to Article 1 (3).

TITLE II

Promoting the development and structural adjustment of the less-developed regions

Article 3

1. Within the context of its contribution to achieving Objective 1 referred to in Article 1 of Regulation (EEC) No 2052/88, the Fund may finance measures for developing and strengthening agricultural and forestry structures, for maintaining the landscape and for rural development.
2. Fund assistance for regions designated under Objective 1 shall comprise particularly measures intended to deal with the backwardness of agricultural structures.

Article 4

Fund assistance for the measures referred to in Article 5 of this Regulation shall in the main take the form of operational programmes including an integrated approach and global grants.

Article 5

Financial assistance by the Fund may relate to the following:

- encouraging retirement from farming in order to restructure agriculture and encourage the installation of young farmers,
- the conversion, diversification, and reorientation and adjustment of production potential,
- if their financing is not provided for by Council Regulation (EEC) No 4254/88 of 19 December 1988 laying down provisions for implementing Regulation (EEC) No 2052/88 as regards the European Regional Development Fund:[8]
- improving rural infrastructures which are necessary for the development of agriculture and forestry,
- measures to achieve diversification, especially those providing multiple activities or alternative incomes for farmers,
- reparcelling and associated work,
- individual or collective land or pasture improvement,
- irrigation, including the renovation and improvement of irrigation networks, the creation of collective irrigation works from existing main channels, the creation of small irrigation systems not supplied from collective networks, and the renovation and improvement of drainage systems,

- encouragement for tourist and craft investments, including the improvement of living accommodation on agricultural holdings,
- protection of the environment and maintenance of the countryside,
- restoring agricultural production potential after natural disasters,
- the development and exploitation of woodland, in accordance with conditions and criteria to be laid down by the Council on a proposal from the Commission, including:
  - afforestation and the improvement and reconstitution of woodland,
  - related work and accompanying measures necessary for the exploitation of woodland,
- in order to increase woodland's contribution to the conservation and protection of the environment and to offer farmers alternative activities and income,
- the development and agricultural and forestry advisory services, and the improvement of facilities for agricultural and forestry vocational training.

TITLE III

Promoting the development of rural areas of the Community in regions covered by Objective 5 (b)

Article 6

Fund assistance for the measures referred to in Article 7 shall in the main take the form of operational programmes, including an integrated approach, and global grants and cover one or more of the operations referred to in Article 5.

Article 7

Without prejudice to the particulars referred to in Article 11 (3) of Regulation (EEC) No 2052/88 and Article 5 of Regulation (EEC) No 4253/88, rural development plans shall include an indentification of the problems of agricultural structures at a relevant geographical level.

TITLE IV

General and transitional provisions

Article 8

Assistance from the Fund of up to 1 per cent of its annual budget, for the measures provided for in Article 5 (2) (e) of Regulation (EEC) No 2052/88 may cover:

- carrying out pilot projects for promoting the development of rural areas, including the development and exploitation of woodland,
- supporting such technical assistance and preparatory studies as are necessary for operations,
- studies to assess the effectiveness and measures provided for by this . Regulation.
- carrying out demonstration projects to show farmers the real possibilities of systems, methods and techniques of production which are in accordance with the objectives of the reform of the common agricultural policy,
- the measures needed for the circulation, at Community level, of the results of the work on and experience with improving agricultural structures.

Article 9

Where appropriate and through procedures suitable to each policy, Member States shall supply the Commission with information concerning compliance with Article 7 (1) of Regulation (EEC) No 2052/88.

Article 10

1. The Council, acting on a proposal from the Commission in accordance with the procedure laid down in Article 43 of the Treaty, shall by 31 December 1989 decide upon the forms of and the conditions for the Fund contribution to measures to improve the conditions under which agricultural, forestry and fishery products are processed and marketed, as referred to in Article 2 (2), with a view to achieving the objectives of Regulation (EEC) No 2052/88 and on the basis of the rules laid down by Regulation (EEC) No 4253/88.

2. With effect from the date of entry into force of the Council Decision referred to in paragraph 1, Council Regulation (EEC) No 355/77[9] is hereby repealed.

However, projects concerning fisheries may still be submitted under that Regulation until 31 December 1990.

3. By way of derogation from paragraph 2, Articles 6 to 15 and 17 to 23 of Regulation (EEC) No 355/77 shall continue to apply to projects submitted by the date of entry into force of the Council Decision referred to in paragraph 1, or as regards the fishery sector, by 31 December 1990.

4. Operational programmes as referred to in Articles 4 and 6 may, as

soon as this Regulation enters into force, include measures for improving the marketing and processing of agricultural, forestry and fishery products, provided they comply with the relevant current provisions.

Article 11

Regulation (EEC) No 729/70, with the exception of the Article 1 (1) to (3) shall no longer apply as regards EAGGF, Guidance Section, subject to the implementation of Article 15 of Regulation (EEC) No 2052/88, Article 33 of Regulation (EEC) No 4253/88 and Article 10 (3) of this Regulation.

Article 12

This Regulation shall enter into force on 1 January 1989.

This Regulation shall be binding in its entirety and directly applicable in all Member States.

Done at Brussels, 19 December 1988.

For the Council
The President
Th. PANGALOS

NOTES

* Appeared in the *Official Journal of the European Communities* 31 December 1988, pp. L374/25–8.
1 OJ No C 256, 3. 10. 1988, p. 19.
2 OJ No C 326, 19. 12. 1988.
3 OJ No C 337, 31. 12. 1988.
4 OJ No L 185, 15. 7. 1988, p. 9.
5 OJ No L 94, 28. 4. 1970, p. 13.
6 OJ No L 185, 15. 7. 1988, p. 1.
7 OJ No L 374, 31.12.88, p. 1 (p. 170 of this volume).
8 OJ No L 374, 31.12.88, p. 15 (p. 197 of this volume).
9 OJ No L 51, 23. 2. 1977, p. 1.

Notice C(88) 2510 to the Member States on monitoring compliance with public procurement rules in the case of projects and programmes financed by the Structural Funds and financial instruments

(89/C 22/03)

1., At its meeting on 4 May 1988 the Commission of the European Communities decided to introduce a system for monitoring compliance with public procurement rules where projects and programmes are executed with assistance from the Structural Funds and financial instruments. The system will enter into force two months following the date of publication of this Notice in the *Official Journal of the European Communities*.

The Commission has taken this decision because it has established that the rules of Community law are not observed in many cases where public contracts financed by the European Community are awarded. Infringements of the 'Works'[1] and 'Supplies'[2] directives have often come to light during examination of grant applications and requests for payment. Such infringements involve failure to comply with rules on tendering procedures, notably:

– awarding public contracts without prior publication of a tender notice in the *Official Journal of the European Communities*,
– splitting up public contracts improperly to evade application of the 'Public Procurement' Directives,
– using the single tender procedure improperly.

2. The failure to comply with public procurement rules in cases where contracts benefit from Community financing weakens considerably the policy on the opening-up of public procurement, one of the priority measures in completing the internal market.

Furthermore, this situation could well prejudice attainment of the Community's sectoral policy objectives. The establishment of infringements may result not only in initiation of proceedings under Article 169 of the EEC Treaty, but also in rejection of request for assistance or suspension and (in some cases) even the recovery of assistance already paid, which can delay or cut short the projects or programmes concerned by the contracts at issue.

3. The system which the Commission has decided to introduce is based on the following principles:

(a) The monitoring of compliance with Community rules must be balanced. The Commission will supervise their proper application both in relation to contracts that benefit from Community assistance and to those that do not. Measures designed to reinforce monitoring of the latter were taken recently.

(b) The monitoring of compliance with the public procurement rules falls not only to the Commission but also to the national authorities. This principle is upheld in particular under the operational programmes which are to become the main form of action under the Structural Funds. Intervention on a programme basis takes shape through the grant of Community assistance for the completion of a series of investments carried out and managed by the national authorities. The very nature of the programme, therefore, calls for decentralized monitoring by the national authorities.

(c) To prevent infringements, it is essential that wide ranging information and awareness campaigns be organized among recipients prior to application of the Community monitoring measures. The rules in force often give rise to different interpretations; the Commission is giving priority to the provision of information to the interested parties on Community law in the field of public procurement.

(d) Since the measures taken following establishment of failure to comply with the public procurement rules may jeopardize the carrying-out or completion of projects or programmes, payment shall not be suspended nor appropriations recovered until the interested party has had the opportunity to submit his comments within the period laid down on a case-by-case basis by the Commission, with the exception of the cases list at 7. Moreover, transparency of the Commission's monitoring shall be ensured through annual publication of the results of the monitoring and the methods used.

(e) To prevent the procedure for checking compliance with the public procurement rules from delaying implementation of a project or a programme, the 'monitoring' has, in so far as possible, been disassociated from the 'payment of advances'. It shall be presumed in paying advances that public contracts have been awarded in accordance with the rules of Community law, unless that presumption is rebutted by contrary facts resulting from examination of the case or the questionnaire.

4. The monitoring system shall comprise measures which aim both to advise recipients of the obligations they assume in receiving Community assistance and to facilitate the monitoring of compliance with public procurement rules.

5. The measures taken to advise recipients shall include:

– an information campaign on Community legislation and widespread dissemination of the Guide to the Community rules on open government procurement[3] in which the Commission has set out its interpretation of the directives on public procurement. This dissemination will be supplemented by direct measures to inform interested parties in accordance with a training programme developed by the Commission in agreement with authorities in the Member States.
– awareness campaigns on the monitoring methods used, mainly the public procurement questionnaire and the payment request form.

6. The public procurement questionnaire is designed to 'guide' applicants for Community financing towards compliance with the rules on public procurement. The answers will also provide the Commission with an effective means of monitoring. They will enable it not only to obtain an overall view of compliance with the key provisions of the directives (advertising, contracts concluded by way of the single tender procedure, excluded sectors, concession contracts, etc.), but also to monitor more thoroughly in cases where there are signs that the public procurement rules have not been adhered to.

The questionnaire will be addressed to applicants for Community assistance. They will be explicitly asked to comply with the public procurement rules when the contracts are to be awarded for the execution of a project or a programme. The contracts covered by the questionnaire are:

– all public contracts with a value exceeding the thresholds in the 'Works' and 'Supplies' directives, and
– public contracts with a value below those thresholds which constitute subdivisions of a single work or supplies of similar goods whose aggregate value exceeds the aforementioned threshold. A 'work' means the outcome of building or civil engineering taken as a whole that is sufficient of itself to fulfill an economic and technical function for the user.

The national authorities should return the duly completed questionnaire to the Commission in respect of each contract awarded:

– when the grant application is submitted by the Member State, in cases where all the contracts have already been awarded when the application is drawn up by the authority/authorities concerned, or
– when a payment request is submitted in cases where all the contracts have been awarded, or

– in any event when the request for payment of the outstanding balance is submitted.

If the questionnaires are not returned, payments will be suspended once notice has been given to the interested party to submit his comments.
7. The payment request form now in use will be amended to include references to public contracts published in the *Official Journal of the European Communities* and a declaration by the Member State concerned to the effect that contracts which do not have to be published have been awarded in accordance with the public procurement directives. On making payment it will be presumed that the contracting authority has complied with the Community public procurement rules. However, payment will be suspended where no references are given to publication of public procurement tender notices in the *Official Journal of the European Communities* and no declaration is made to the effect that the public procurement directives have been complied with, in the case of contracts not requiring notice publication.
8. The legal basis for monitoring *sensu stricto* is to be found in Article 5 of the EEC Treaty and in the clauses which commit recipients to compliance with Community legislation. It will be carried out by the Member States and by the Commission, notably on the basis of the public procurement questionnaire and the payment request form.

– The national authorities will first verify the answers given to the questionnaire and in the payment request form. Timely national monitoring will expedite considerably payments relating to a project or programme.
– The Commission, for its part, will verify the tender notices published in the *Official Journal of the European Communities* and make sample checks on the proper application of all the public procurement rules, notably those concerning the qualitative selection of tenderers and the award of contracts.

9. Both suspension and recovery of payments shall be effected in accordance with the specific rules of each Fund or Community financial instrument.
If failure to comply is established, proceedings may be instituted under Article 169 of the EEC Treaty, even after completion of the financing operation.
10. The monitoring system shall be differentiated by project or programme:

(a) For projects, the decision granting assistance must include suspension or repayment clauses or similar clauses. These clauses shall refer to the need to comply with Community law on public procurement, not simply the obligation to publish in the *Official Journal of the European Communities*.

(b) For programmes, the awareness campaigns, checking and follow-up to the application of the public procurement rules will be shared between the national authorities and the Commission. Subject to adoption of the proposal for a regulation on the reform of the Structural Funds, compliance with the public procurement rules will be ensured in the following way:

- when preparing the Community framework for supporting the development or conversion of a region and when the decision is being taken on an operational programme, the Commission will organize an awareness campaign and ensure that the clauses concerning compliance with the public procurement rules are written into the programme contract or in the corresponding draft decision.

- when the operational programmes are being launched and when they are in progress the national authorities will be primarily responsible for making the contracting authorities aware of the rules and performing the necessary checks on each project without prejudice to the monitoring carried out by the Commission's authorizing departments and financial control.

- when payment of the outstanding balance is requested for a programme instalment in the case of contracts awarded pertaining to a project completed during the instalment period in question, the Commission will verify publication of tender notices in the *Official Journal of the European Communities* and subsequently make sample checks on compliance with the public procurement rules on the basis of the answers given to the questionnaire returned to the Commission by the national authorities when requesting payment of the oustanding balance.

For projects implemented over two or more instalment periods, these verifications and checks will be carried out in conjunction with examination of the request for payment of the oustanding balance for the instalment period in which the project is completed.

In the event of failure to comply with the public procurement rules, recovery will be undertaken in accordance with the relevant administrative rules.

To ensure that the public contracts to be awarded under these programmes are transparent, details concerning certain features (for example, infrastructure works, construction of training centres, research centres, supplies) will be published in the *Supplement to the Official Journal of the European Communities* by way of preliminary information to interested Community contractors or suppliers in accordance with the relevant rules of Community legislation in force.

(c) The Commission will also monitor compliance with the public procurement rules on the spot while performing other checks connected with the proper material and financial execution of projects or programmes in receipt of Community assistance.

11. For European Investment Bank loans, the Commission will take account of the results of the EIB's own *ex ante* monitoring procedures in respect of projects subject to the consultations referred to in Article 21 of the Protocol on the Statute of the EIB.

12. For projects and programmes that give rise to contracts falling under sectors not covered by the directives in force (water, transport, energy and in the case of the 'Supplies' directive, telecommunications) the recipient may undertake, in a specific clause to open up contracts to Community competition, without, however any additional eligibility criteria being introduced for the granting of assistance. In particular, in the case of contracts for which EIB, Euratom or ECSC loans are granted, recommendations encouraging the opening-up of contracts shall be included (when not already the case) in the contract document.

To that end, and pending adoption of the directives now before the Council,[4] the Commission intends to give, by way of an incentive, (wherever numbers of applications of the same type are excessive and all other things being equal) priority to applicants for assistance who open up contracts to Community competition or who undertake, in writing, to do so by publishing the tender notices for the contract concerned in the *Official Journal of the European Communities* and by awarding these contracts on the basis of non-discriminatory criteria.

These tender notices must contain the following minimum details:

- name and address of the contracting authority,
- purpose of the contract,
- time limit for reception of tenders or requests to participate,
- criteria for qualitative selection.

13. The monitoring system outlined above will enter into force two

months following the date of publication of this notice in the *Official Journal of the European Communities*.

In the meantime the Commission will undertake the measures required to bring it into effect, information and training for the interested parties, verification of advertising, pilot surveys, investigation of infringements, while maintaining a balance in the monitoring as between public procurement financed from the structural Funds and financial instruments and public procurement which is not so financed.

NOTES

* Appeared in the *Official Journal of the European Communities* 28 January 1989, pp. C22/3 – 6.
1 Directive 71/305/EEC, OJ No L 185, 16. 8. 1971, p. 5.
  Directive 72/277/EEC, OJ No L 176, 3. 8. 1972, p. 2.
  Directive 78/699/EEC, OJ No L 225, 16. 8. 1978, p. 41.
2 Directive 77/62/EEC, OJ No L 13, 15. 1. 1977, p. 1.
  Directive 80/767/EEC, OJ No L 215, 18. 8. 1980, p. 1.
  Directive 88/295/EEC, OJ No L 127, 20. 5. 1988, p. 1.
3 OJ No C 358, 31. 12. 1987, p. 1.
4 Proposal for a Council Directive on the procurement procedures of entities providing water, energy and transport services: COM(88) 377 final of 11 October 1988; Proposal for a Council Directive on the procurement procedures of entities operating in the telecommunications sector: COM(88) 378 final of 11 October 1988.

Index